23.95

Gender and Political Economy

Gender and Political Economy

Incorporating Diversity into Theory and Policy

Ellen Mutari   **Heather Boushey**

William Fraher IV

M.E. Sharpe
Armonk, New York
London, England

Copyright © 1997 by M. E. Sharpe, Inc.

All rights reserved. No part of this book may be reproduced in any form without written permission from the publisher, M. E. Sharpe, Inc., 80 Business Park Drive, Armonk, New York 10504.

Library of Congress Cataloging-in-Publication Data

Gender and political economy: incorporating diversity into theory and policy / [edited by] Ellen Mutari, Heather Boushey, and William Fraher IV.
p. cm.
Includes bibliographical references and index.
ISBN 1–56324–996–0 (alk. paper). —
ISBN 1–56324–997–9 (pbk. : alk. paper)
1. Feminist economics—Congresses. 2. Women—Economic conditions—Congresses. 3. Women—Employment—Congresses.
I. Mutari, Ellen, 1956– . II. Boushey, Heather, 1970– .
III. Fraher, William, 1971– .
HQ1381.G38 1997
306.3'6—dc21
96–40285
CIP

Printed in the United States of America

The paper used in this publication meets the minimum requirements of American National Standard for Information Sciences— Permanence of Paper for Printed Library Materials, ANSI Z 39.48-1984.

BM (c)   10   9   8   7   6   5   4   3   2   1
BM (p)   10   9   8   7   6   5   4   3   2   1

Contents

List of Tables and Figures	vii
Acknowledgments	ix
1. Introduction: The Development of Feminist Political Economy *Ellen Mutari and Heather Boushey*	3

Part I Dissolving Dichotomies: New Approaches to Social Reproduction and Labor Supply

2. Family Troubles *Brian Cooper*	21
3. Female Labor Supply During Early Industrialization: Women's Labor Force Participation in Historical Perspective *Margaret S. Coleman*	42
4. Gender, Sexuality, and Sexual Orientation: All in the Feminist Family? *M.V. Lee Badgett*	61
5. A Structural Connection Among Race, Gender, Class: Marx's Political Economy Without the Subject *Teresa Brennan*	78
6. Class, Gender, and Culture: A Discussion of Marxism, Feminism, and Postmodernism *Ann Davis*	92

Part II Engendering Production: The Social Construction of Low-Wage Labor Markets

7. Comparable Worth in a Restructuring Economy: Discourse and Counter-Discourse *Ellen Mutari and Deborah M. Figart*	115

8. Women and Labor Market Flexibility: The Cases of Japan and the Former West Germany in the Postwar Years
   David Kucera — 131

9. Race, Class, and Occupational Mobility: Black and White Women in Service Work in the United States
   Marilyn Power and Sam Rosenberg — 150

10. Embracing Discrimination? The Interaction Between Low-Wage Labor Markets and Policies in Aid of the Poor
    Heather Boushey — 170

11. Reversing the Great U-Turn: Pay Equity, Poverty, and Inequality
    Deborah M. Figart and June Lapidus — 188

Bibliography — 207
About the Editors and Contributors — 235
Index — 238

List of Tables and Figures

Tables

3.1	Seamstress Employment Estimates for Four Cities	53
3.2	Estimate of FLFP in Massachusetts and Boston, 1833	55
8.1	Japan: Regression Results, 1952–1990	139
8.2	West Germany: Regression Results, 1952–1990	142
8.3	Confidence Interval Results, 1952–1990	144
8.4	Average Annual Growth Rates of Labor Force Participation and Employment in Japan: Comparing the 1987–1991 Upswing and the 1991–1993 Downswing	145
8.5	Standard Deviations of Logarithmic Growth Rates of Total (Men plus Women) Labor Force Participation and Employment, 1952–1990	147
8.6	Standard Deviations of Logarithmic Growth Rates of Women's Labor Force Participation and Employment, 1952–1990	148
9.1	Percentage of Black and White Women Employed in Service Occupations, 1960 and 1994	151
9.2	1988 Occupations of White and Black 1972 Service Workers	154
9.3	Occupational Ranks in 1972 and 1988 of 1972 Service Workers	155
9.4	Occupational Mobility by Rank, 1972–1988	157
9.5	Number of Children per Family by Race, 1972 and 1988	159
9.6	Educational Attainment by Race, 1972 and 1988	160
9.7	Rank in 1972 and 1988 by School Attendance	161
9.8	Father's Occupation in 1968 for Women in Service Occupations in 1972	162
9.9	Top Four Service Occupations by Race, 1972	164

9.10	Education, Presence of Children, and Mobility by Occupational Rank for White and Black Women Working as Domestic Workers in 1972	165
11.1	Decomposition of Inequality Indexes	199
11.2	Dissaggregated Measures of Inequality	201

Figures

8.1	Japan: Measures of Women's Relative Labor Force and Employment Volatility	140
8.2	West Germany: Measures of Women's Relative Labor Force and Employment Volatility	143
11.1	Hourly Wages Before and After Comparable Worth	196
11.2	Female-to-Male Median Wages	197
11.3	Relative Decrease in Wage Dispersion and Inequality	198
11.4	Lorenz Curves for Women	202

Acknowledgments

The conference that originally brought these papers together, Gender, Race, Economics, and Public Policy, took place due to the enthusiasm and initiative of the economics graduate students at the New School for Social Research. Their commitment to the project of integrating gender and race analysis into political economy was the seed from which this project germinated. We would like to extend our gratitude to the organizations at the New School for Social Research that were supportive of the conference. The New School Diversity Initiative, the Graduate Faculty Student Union Fee Board, and the Economics Student Union all supported the conference financially. The conference itself occurred at a difficult time for the program. David M. Gordon, a senior member of the faculty and intellectual pioneer in political economy, passed away only weeks before it was held. The conference, which helped reinvest many with a spirit of intellectual purpose, was dedicated to his memory. The lively discussion and commentary of those who attended was of great assistance to us as editors in developing this project.

Following the enthusiastic response to the conference, department chair John Eatwell suggested that we contact M.E. Sharpe about publishing the conference proceedings. We are grateful for his guidance in developing this project, as well as that of our editor Stephen J. Dalphin. Others also provided invaluable editorial comments and suggestions in assembling this book, among them Deborah Figart, Ellen Houston, Gerard MacDonald, William Milberg, and Thomas Palley. The contributors were delightful to work with, responding valiantly to our efforts to bring this to print while the research was still fresh.

Finally, we are thankful for the larger community of feminist scholars whose work continues to enlighten us.

Gender and Political Economy

1

Introduction

The Development of Feminist Political Economy

Ellen Mutari and Heather Boushey

Feminist economics has experienced a recent flourishing of interest and research activity. The key characteristic of this emerging research is a critical stance toward many of the premises, categories, and methods of neoclassical economics (see, for example, Ferber and Nelson 1993; Kuiper and Sap 1995). Taking a cue from the work of feminist philosophers of science, feminist economists view economic discourse as a social practice with concrete historical origins. This new feminist work augments the important contributions of empirical research on women's economic experiences by challenging the gendered assumptions guiding the neoclassical paradigm.

More than the other social sciences and humanities, economics has been a discipline dominated by a reigning paradigm. The wide-ranging theoretical and policy interests of the early classical political economists (such as Adam Smith, David Ricardo, and Karl Marx) were subsumed into a "scientific" quest for natural laws. Neoclassical economics, defined as the study of the allocation of scarce resources toward the satisfaction of human desires, narrowed the scope and tools of economic inquiry. Yet there has always been a sizable contingent within the discipline that has embraced broader theoretical approaches and methodologies, including Marxists, institutionalists, social economists, and post-Keynesians. Like feminist thought, political economy is less rigid in its disciplinary boundaries. Further, most political economists reject the naturalization of the economy as an ahistorical, disembodied entity. They also question the form of economic rationality posited by neoclassicals as the basis of behavior (see, for example, Block 1990).

Feminist economics, and more specifically feminist political economy, recognizes this shared critical perspective toward mainstream theoretical constructs, but also asserts that feminist analyses provide unique contributions to economic and social theory. Feminist political economy is in many ways an act of synthesis—the creative combustion of insights drawn from diverse intellectual standpoints in the hopes of generating new illumination. Because feminist political economists take inspiration from so many sources, their work reflects a range of interests, principles, and methodologies.

Gender and Political Economy presents some of these diverse approaches to feminist political economy in dialogue with progressive economic theory and public policy. It is an outgrowth of a conference held at the New School for Social Research in New York City in April 1996. The conference on which this volume is based provided a forum to explore how feminist political economy provides greater insight into economic theory and produces fruitful ways of approaching policy. The goals of the conference and of this volume are to extend the boundaries of political economy by incorporating gender in interaction with class, race, and sexuality. This compilation includes a broad range of authors representing diverse perspectives—including a new cadre of feminist political economists who build on the work of their feminist forebears.

The contributors utilize gender analysis in reformulations of political economic theory, empirical studies of women's economic activity, and proposals for broadening public policy agendas. Parallel to the feminist critique of neoclassical economics, the development of gender-blind categories in political economy, most especially the category of class, is challenged by feminist political economists. Exposing the limits of gender-blind analyses, they demonstrate the centrality of gender in understanding the functioning of the macroeconomy and labor markets as well as the household.[1] Gender itself is presented as a complex construct. Therefore, these studies emphasize the historical contingency of gender and its reformulation during periods of economic transformation. Yet gender alone is also insufficient. The authors are attentive to gender's intersections with class, race, and sexuality.

The Development of Feminist Political Economy

In the United States, contemporary feminist political economy emerged with the second wave of feminism out of the civil rights and antiwar struggles of the 1960s.[2] Feminists, along with others influenced by this grassroots New Left politics, grappled with their relationship with the intellectual tradition that seemed to provide important insights into the process of social change: Marxism. At a time when the line between academic and political discourse was blurred, political economists were among those most involved in these discussions. The early "Marxist-feminist debates" centered on the appropriateness of certain key Marxist categories in analyzing women's experiences in and out of the labor force. For example, the domestic labor debate posed the question of whether Marx's labor theory of value could be applied to reproductive labor in the home (see, for example, Seecombe 1974; Gardiner 1975; Himmelweit and Mohun 1977; Folbre 1982).[3] Did women's domestic labor create surplus value and, if so, for whom? Similarly, feminist political economists debated whether Marx's concept of a reserve army of labor, that is, a pool of marginally employed workers who were used to pressure wages downward, could be applied to married women (Benston 1969; Bruegel 1979; Humphries 1983; Power 1983).

Implicitly and explicitly, these discussions addressed (1) the role of women's paid and unpaid labor in the perpetuation of capitalism, and (2) the relative primacy of class or gender interests. Who benefited from women's unpaid housework: men as husbands, or capitalists who needed their workers nurtured and sustained? Who benefited from women's low wages and secondary status as workers: husbands or capitalists? In retrospect, these questions appear unnecessarily reductionist. If the classic feminist critique is that many theories attempt to "add women and stir," (Andersen 1988), some early efforts by political economists can be accused of adding *reproduction* and stirring. The domestic labor debate also tended to reify a particular model of gender relations, the male breadwinner and the female homemaker, ignoring historical and cultural variations.[4] Nevertheless, the influence of these early discussions continues to be felt. One lasting effect of these debates was the systematic recognition of the economic contribution of domestic labor in regenerating labor power as a productive input. Challenging the dichotomy between "work" and "leisure," attention was drawn to unpaid work in the home. Methodologically, the Marxist-feminist debates highlighted the systematic nature of women's secondary economic status, rather than suggesting that it resulted from individual choices or prejudices.

Yet many feminists remained dissatisfied with analyses that appeared to subsume women's issues within Marxist analysis. In a series of landmark articles, Heidi Hartmann (1976, 1979, 1981) suggested that reliance upon Marxist categories (such as class, reserve army of labor, and wage labor) could not explain why women were the ones who did domestic labor or occupied low-wage jobs. Marx's analytic categories were gender-blind. Hartmann proposed a systematic analysis of relations between women and men that utilized materialist methodology rather than specific class-based categories. Drawing upon the work of radical feminists, she utilized the concept of *patriarchy* as a social and economic structure that interacted with capitalism. Hartmann's (1979) oft-cited definition of patriarchy as "a set of social relations between men, which have a material base, and which, though hierarchical, establish or create interdependence and solidarity among men that enable them to dominate women" remained influential for a new stream of socialist feminist thought (see, for example, Eisenstein 1979; Sargent 1981).[5]

Socialist feminists viewed capitalism and patriarchy as distinct, autonomous systems, and analyzed the nature of their interaction. Thus, Hartmann proposed a solution to the dilemma (for both neoclassical and traditional Marxist perspectives) of why capitalism had not eradicated labor market inequality: the conscious organization of male workers to maintain relative privilege in the labor market and household. Protective legislation, the family wage, and the development of job segregation were historical examples of institutionalized solutions that enabled mutual accommodation between capitalists and male workers. Sylvia Walby (1986) argued that the contemporary relationship between capitalism and patriarchy has been fraught with tension, as domestic patriarchy competes with public capital for women's labor. Part-time work for married women was one resolution of this tension in the postwar period—a "new form of compromise" (Walby 1986, 207). In her early writing, Zillah Eisenstein (1979) portrayed the process of mutual accommodation as leading to a fusion into one system, which she termed capitalist patriarchy.

Some feminist political economists critiqued socialist feminism (or dual systems theory) for positing capitalism and patriarchy as autonomous systems. Instead, Jane Humphries and Jill Rubery (1984) presented a theory of the "relative autonomy" of *social reproduction,* building on the methodological approach of French Marxist Louis Althusser. They viewed the interaction between production and reproduction as a dialectical and historically contingent process (see also Benería 1979). Utilizing Humphries' previous research on the historical evolution of the family wage, they disputed the tendency of both Marxists and socialist feminists to portray family structure as accommodating the needs of capitalism (see also Humphries 1977a, 1977b). In contrast, Humphries and Rubery asserted that family structure constrained capitalist development. The institution of a family wage for male breadwinners resulted from efforts by working-class families to minimize the family members' involvement in wage labor—which, in the nineteenth century, was more exploitative than emancipatory. Restricting women's labor supply was a deliberate working-class strategy to pressure up the male wage, enabling families to survive on one income.

The strength of this analysis was its focus on the historical process of defining family structure. Humphries (1977a, 1977b) rejected depictions of working-class women as passive victims of patriarchal conspiracies, differentiating the short-term benefits of the family wage from its long-run reinforcement of women's powerlessness. However, Veronica Beechey (1988) has noted that Humphries and Rubery's framework presumed families make rational decisions about labor supply based upon an economic calculus in which there are unitary interests among family members. As Folbre (1993, 328) has pointed out, conflict within households and the collective interests of men and women across classes, in addition to the role of social reproduction, are key feminist insights that need to be incorporated into political economy.

Dual systems approaches, grounded in feminist analysis of patriarchy in the household, continued to face criticism in the 1980s. Perhaps the most inescapable problem confronting socialist feminists was their trivialization of racism and colonialism. Thus, socialist feminists found themselves accused of doing unto people of color as Marxism had done unto them (hooks 1981; Joseph 1981). Further, many of the issues addressed by early feminist political economists generalized from the experiences of white women in industrialized countries. The emphasis on married women's unpaid domestic roles ignored the extensive labor force participation of both married and single black women. Women of color affirmed the importance of families as a source of strength in a racist society (Zinn 1987; Dill 1988). While much of this work on race was authored by sociologists, political economists researching Third World women and the process of economic development emphasized the dynamic nature of the gender division of labor (Benería and Roldán 1987; Sen and Grown 1987).

In the 1988 introduction to her book originally published in 1980, Michèle Barrett reflected on the theoretical challenges that had been posed in the intervening years:

> *Women's Oppression Today* is not a book that was unduly exercised by these questions. In terms of the substantive argument of the book, ... the major problem lies in the treatment (or lack of it) of issues of ethnicity, race and racism. ... More significantly, some of the theoretical formulations of the book I would now regard as ethnocentric: perhaps the strongest example of this would be the analysis of the 'male breadwinner-dependent wife system' which does not in fact apply to the black British population of West Indian origin to the same extent as it does to the dominant white ethnic group. (1988, vii)

Barrett goes on to critique her prior emphasis on "'the family' as the major agency of women's oppression and hence unilaterally oppressive, and the consequent tendency to underplay the role of state coercion and violence" (vii).

From the added dimension of racial analysis came several theoretical advances. Feminists rejected the dichotomy between families as a site of power imbalance (as in the work of Hartmann) and families as a site of resistance to domination (as in the work of Humphries). Variations in household structure and women's economic activity were accentuated (Glenn 1987). The difficulties in generalizing about women's experiences led to philosophical critiques of "women" as an analytical concept (Barrett 1988, vi, on the work of Gayatri Chakravorty Spivak). The multiplicity of women's experiences and prevailing ideologies about gender roles became the starting point of many analyses. As articulated by Sen and Grown (1987, 18–19), "While gender subordination has universal elements, feminism cannot be based on a rigid concept of universality that negates the wide variation in women's experience. There is and must be a diversity of feminisms, responsive to the different needs and concerns of different women, and *defined by them for themselves.*"

Not only did the male breadwinner model of family life exclude the concrete experiences of women of color, it has appeared less and less representative of white family structure. Thus, social, economic, and political changes were increasingly visible in the 1980s. The shift of manufacturing to newly industrialized countries, the expansion of the service and information sectors, global market integration, and the demise of Keynesian welfare states in the West became fodder for new directions in political economy in general, and feminist political economy in particular. The process of restructuring economic, political, and social institutions, historically and contemporarily, became important intellectual projects. As exemplified by the contributions to this volume, the process of constructing and reconstructing gender relations was analyzed as one dimension of this historical change (see also Benería and Stimpson 1987; Jenson, Hagen, and Reddy 1988; Rubery 1988).

The concept of patriarchy became increasingly weighted down by all of this diversity and historical change. It seemed more and more difficult for one system, no matter how broadly defined, to incorporate all of the variations in women's and men's experiences (Lorber 1994, 3). Although patriarchy continues to be used as "a popular shorthand term for systemic male dominance" (Cockburn 1991, 8), *gender* has become a core analytical tool. Drawing upon interdisciplinary work in gender studies, feminist contributions to political economy are grounded in an understanding of the social construction of gender. As elaborated by historian Joan Scott (1988), gender as an analytical category is used to reject biological determinism and the tendency to naturalize a socially constructed gender order. While the gendered division of labor is central to the material dimensions of patriarchy, gender theory has also embraced the importance of culture and ideology as social determinants, not mere "superstructure" (Amott and Matthaei 1991). Since the social construction of gender is located in ideology as well as society's institutional structures, this approach has been termed "post-structuralism."

Post-structural accounts of the interaction of gender, race, and class (and, more recently, sexuality, nation, and age) permit researchers to address complex variations in institutional arrangements and social norms. The recent work of Nancy Folbre (1994) is exemplary of this approach. Folbre conceptualizes gender, race, class, nation, sexuality, and age as "structures of collective constraint" rather than as autonomous systems, in order to highlight the interaction between different dimensions of collective identity and action (53). She also maintains room for a structural definition of patriarchy as "a variable set of structures of collective constraint based on gender, age, and sexual preference (74)." Feminist political economists inspired by radical institutionalism have also contributed to theoretical developments in this area (Peterson and Brown 1994). Because institutionalist theory has traditionally rejected the pursuit of universal laws of causation as well as narrow concepts of materialism, there is an affinity between institutionalism and postmodern gender theory.[6]

One strength of contemporary gender theory lies in its reading of gender in all aspects of social organization. Transcending the identification of gender solely with reproduction and the household, these approaches acknowledge that economic concepts and structures are gendered. For example, nineteenth-century concepts of class were themselves gendered since they often embodied ideas of masculinity, such as physical strength and being a breadwinner (Scott 1988). The organization of this volume reflects this desire to dissolve dichotomies by engendering production, that is, to emphasize the permeance of gender, interacting with class, race, and sexuality, in all aspects of economic life.

Overview of This Volume

The essays in Part I contest conventional depictions of the gendered division of labor between production and reproduction. Eschewing the tendency of earlier writers to universalize women's and men's experiences, these authors explore both the stability and variability of women's economic activity. They also problematize the concept of "family" so often taken as given in both neoclassical and Marxist analysis. Dissolving the dichotomies between work and family, production and reproduction, and gender and class, these contributions deconstruct economic assumptions that mask the complex interaction of gender, race, class, and sexuality. In each of the contributions, the introduction of new categories of analysis (gender, race, class, sexuality) implies that we must actually alter theory itself—or de-universalize what have been taken as economic laws or principles. This not only provides greater insight into the experiences of marginalized groups but also deepens our understanding of economic categories themselves.

Brian Cooper's chapter explores the interrelationship between the ideological developments regarding the family, gender roles, and political economy in England during the early nineteenth century. Popular writings on political economy during this period were self-conscious exercises in social construction, designed to create appropriate economic subjects differentiated by gender, class, and race. For the middle class, these texts simultaneously constructed the concepts of rational economic man and domestic woman as virtuous economic agents. Some writers also attempted to "educate" the working class in the premises of political economy, especially in reaction to the growth of radical presses. Cooper depicts this period as a time of flux and transition, with social stability threatened by two anarchic principles: money and desire. In the emerging commercial economy, money was displacing property as the source of economic status; alienability of property required proper economic behavior if social stability was to be maintained. The marriage market, traditionally a means of stabilizing property relations, was destabilized by desire. As in the world of Jane Austen's novels, virtuous (heterosexual) love combining "sense" and "sensibility" was part of the solution. Thus, domestic economy and political economy were intertwined.

The focal point of Cooper's analysis is a contrast between two examples of these popular writings, both of which draw upon the public's interest in utopian travel tales, in the tradition of Daniel Defoe's 1719 novel, *The Life and Adventures of Robinson Crusoe*. Over a century later, two English writers, Harriet Martineau and Jane Haldiman Marcet, present contrasting shipwreck tales that provide alternative models for solving the "family troubles" of the early nineteenth century. Martineau's *Life in the Wilds* (1832) imagines a utopia based upon communal property and housework, however one with the sexual division of labor left relatively intact. Marcet's "The Three Giants" (1833) naturalizes an extensive division of labor, both within individual households and the community at large. The first story acknowledges the productive contribution of household labor, while the latter divorces the women in the household from the (male) economic subjects of the productive economy. Cooper argues that these tales illustrate the instability of the categories of "family" and "household" and the process of defining gender roles.

A different angle on this same historical period is provided by Margaret Coleman's empirical study of women's paid labor in the industrializing Massachusetts economy. Shifting the focus from middle class to working class, Coleman contrasts the gender ideology of "woman as homemaker" with evidence of women's extensive labor force participation. Her empirical estimate that 45 percent of Massachusetts women participated in nonagricultural paid labor in 1833 contributes to an important literature demonstrating the centrality of women's paid work to early capitalist development. This research is divided between those, such as Coleman and Christine Bose (1987), who stress the constancy of women's labor force participation and advocates of the "U" hypothesis who argue that married (white) women's labor force participation declined in the late nineteenth century before increasing in the twentieth century (see Scott and Tilly 1975; Goldin 1990; Horrell and Humphries 1995; as well as Mutari and Figart in this volume). Following Bose, Coleman focuses on the invisibility of women's work in rural and informal labor markets, leading to an undercount of women's paid employment.

Coleman's research contributes to dissolving dichotomies by grounding her analysis of women's labor supply in the social construction of labor as well as reproduction. The meaning of wage labor in the early days of the U.S. republic has to be understood in a historical context where most manual labor was either indented or enslaved. As in Cooper's analysis of England during the same period, money destabilized the existing social order. As barter markets were replaced by a cash economy and rural debt increased, women's wage labor was a way to reconcile households' desire for currency with the devaluation of wage labor. Ideology, not material incentives, was used to increase women's labor supply.

The implication of both of these analyses (as well as the chapter by Ann Davis) is the historical contingency of the nuclear family based upon a male breadwinner and a full-time female homemaker. M.V. Lee Badgett also points to the inadequacy of economic models and theories that assume a universal family form. In so doing, she evaluates neoclassical models of the family, as well as many radical, institutionalist, and feminist analyses. Asserting that gender and sexuality are analytically separable though empirically intertwined, Badgett critiques attempts to subsume lesbian, gay, and bisexual relationships into gender-based analyses. Instead, she challenges feminist economists to explore the diversity of family forms.

This chapter is representative of the very recent emergence of sexuality as a topic within political economy (see also Badgett and Williams 1992; Anderson 1993; Matthaei 1995). As with early feminist attempts to analyze the nuclear family, the economics of sexuality has challenged conventional boundaries of economic discourse. Badgett maintains that "expanding the economic theory of the family should involve *analyzing* that which is normally *taken as given* in economic models, i.e., the range of functions performed by families, the legally and culturally sanctioned idea of what constitutes a family, and the roles of individuals within the family." She notes that society is once again in a historical period where cultural definitions of and public policy toward the institution of family are in flux; heterosexual and lesbian feminists need to work together to reinvent family.

The final two chapters in Part I draw upon tools within Marxian political economy while integrating contemporary theoretical concerns. While both place issues of social reproduction at the heart of their analyses, they come to radically different conclusions regarding the usefulness of the labor theory of value and the structural versus post-structural frameworks. Teresa Brennan boldly rejects the contention that labor is the sole source of value. For Brennan, energy is the resource that transforms matter in production; nature, as well as humans, is a source of energy. Within her revised, environmentally sensitive value theory, controlling the time it takes to reproduce various sources of energy is key to generating profits.

Brennan's structural connection between race, gender, and class lies in the distinctive relationship of women and of particular racial/ethnic groups to the process of reproduction. Women have been charged with responsibility for generational reproduction of the labor force, while migrating racial and ethnic groups provide an alternative means of replenishing the labor supply. Migration provides a shorter time line for the reproduction of labor as a source of energy than biological reproduction. However, one conclusion Brennan draws is that both groups are impoverished precisely to minimize the cost of reproduction.

In contrast, Ann Davis notes that Marx's own critique of political economy can incorporate women's domestic activity in the reproduction of labor power into the circuit of production. Theoretically, she moves beyond the duality of capitalism as an economic system and patriarchy as a system of gender relations (dual systems theory) to acknowledge instead how capitalism integrates the ideology of women's labor at home into the logic of economic development. To undertake her analysis, Davis must also therefore reject the supremacy and separation of the material base of the economy from the ideological superstructure. Drawing upon the insights of post-structuralism, she returns to the theme of families in flux.

Presenting a historical periodization of domestic ideology and gender roles, Davis argues that there is a coincidence between major shifts in the social construction of gender and substantive economic dislocations. When capitalist economies undergo structural transformation, the ideological drive to sustain institutional norms in the home helps to control the contradictory effects of the market's hegemony over most aspects of capitalist life. Thus, the appearance of a separation between the economy and the household, and the gender ideology of separate spheres, can be traced to the rise of capitalism and the formation of a working class in the United States and Great Britain. Echoing Cooper, she finds that middle-class women played an active role in articulating and disseminating gender ideology. Providing a transition to Part II, Davis suggests that economic periodizations such as those found in the social structure of accumulation literature need to be attentive to changes in domestic ideology and household forms.

The historical analyses in Part I focus on the evolution of the ideology of separate spheres despite women's extensive paid and unpaid contributions to economic production. The authors in Part II provide further evidence of the centrality of women's paid labor in the so-called "advanced" industrial economies of the late twentieth century. In particular, these studies substantively contribute to recent research on the gendered aspects of employer strategies for restoring profitability during economic restructuring (Jenson, Hagen, and Reddy 1988; Rubery 1988; Bakker 1994, 1996). Macroeconomic stability and business profitability are dependent upon the gendered and racialized nature of low-wage labor markets; attention to gender and race yields solid empirical work. These investigations indicate that a complete understanding of gendered economic subjects necessitates moving beyond the supply side and the domestic division of labor; production is gendered by managerial strategies and institutional arrangements embedded in the structure of employment.

Opening Part II, Ellen Mutari and Deborah Figart explore the transition from the postwar gender order—based upon the extension of the male breadwinner model into the white working class—to an emerging regime based upon intensified feminization of employment. The theoretical context for their discussion is the contention that economic restructuring is a gendered process. For example, the pursuit of flexible employment, wages, and working conditions transforms jobs from "male" (stable employment with promotion opportunities and a family wage) to "female" (low-wage, dead-end, contingent labor). Social structure of accumulation and regulation views of contemporary restructuring have neglected this dimension of the institutional arrangements supporting accumulation.

Providing evidence that gender relations are in a period of redefinition, Mutari and Figart focus on the movement to raise wages for female-dominated occupations as a potential site of contradiction among conservatives and thus a significant arena for progressive economic and social change. Pay equity directly challenges feminization strategies predicated on the flexibility of women's low-wage labor, as revealed by a discourse analysis of the arguments against comparable worth. Right-wing ideology is caught between supporting the male breadwinner model and defending the ability of market forces to accommodate the career aspirations of professional women. The reality of working women's complex relationship to their jobs is rendered invisible. The authors advocate a counterdiscourse that links pay equity to a redefinition of gender roles and a broad living wage movement.

The gender implications of contemporary flexibility strategies are also the subject of David Kucera's study of labor market flexibility in Japan and the former West Germany. According to flexibility advocates, Europe's relatively high unemployment is due to a lack of labor market flexibility. In contrast, the United States and Japan have maintained macroeconomic stability by pursuing alternative flexibility strategies; Japanese companies rely upon flexible production techniques (such as just-in-time manufacturing) while U.S. businesses have sought flexibility in employment relationships by varying hours of work and lowering wages. Kucera critiques this overly simplistic dichotomy, establishing that the Japanese economy is dependent upon the flexible employment of women workers to maintain the appearance of low unemployment.

Because most studies exploring Japan's relatively low unemployment rates have focused on the experience of male workers, they have missed the role played by women workers in buffering the impacts of macroeconomic instability. Kucera's work exposes the limitations of gender-blind research and reinforces the need to disaggregate data. Kucera differentiates the periods before and after 1973, frequently viewed as a turning point between the postwar period of stable accumulation and declining global profitability (Kotz, McDonough, and Reich 1994). He finds increased employment volatility for Japanese women in the post-1973 period, providing further evidence of the gendered impact of contemporary flexibility strategies.

Recent research suggests that the impact of gendered restructuring strategies has been to narrow gender-based wage differentials through a process of "harmonizing down" (see Armstrong 1996). At the same time, class and racial differences between women have intensified (Wagman and Folbre 1988; Badgett and Williams 1994). Marilyn Power and Sam Rosenberg focus on differences in opportunities for occupational mobility among young black and white women working in service sector jobs. They find that service occupations provide a temporary means of support for young white women who frequently move on to professional and technical occupations after pursuing additional education. Black women are more likely to stay in service work; however, when they exit the job category it is more often for blue collar occupations.

Rather than treating race, class, and gender as independent variables, Power and Rosenberg's methodology enables them to focus on the complexity of the interaction of these forces in women's employment life stories. This is especially evident in their comparison of the career paths of white and black domestic workers and waitresses. Because of the centrality of feminized and racialized service work in the deindustrializing U.S. economy, Power and Rosenberg's research provides important insights into employment prospects in the era of flexibility. While some workers will be able to take advantage of flexible employment relations to attain greater economic security, many women will face barriers to career mobility. Family class background and early childbearing, as well as racial discrimination, increase these obstacles.

Heather Boushey continues this inquiry into low-wage labor markets by examining the relationship between government poverty policies and employment discrimination. Synthesizing two research streams—Marxian theories of labor market discrimination and historical analyses of the development of poor relief—Boushey concludes that both the labor market and relief programs have reinforced the gendered and racialized character of low-wage labor markets. In fact, the interaction of miserly welfare allocations and low wages has enabled employers to maintain women, especially women of color, as a flexible labor supply.

Boushey introduces the state and public policy formation as yet another site for the institutionalization of gender and race inequality. Her historical analysis of the 1935 passage of Aid to Dependent Children (later renamed Aid to Families with Dependent Children) as part of the Social Security Act indicates how gender ideology is itself racialized. A stated goal of the program was maintenance of the domestic code by enabling "deserving" mothers, that is, widows and those abandoned by their husbands, to be full-time homemakers. Yet, by deliberately excluding minority-concentrated occupations at the behest of Southern employers and politicians, women of color were excluded from the dominant gender order. Gender was differently constructed by race; white women were homemakers while women of color were workers. The absolute starkness of this contrast can be seen by noting that domestic service was one of the occupations excluded under the original Social Security Act, illustrating that the racial division of labor between women centers on paid versus unpaid reproductive labor (Glenn 1992).

Part II ends by returning to a discussion of pay equity as a strategy for addressing some of the worst effects of contemporary economic restructuring. Why aren't political economists talking more about pay equity? Is it because it does not challenge hierarchies within the labor market and in the capitalist economy? Deborah Figart and June Lapidus show otherwise. The authors find that the benefits of implementing a comparable worth policy nationwide are far greater than previously imagined. By calculating five indexes of inequality, they find that comparable worth would decrease overall earnings inequality, inequality between women and men, and inequality among women. The decline in inequality holds across choice of index. Decomposing the overall inequality, as the authors do, leads to better-informed policy decisions.

The codetermination of gender and class are hammered home in this study. Figart and Lapidus demonstrate that inequality is not simply an aggregate phenomenon, but one that plays out in terms of gender. The studies by Kucera and Boushey warn us that gender-blind policy may indeed be gendered in its impact, while the lesson of Figart and Lapidus's work is that gender-targeted policy can alleviate problems that are commonly viewed as gender-neutral. Thus, their chapter exemplifies how the incorporation of gender reinvents the purpose and effect of economic policy.

In addition to refining theory, feminist political economy leads to prescriptive visions for public policy and social change. Not only do the theoretical models and assumptions of neoclassical economics need to be challenged, but so do current economic institutions and structures. It is not only economists' ideas about how market economies operate but the actual historical development of market systems that are implicated in the contemporary gender order.

Notes

1. Both traditional Marxist and neoclassical theory have been used to argue that the emergence of capitalism and the rationality of market relations tend to undermine the social and cultural basis of patriarchy. Both views tend toward reductionism (see Folbre 1994). For a debate over the attributes of markets and alternative feminist perspectives on markets, see *Feminist Economics* 2, 1 (Spring 1996).

2. The following represents one perspective on the evolution of feminist political economy, admittedly focused on English-language writings from the United States and Great Britain—not all of them by economists.

3. Marx had developed the labor theory of value into an analytical tool for defining exploitation. The labor theory of value answers the question posed by the circuit of capital: Why does the end result of the production process have greater exchange value than the sum of the value of its inputs? While modern economics texts attribute the origin of profits to entrepreneurship, Marx, like Adam Smith before him, believed only labor could create value. However, the wage, set through a socially contingent process, is less than the value created by the worker. Capitalists are only able to extract this surplus value because the historical transition to capitalism has rendered workers relatively powerless.

4. An exception to this would be historical debates about the role of class and gender interests in the emergence of the family wage as ideology and economic policy (see, for example, Humphries 1977a, 1977b; Hartmann and Markusen 1980; Sen 1980; May 1982; Lewis 1984).

5. While the distinction between Marxist feminists and socialist feminists has always been in the eye of beholder, one way to differentiate them is to rely upon Hartmann's differentiation between Marxist categories and Marxist method. Thus, the term Marxist feminist would apply to those who analyze women's experience using categories developed within Marxist theory, while socialist feminists rely more generally upon historical materialist methodology.

6. Postmodernism, a broader label for an intellectual perspective that challenges the authenticity of universalizations, provided a rubric for incorporating many of these insights. Developed primarily outside the economics discipline, postmodernism emphasizes that power is constructed through language and knowledge (Nicholson 1990; Bryson 1992).

Part I

Dissolving Dichotomies

New Approaches to Social Reproduction and Labor Supply

2

Family Troubles

Brian Cooper

In the mid-seventeenth century a young middle-class Englishman goes to sea against his parents' wishes. Seized off the coast of North Africa, he endures slavery, escapes, and makes his way by boat along the west coast of Africa accompanied by a young boy. Rescued by Europeans, they set forth to Brazil where he sells the boy and begins a profitable new life as a plantation owner. Ever restless, he joins neighboring plantation owners in outfitting a trading and slaving vessel bound for Africa. The boat is shipwrecked on the reefs of an uninhabited desert isle off the coast of South America, with our Englishman the sole survivor. Utilizing his wits, his religious faith, and material salvaged from the wreck, he manages to impose a one-man civilization on the island for twenty-six years. His isolation from human companionship is broken when he rescues and civilizes a young cannibal. After three years together they escape to Europe where he finds his Brazilian property has made him wealthy. Back in England, he assumes the settled life of a family man but, as the narrative ends, he is off adventuring again.

Such is the first part of the novel *The Life and Adventures of Robinson Crusoe* (1719) by Daniel Defoe. I address the following question: How did Crusoe come to represent for economists an educational tool par excellence, the archetypal rational economic individual? In fact, writers on economics did not immediately and universally recognize Crusoe as "economic man" (White 1987). The economists' Crusoe is characterized by a set of absences—a lack of social relations and history—that are less the product of the novel than of elisions in economists' usages of Crusoe only since the 1870s. Rather, the economic calculations of the fictional Crusoe are imbricated in systems of racial, sexual, and colonial domination (Grappard 1995).

The demurral of Maria Edgeworth, a prominent writer of fiction and of works on education and economics at the turn of the nineteenth century, on the educational value of travel and voyage literature, of which *Robinson Crusoe* is a part, is instructive on this point.[1] For Edgeworth, teaching children (and adults) economy and prudence necessitated a wise choice in reading material. Edgeworth cast doubt on the fitness of travel and adventure literature as an example for children to imitate on two points that we can easily apply to *Robinson Crusoe:* first, adventures like Crusoe's represent a temperament ill-suited to teaching the "sober perseverance necessary to success"; and, second, Crusoe's ongoing lack of foresight bears little in common with the reckonings of an ideal "rational probability of success," the idea of which Edgeworth elsewhere attributes to Adam Smith (1811: v. 1, 431).

These criticisms remind us of the commonplace that economists not only seek to describe the world, but also seek to make the world (and its economic agents, real or fictional) fit their descriptions. Rewrites of *Robinson Crusoe* composed in the 1830s by two English writers—*Life in the Wilds* (1832) by Harriet Martineau (1802–76) and "The Three Giants" (1833) by Jane Haldiman Marcet (1769–1858)—illustrate this process. These two Robinsonades—a literature not restricted to imitations of *Robinson Crusoe* but including voyage and shipwreck narratives, voyages to isolated lands, and more generally, narratives on colonial settlements that depicted various stages of social development (Gove 1941; White 1987)—make Crusoe safe for economics and economics safe for children, and, critically, the masses. Both tales thread the doctrines of political economy into a standard theme of the Robinsonades, to wit, a shipwreck or some other disaster offers the European survivors an opportunity to build a new society. Both tales echo Adam Smith's concerns over the presence of money as a veil to the true perception of value, and the claim that the workings of the division of labor constitutes the engine of social progress.

These stories reflect as well the acknowledgment in the 1820s and 1830s among political economists and their supporters of the value of mass education in the doctrines of political economy. Education would serve the end of creating better economic subjects, and would consequently ease the acceptance and operation of political economists' policy proposals. Presumably, once knowing the principles of economics, a reader or listener could match her or his behavior to the ideal examples on the written page, thus hastening the day when the natural laws of political economy would hold sway.

I maintain these tales turned *Robinson Crusoe* into literature that was useful precisely to the extent that they did not glorify individuals abstracted from social relations. Instead, they embed the story of Crusoe in a web of family, class, and racial relations. Both stories reimagine the nation as a harmonious community, a set of neatly meshed and orderly family relations, free from the class and party divisions wracking England at the beginning of the 1830s.[2] Both confront the Malthusian anxiety over the threat of overpopulation that shaped much of the debates over political economy and public policy in England in the first half of the nineteenth century. By making a virtue of travel, in the form of emigration, the fictional utopian communities depict successful resolutions to the putative collective lack of foresight that caused the Malthusian problem of numbers.

The stories imagine the race of English spreading itself over the globe, occupying empty but fertile colonial spaces, and, in the process of solving the Malthusian population dilemma, becoming a new race. Here, we must understand that until at least the 1860s, most English considered race an environmental concept, denoting a people of a particular time and place or even of a particular occupation (Stocking 1987). A vision of surplus population occupying empty colonial spaces was one held by many anti-Malthusians as well. G. Poulett Scrope, a contemporary essayist on political economy who was corrosively critical of Martineau's Malthusianism in general and dismissive of the literary and educational value of *Life in the Wilds* in particular (Scrope 1833), nonetheless wholeheartedly endorsed the idea of emigration as a means to drain off excess population. Scrope relates with wonder travelers' accounts of the Americas and Australia, lands of "superabundance" where the "very reverse of the Malthusian axiom prevails," where "meat becomes a drug," and where, in places, food was so plentiful that livestock was butchered, not for meat, but for hides, skins, tallow, and even as fuel for limekilns (Scrope 1831, 102).

What these utopian visions overlooked, as the sources of class conflict drain off in the tide of emigration, of course, is any reference to the fate of native populations and other colonial powers that come into contact with English colonists; others are simply pushed to the margins. Thus the problems raised by emigration as a solution to the poverty of the working classes reduce, at the stroke of a pen, to quibbles over the will and the means to emigrate.

If both stories solve the population problem by conjuring a stream of emigrants, they do so by invoking radically different conceptions of family and the relationship of "domestic woman" to "economic man." Proper family behavior as exhibited by these two ideals formed the other axis of Malthusian solutions to population pressures. *Life in the Wilds* stresses the operation of Malthusian moral restraint through delayed marriage. Only when the settlers establish self-sufficiency can a young, hard-working couple marry. "The Three Giants," on the other hand, emphasizes a less controversial and more positive tenet of later Malthusian doctrines: the pressures of feeding a family may act as a spur to individual initiative. *Life in the*

Wilds portrays a cooperative community where work is distributed equally according to socially agreed-upon conventions. "The Three Giants," on the other hand, draws the line for social responsibility almost exclusively around the nuclear family, a natural, hence unexamined category in the story. Further, where in *Life in the Wilds* household labor is shared communally, without a strict division of labor by sex, and there is no economic disadvantage in terms of knowledge or rewards entailed by the division of labor, in "The Three Giants" the sexual division of labor ensures less than full economic subjectivity for women.

Family Troubles

This is one sense in which the tales produce "family troubles" for economics. The stories indicate the myriad possibilities publicly discussed in the 1830s for classifying and analyzing the categories family and household, within and beyond that of the prudent heterosexual couple espoused by Thomas Malthus. Given the erosion of eighteenth-century status distinctions that had identified "family" with "blood," single individuals, like Crusoe, could constitute a "family"; cooperative schemes, such as those utopian communities supported by William Owen, could order relations as an "extended family"; and the entire English nation could be identified, as in *Life in the Wilds,* as "that larger family." If the alternative textual conceptions of the economic roles of men and women lay open to widely different interpretations, so too did the categories "family" and "household."

The stories signify "family troubles" in a more obvious yet less literal sense. They are fictions meant to illustrate economic truths. They blur the boundaries that established separate literatures for women and men in this period. They certainly do conform to prevailing ideologies that defined women's roles as educators and as inculcators of virtue. Yet they also exploited the fact that such a definition of women's roles allowed women's sphere to be limitless, and could sanction for women constrained yet visibly public roles previously reserved for men. The tales thus had the paradoxical effect of strengthening and breaching the wall of separate spheres.

The stories also attest to the fact that the term "science" in English had not yet attained by the 1830s the distinct and separate status we understand today, but was still considered a branch of literature (Williams 1987, 10–11). It is true that by the 1830s, economics had begun to carve out its own discursive space, organized roughly around the analysis of wealth, production, consumption, and distribution, apparently lacking in moral considerations, and expressly opposed to fictions (Dentith 1983). Critiques of utilitarianism such as that by Dickens in *Hard Times* are familiar grist for the mill for historians (Ryan 1981). But I believe we should extend the scope of our discussion of economics as rhetoric, discourse, or narrative (McCloskey 1985; Klamer 1988; Strassmann 1993) to literatures that embrace alternative economic visions in this period. Malthusian economics especially can be viewed as sharing a moral object, the desire to temper passion by reason, with discourses such as educational treatises, conduct books, and fictions such as polite novels and travel literature. A principal purpose of Malthusian economics, then, was to shape men, women, and children into virtuous beings by employing a vocabulary, in common with these other discourses, of prudence, thrift, and sobriety (Waterman 1991; Hilton 1988).

The stories of Martineau and Marcet, designed to influence individual conduct and public policy, employ devices from discourses not usually considered, from the vantage point of late-twentieth-century economics, to constitute part of the family of economics. Part of my aim is to take the economics of these other discourses seriously. The result of such a repositioning of the discourse of classical political economy is not only to broaden but to question the boundaries of economics past and present (Amariglio, Resnick, and Wolff 1990). It is not just economists but economic agents who seek to describe the world and make it fit their descriptions. And they often do so in explicit acknowledgment of the public posturings of economists. As economists seek to describe, explain, and educate in order to remake the world, they may direct their writings principally toward policymakers, but they ignore the economics of their subjects at their peril.

The remainder of this essay places the rage for instruction in political economy, considered as a moral science, in the context of the dramatic growth in the publication of educational tracts in the beginning decades of the nineteenth century in England (Brantlinger 1977, Ch. 1). I then look at the commentary on domestic woman and economic man in conduct books and works on education. In terms of public policy, the marriage of these two ideal individuals, by balancing passions and interests through the concept of "virtuous love," would solve two problems: the alienability of capital, and the threat of overpopulation.

The final section places the rereadings of Crusoe by Martineau and Marcet in the context of virtuous love and more general concerns over proper economic behavior and the determination of economic value, as expressed by Adam Smith and Thomas Malthus. The stories illustrate that, just as is the category economics, classifications such as race, gender, and class are not immutable but constructed (Williams 1991, 10–11). While both Martineau and Marcet bring domestic woman into the realm of economic man and outfit their ideal marriages with the equipage of what

Foucault dubbed the "Malthusian couple" (Foucault 1990, 105)—each is sober, industrious, and prudent—they sanction quite different behavior within this category. Where Marcet portrays a new world in which women remain dependent upon men, Martineau imagines reasoned economic behavior and economic independence and equality for women and men. And where Martineau's utopia satisfies all the criteria for a radical reimagining of society (cooperative economic relations and the absence of ranks), Marcet confines her text to a much less radical but still fantastic vision of a society that preserves economic difference between men and between husbands and wives, yet ensures economic prosperity for all.

(Virtuous) Love and Property

In the emerging commercial society of eighteenth-century England the bases of marriage, love, and money were seen as anarchic principles. Simultaneously universal and random, love and money attach themselves willy-nilly to any person or object. Each retains the capacity to level ranks and upset the status quo. In the mid-eighteenth century, prior to the Malthusian anxiety over the threat of working-class overpopulation, efforts to reconcile love and money focused on upper-class concerns over the possibility of (upper-class) underpopulation. Family management, particularly proper marriage matches and strict legal provisions on the settlement of property, were designed to ensure stability of generations, and the stability of property over generations.

Yet the certainty of the alienable nature of capital, combined with the uncertain and invisible movements of love, made reliance on the marriage market as a means to stabilize property a risky strategy. In the first half of the eighteenth century, the proliferation of cases of dubious or secret marriages, as well as apparent bigamy—all considered "clandestine" marriages—made uncertain the legal and morally right distribution of property between generations. For the landed gentry such uncertainty in family status jeopardized the guarantor of autonomous political participation. The increase in bachelordom among the landed gentry added to the sense of crisis among the ruling classes (Stone 1977, 43–44; Stone and Stone 1984, 276–77). The nineteenth-century Malthusian debates completely reformulated the locus and mathematics of this class anxiety. Rather than too few of the aristocracy reproducing, the fear was that the unchecked reproduction of the lower classes would ultimately eat up England's productive capital in poor relief expenditures. But in both cases stabilizing family in order to stabilize population (or a specific portion of it) and capital, was seen as vital to the health of the social state.

The concept of virtuous love was the product of much political and cultural work of the second half of the eighteenth century that sought to buttress the upper-class family against the destabilizing tendencies of love and money. This theme underscored, for instance, the parliamentary debate over Lord Hardwicke's Marriage Act (1753), where "considerations of love and marriage were embedded in those of money and property"[3] (Harth 1988, 133). The act introduced state recognition of marriages, and the provisions form the basis for state regulation of marriages to the present day (Barker 1978; Harrison and Mort 1980). By codifying procedures to be met for state recognition of marriage and penalties for failure to adhere to the letter of the law, supporters of the act sought to control or limit the circulation of capital by limiting the circulation of love to that designated "virtuous love."

What, exactly, is virtuous love? Virtuous love is love married to prudence. Such a combination allowed virtue and sentiment to tame the passions and establish an equilibrium between the interests of love and the interests of money. Time and visibility were the critical factor in taming desires that might otherwise lead one to rush headlong into marriage. The Earl of Hillsborough avowed that the month-long waiting period included in the act's provisions would, as a brake on the passions, facilitate prudential love, "a sedate and fixed love ... founded upon judgment and discretion." The Earl deemed the alternative—"a sudden flash of passion which dazzles the understanding, but is in a moment extinguished"—a faulty and impermanent foundation for marriage. Passage of the act, by making public all marriages and voiding clandestine ones, would, supporters maintained, ensure the stability of the nuclear family, and the certainty and legitimacy of inheritances. The nuclear family, with "mutual love ... fixed upon a solid foundation" of time, both regulates and is an outcome of the regulation of sexual desire and money (cols. 62–63).

Key components of the struggle to regulate sexual desire and the desire for property through "virtuous love" were the retention of male prerogatives over property and the economic dependence of women. This was reinforced in the eighteenth century by the developing body of property law, which included the increased use of strict settlement. Strict settlement, a provision to set aside capital to guarantee sums for younger children, could plausibly be seen as a device to strengthen primogeniture by limiting the other heirs' interest in the eldest son's property rights. In fact, in the mid-eighteenth century, when contract law was briefly applied to women's rights to own and dispose property, the results were socially intolerable. Courts quickly reverted to patriarchal legal structures, depriving married women of full ownership of property (Staves 1990).

The concept of virtuous love also received wide circulation through cultural productions, such as Samuel Richardson's *Pamela* (1740), one of the claimants to the title of the first English novel. The novel, so popular it set off a Pamela vogue, arose out of Richardson's efforts to compose a manuscript that would combine instruction on the forms and styles of letters with prescriptions for individual conduct. It details the efforts of Pamela, a servant girl of fifteen, to fend off her master's attempts to seduce her. Pamela's defense of her virtue ultimately wears down and transforms her master, Mr B, and he eventually marries her; thus, Pamela gets to keep her virtue and get the gold. Though the marriage of Pamela and Mr B in the novel reasserts women's economic vulnerability, what contemporary readers found most extraordinary was the manner in which *Pamela* apparently inaugurated a new model of household behavior, one where female virtue tames sexual passion rather than being overwhelmed by an assertion of aristocratic privilege (Armstrong 1987; Harth 1988).

The idealization of Pamela did not go uncontested. The concept of virtuous love as a brake on unions founded upon either unbridled passion or mere interest found its most passionate critic in Henry Fielding, who thought the proposition that Pamela could fend off Mr B's advances by dint of mere virtue alone absurd enough to publish two novels, including the parody *Shamela* (1741). Despite Fielding's efforts to fashion an aristocratic alternative, however, Richardson's model of the novel triumphed.

The delaying stratagems of Pamela and the month-long waiting period legislated by the 1753 Marriage Act, a period designed to allow the operation of prudent reflection, appear as precursors, writ small, of the years-long delays in marriage advocated by Malthus in his doctrine of moral restraint. Malthus, in fact, did weigh in on the debate over the management of desire through virtuous love. In the first edition of *An Essay on Population* (1798), Malthus, despite praising its pleasures (Ch. 11, para. 1), not surprisingly expresses doubts that virtuous love serves the purpose of forestalling unhappy and unfortunate marriages. The realization of the loss of rank and prestige that would ensue for both man and woman upon the formation of a family would prevent a "man of liberal education, but with an income only just sufficient to enable him to associate in the rank of gentlemen ... from following the bent of his inclinations in an early attachment." Yet Malthus concludes that "others, guided either by a stronger passion, or a weaker judgment, break through these restraints, and it would be hard indeed, if the gratification of so delightful a passion as virtuous love did not sometimes more than counterbalance all its attendant evils. But I fear it must be owned, that the more general consequences of such marriages, are rather calculated to justify than to repress the forebodings of the prudent" (1798, Ch. 4, para. 10–11). Malthus attributes to virtuous love the exact opposite characteristic its supporters had given it: it is imprudent.

In the 1803 and the final (1826) editions, however, Malthus seeks to wed the concept of virtuous love to moral restraint. He writes: "After the desire for food, the most powerful and general of our desires is the passion between the sexes, taken in an enlarged sense. Of the happiness spread over human life by this passion, very few are unconscious. Virtuous love, exalted by friendship, seems to be that sort of mixture of sensual and intellectual enjoyment, particularly suited to the nature of man, and most powerfully calculated to awaken the sympathies of the soul, and produce the most exquisite of gratifications" (Book IV, Ch. 1, para. 10). That Malthus initially held virtuous love to be no virtue, and then recanted, calling it a proper mixture of the "sensual and [the] intellectual," indicates just how unstable this stabilizing concept was. What is important here is not whether but how the concept worked. It allows us to position economics as part of a debate that involved texts as various as the record of legislative efforts to regulate marriage, the "first" English novel, and, as we shall see next in considering conduct books, the role of domestic woman as a complement to economic man. These were ideal, and yes, virtuous, economic agents who could successfully manage the bodily desires that so preoccupied Malthus and his popularizers, Martineau and Marcet.

Domestic Woman and Economic Man

Did *Pamela* "[sever] the language of kinship from that of political relations, producing a culture divided into the respective domains of domestic woman and economic man" (Armstrong 1987, 60)? An examination of the role that classical political economy plays in the process of creating subjects runs into the problem that economists had very little to say on the position of women. These textual absences place me in the position of asserting, like a good deconstructive critic, that political economists' silence about the family speaks volumes. Eighteenth- and nineteenth-century conduct books and domestic fiction help fill in the picture of "domestic woman." Combining these with texts in the emerging social sciences allows us to flesh out more fully the processes by which each helps establish identities and subjectivities. These texts establish protocols defining and prescribing individual conduct for women and men. They do so in order to uncover and construct the laws regulating the organization and functioning of individuals within society.

Home, women's sphere, defined by the ideologies of domestic spheres and social paternalism (Davidoff and Hall 1987, Ch. 3), was, theoretically, separate, and identified with different written forms of representation than political economy. Nonetheless, it was not really materially separate, in terms of production and consumption, from the sphere of man, the market.

Women and men played a role in both spheres by contributing and managing resources. Women's financial resources and management skills in husbanding men's income were crucial elements in both establishing the necessary capital for businesses and maintaining middle-class households in nineteenth-century England (Davidoff and Hall 1987).

Indicative of this permeability, Martineau, as already noted, directly compares political economy to domestic economy in the Preface to *Illustrations of Political Economy* when she describes the evolution of an understanding of political economy as not quite equivalent to household economy. But this is a commonplace. James Mill, for example, opens the third edition of *Elements of Political Economy* (1826) by citing the analogy between domestic economy and economy: "Political Economy is to the State, what domestic economy is to the family." The metaphorical link between the two spheres derives, of course, from the lexical connection between the discourses of domestic and political economy. The ancient Greek root for "economics," *oikonomos,* meaning "household management," which applied to both family and national budgets, provides a direct linguistic link between the domestic and political economies.

For Aristotle, the household consisted of servants and the biological family. Household also constituted the circuit of production and consumption, and the natural limit to exchange. The limits to the natural, Aristotelian household immediately suggest that the link between household management and economics provides two analytical problems for political economy in this period. The first lies in specifying the relationship between an individualistic ethos of "economic man" and that of the household unit. The second lies in specifying the relationship between family and economy. The notion of family as problematic analogy for society reaffirms the importance of family to social reproduction, and its connection, through biological reproduction, to the determination of the wealth of nations. This link is not simply metaphorical, an artifact of language, but empirical and theoretical. In the first half of the nineteenth century, demographic statistics offered the best evidence for evaluating the relative progress, stagnation, or retrogression of nations. On the theoretical side, the causal determinants of these demographic statistics were the source of much speculation. The determinants were as much behavioral as physical: good (bad) families aggregated up to strong (weak) nations.

Despite these links between domestic economy and political economy, political economists up to the publication of John Stuart Mill's *The Subjection of Women* (1869) rarely had anything to say about the place of women in market society, or the gendered aspects of work, family, and the discursive forms meant to represent them. The analogy between political and domestic economy is made then dropped. Malthus, for example, sought to define changes in population not in terms of the political economy of the interactions within the family, but in terms of family formation as a manifestation of "man's compound nature," the mind–body or reason–passion split. And population analysis is most definitely about "man." In the first edition of *Essay,* women's bodies, if present at all, constitute passive, dependent vessels. Even working-class women's bodies only come into being after the birth of a child, and then as absent maternal presences. Obviously this represents an idealization: women's bodies certainly were evident in real life. The writings of English political economists implicitly (by omission) devalue the economic presence of women.

Conduct books, and polite novels, by way of contrast, explicitly prescribe behavior. These forms establish male and female identity by a process that sublimates desire, and that smooths, privatizes, and internalizes the conflicts of the marketplace, the social contract, by displacing them onto the sexual contract, that is, the marriage market, and in the details of household management (Armstrong 1987, Ch. 1 and 2; Pateman 1988). These forms of writing represented the ideals of a virtuous marriage and well-kept household as objects within the reach of any man or woman. Conduct books for the upper classes became widely popular during the beginning of the eighteenth century, a period in which the increasing anonymity of mercantile transactions contributed to the shattering of fixed social distinctions based on hereditary status (these included distinctions of both dress and comportment, such as Elizabethan sumptuary codes, for example), and to the rise of economic distinctions (Earle 1989, Ch. 1). Proper conduct signified good moral standing, and was increasingly relied upon to establish trust in the absence of trustworthy personal knowledge.

Conduct books written mainly by and for middle-class women became a significant literary genre in the late eighteenth and early nineteenth centuries on the heels of the Evangelical revival. In the early nineteenth century these discursive forms served as the ground for middle-class identity through the establishment of comparative (intra- and interclass) distinctions (Armstrong 1987; Morgan 1994; Langland 1995). Literary representations of the ideal, desirable woman composed of psychological attributes (virtues) and available to anyone of good moral standing helped contest what was principally but not exclusively an aristocratic ideal embodied in status and family name. Disruptions both domestic and international contributed to the growth of these works. Anxieties over women's freedom of action fostered by the growth of towns and the growth of middle-class female leisure were exacerbated by the necessity for women to take a public role in the wars against France that began in 1793. By contributing time and money to the war effort, "British women showed themselves willing to leave the confines of their homes to defend their security within them" (Colley 1992, 266). While reaffirming the duties of women as essentially private, conduct book writers such as Thomas Gisborne and Hannah More maintained that the defense of the home validated a visible civic role for women in the defense of the realm (Colley 1992, Ch. 6).

Eighteenth- and nineteenth-century conduct books helped define the boundaries of women's roles and the responsibilities of both sexes toward one another. If conduct books helped construct the outlines of ideal subjects, both middle-class and aristocratic, both female and male, they also contributed to the rise of the polite novel, a form produced and aimed, again, at a mostly female readership, at the beginning of the nineteenth century in England. The development of the polite novel and etiquette books, which appeared for the first time in profusion in the 1830s, inscribed social distinctions as class distinctions. These nineteenth-century literary forms help define who is a (middle-class) subject fit to be deemed "economic man"—as mediated through "domestic woman"—as opposed to aristocrat or "workie" (Armstrong 1987, 60–69, 94; see also Langland 1992; Curtin 1987).[4] The polite novel highlighted economic individualism (derived, in part, from Puritan ethics of individualism) in courtship and the difficulties of females to act as independent economic agents, even in the marriage market (Watt 1957; but see Scheuermann 1993). One noted historian of the novel describes this historically specific phenomenon of replacing women's bodily desires with purely psychological attributes (virtues) in novels as the "decarnalisation of the public feminine role" (Watt 1957, 163). This process was to be internalized by middle-class women and, if possible, working-class women through the former's instructional visitations. Among the attributes to be internalized were those synonymous with religious and political economic prescriptions for proper, productive, individual and family behavior—discipline, foresight, prudence, sobriety, thrift. Again, internalization and discipline were to be principally directed at women—by conduct books and polite novels—and by women, through the aforementioned visiting.

These educational works also served to articulate ethnographic observations of racial difference, where "race" is determined as much by environmental factors as by physiological difference. Maria Edgeworth, in the final chapter of *Essays in Practical Education* (1811), "Prudence and Economy," draws on travelers' reports to indicate the influence of race and institutions of property on economic language and action. She articulates differences in British economic subjectivity and discourse by indicating the sources of a lack of prudential behavior among colonial Others, in this case planters and slaves in the West Indies. Imprudence, extravagance, and speculation typify their behavior, as a result of the "uncertainty as to the tenure of property, or as to the rewards of industry." Edgeworth quotes from a work on the history of the West Indies to the effect that, "Prudence is a term that has no place in the negro-vocabulary.... The idea of accumulating, and of being economic in order to accumulate, is unknown to these poor slaves, who hold their lands by the most uncertain of all tenures." Edgeworth concludes, "Is it wonderful that the term prudence should be unknown in the negro-vocabulary?" (vol. II, 406–7).

Edgeworth immediately relocates the example from the West Indies to London, noting that the "very poorest class of people in London," who "are it is said, very little disposed to be prudent," constitute the chief consumers of certain seasonal luxury goods ("oysters, crabs, lobsters, pickled salmon, &c") when they first appear on the market (408).[5] Unlike the middle classes and those immediately beneath them, the very poor cannot wait until the prices moderate. Despite her avowal that the illustrations are "far-fetched," Edgeworth's disapproving citation of West Indies planters and slaves literally brings home the empire, placing it in the streets of London.

Class is a relational category, and the English often drew upon racial distinctions to delineate class differences. The final lesson to be drawn from these examples is clear. Only the stability and certainty of property, an attribute belonging not to those with the "greatest affluence" but to the middle ranks (and those aspiring to such ranks), allows one to develop the habits and the very language of prudence and economy. Hence, the text concludes, "the little revenue of young people ought to be fixed and certain."

Edgeworth invokes the West Indies as a fleeting but potent reminder that the instability and insecurity of property can derange the civilized English planters and deprive the slave of the capacity to even *imagine* and *speak* of the economic. Likewise, Jane Austen mentions only in passing the plantations in Antigua that form an integral part of *Mansfield Park* (1814). In the novel, order and stability, the result of proper household management, can only be restored to the Bertram estate concomitant with its establishment at the Antigua property that financially underpins it. Austen easily references, yet distances (by studiously brief, casual allusions) the fact of empire. The text typifies the power of cultural productions to acknowledge and simultaneously place at a distance the unpleasant aspects of the presence of an empire inextricably bound up in everyday, domestic life (Said 1993, 80–97).

Political economy, too, relied upon and contributed to English ethnographic visions of difference in the eighteenth and nineteenth centuries (Hunt 1993; Stocking 1987, Chs. 1, 2, and 3; Herbert 1991, Ch. 2). Before political economy could become part of the educational curriculum, however, its proponents had to struggle against its novelty. The initial efforts at spreading the largely unknown doctrines of classical political economy, which appeared mainly in university lectures and journal articles, in the first two decades of the new century, were aimed principally at the educated middle classes (Fontana 1985). G. Pryme, in *A Syllabus of a Course of Lectures on the Principles of Political Economy* (1816), laments that "the many important truths which Dr Smith has established and their application to subsequent events are alike neglected and unknown due to a failure to realise the utility of their widespread dissemination" (1).[6]

In the same year, Mrs. Marcet, wealthy dinner confidante of David Ricardo and friend of Maria Edgeworth, published *Conversations on Political Economy*. Marcet had considerable experience in educational efforts: a decade earlier she had published what was to become the most popular book on chemistry in the first half of the nineteenth century, *Conversations on Chemistry* (1806). In *Conversations on Political Economy,* Marcet sought to negotiate the tensions that arose from depicting the workings of political economy as a science, as an art (that is, as a tool for public policy), and as a discipline safe for women and children. The rhetoric she employs to meet these objectives sounds like nothing so much as the admonitions of a conduct book. If women must stay within the private sphere they must ensure that they exercise their moral influence outside it. Where Hannah More admonishes women to hone their intellect in order to employ their influence to promote "the well-being of . . . states . . . and the virtue and happiness, nay perhaps the very existence of . . . society," (1799, 5), in *Conversations on Political Economy,* Mrs B claims that sharpening one's reason with an education in the principles of political economy will "tend to promote the happiness of nations, and the purest of morality" (19). Adherence to the doctrines of political economy not only advances the cause of both reason and sentiment and promotes the health of nations, it is consistent with the private duties of women. Mrs B, in response to her student Caroline's query as to whether political economy should be taught to children, cites the bad legislation and bad policies resulting from defective knowledge of political economy, and observes "I would wish that mothers were so far competent to teach it, that their children should not have anything to unlearn" (9). She approvingly cites the example of Edgeworth's "Cherry Orchard," a tale on the division of labor. The story, Mrs B asserts, proves that "no one, I should think, would esteem such information beyond the capacity of a child" (9).

Marcet explicitly denies such a "capacity" to the working classes in *Conversations* (114). By the late 1820s, however, sentiment had changed. This shift toward educating the working classes was due, in part, to the presence of a radical working-class press opposed to the doctrines of classical political economy (Webb 1955, 100; Thompson 1984). Works pumped out by individuals such as Martineau, and organizations such as The Society for the Diffusion of Useful Knowledge were premised on the idea that the working classes needed an education in the true principles of political economy, not the falsehoods uttered in the radical presses. When Nassau Senior contended, in 1827, that the chair of political economy he occupied at Oxford afforded an opportunity "of innoculating the minds of a class, whence, in after-life, a great portion of the governing body in this country is drawn, with the principles of so beneficial a science," he also cited the need for those principles to be "diffused throughout the community; [they] must attract the notice of the mechanic and the artisan and penetrate into the cottage of the labourer" (Senior 1827, 189, 183). Marcet herself compiled *John Hopkins's Notions on Political Economy* (1833) expressly to instruct rural laborers on the principles of political economy.

If disseminators of political economy had to contend with the suspicion among the educated classes that the science was cold, dry, and abstract, and that, in its utilitarian guises, it assumed exactly those aspects about human nature that it should study, these same propagators faced the additional charge from the working-class press that they were supporting class interests inimically opposed to those of the working classes. The psychological attributes of prudence, restraint, foresight, desire tempered by reason, and so on, a staple of conduct books and domestic fictions, were extended to working-class females and males as a behavioral standard in the doctrines of political economy. Whether one measured up to these standards of true economic subjectivity or not, the measure of success or failure would remain individualized, internal, and privatized rather than inherent in the structure of economic forces beyond any one individual's control. This same process worked in popularizations of Malthusian models: aggregated, the many individual actions of the ignorant and imprudent dictated failure for the masses. To be sure, Ricardo, Senior, and James Mill also attacked the position of landowners as an unproductive class squeezing, through rent, profits and, indirectly, wages. But the Malthusian implication that the working classes had only themselves to blame had become the centerpiece of the vociferous attacks on classical political economy in the working-class press by the early 1830s, making the labors of popularizers like Marcet and Martineau all the more difficult.

Rethinking *Robinson Crusoe*

One way political economists sought to avoid the criticism of the working classes implicit in Malthus's population theory was through the use of fictive utopias. Harriet Martineau, a radical Dissenter with a fervent belief in equal opportunities for women, chose to open her popular series *Illustrations of Political Economy* with *Life in the Wilds*. The series, inspired by Mrs. Marcet's *Conversations on Political Economy,* was dedicated to "such parts of [political economy] as lead directly to important practical results" (Mill 1834). Each tale was devoted to illustrating the operation of a different principle of economics in real life, and to that end Martineau endowed characters with what she called "embodied principles," good and bad, to carry the action of the stories (1877, 1). *Illustrations* was designed to instruct readers of all classes and ages to emulate the ideal characters in the tales and shun the example of the bad. By extending the reach of woman as educator beyond the domestic sphere, these political economic "conduct books," if we may call them that, earned Martineau the moniker "instructress to the nation." While it is doubtful that she created a universal audience through her series, she did achieve literary fame and not a small measure of notoriety for her efforts.

Life in the Wilds recounts events in a South African frontier settlement as colonists from England rebuild in the wake of a devastating attack by "Bushmen" (San tribesmen). The raiders destroy all the settlers' possessions, avenging, in Martineau's words, the original sin the first Europeans visited upon the natives. The natives are never seen: the raid occurs before the story opens. The Dutch, recent losers to the British for control of the Cape colony, are absent from the story as well. As part of the reimagination of community, the tale is drained of all violence among Europeans, and between Europeans and natives. Populating and taming a deserted land is a distancing convention of travel writing of this period, a method employed to wipe away the stains of violence that marked colonialism and the extension of markets while simultaneously glorifying the conquest of nature (Pratt 1992).

Natives are "present" albeit not as actual bodily presences. Lacking tools, the settlers must rely on the available natural resources to survive. But they must also improve upon their knowledge of native technologies to surpass the level of civilization (signified by domestic comforts) attained by the natives. The English are able to do so, building better versions of the natives' huts, for example, because they are intellectually superior. This superiority is not, however, innate. In the only reference to the original depredations that drove the "Bushmen" from the land, a passage that opens the tale, Martineau notes that Europeans might suffer the same physical and intellectual stunting if forced to endure the hardships that afflict the "Bushmen" (25–27).

Race, then, is an environmental concept in the tale. The advance of an autarkic civilization in *Life* unfolds in stages consonant with the exploitation of the division of labor and comparative advantages, as in *Crusoe* when Friday and Crusoe divide their work. Amending a page from Adam Smith, *Life* also suggests that the increasing division of labor entails beneficial consequences for the household economy:

> "So with them [the children] the division of labor has led to the invention of machinery," said the captain. "A certain consequence," replied his friend. Men, women, and children, are never so apt at devising ways of easing their toils as when they are confined to one sort of labor, and have to give their attention wholly to it. . . . [The women] have divided their labors according to their talents or habits, and daily find the advantages of such a plan. . . . [I]t is clear that if each person had only one method to practise and was not disturbed when once her hand was, the work of every kind would go on faster. . . . [B]etween this division of labor and the little contrivances to which it gives occasion, we are certainly better waited on and taken care of by our wives and companions than if each had to do all the offices of one household. (126–27, 129)

Women and children exploit the gains to be made from the division of labor, and are as much economic creatures as are men. In fact, the women and children catch on to the advantages of specialization more quickly than the men do.

The division of labor by sex and age is not absolute. Mrs. Prest, who does the cooking for the settlement, is often aided by her husband. And when men, conscripted for the arduous job of digging irrigation trenches, take a daily afternoon break, they often pursue other tasks with the women and children, such as flax preparation, looking for fruit and honey, and so on (80). Unlike Crusoe, who prior to the arrival of Friday is in his own person synonymous with the economy, and who quickly sets up his individual household with its feminine housekeeping conventions, much of the action of *Life* is explicit about the necessity and efficiency of communal property and communal housekeeping. Even by the opening of the final chapter, when the settlers have copied indigenous technologies and put up rude shelters for individual households, the bulk of the household work remains communal.

At the close of *Life,* barter trade with Capetown resumes and machinery, tools, and diverse supplies arrive by wagon. The settlers distribute the goods as communal property in a public ceremony. Within the community there is as yet no need for money or exchange and its power to obscure the true relations of value and to establish and disestablish ranks. The raid, while a disaster, has the positive effect of leveling ranks and revealing "a new test of rank . . . the comparative utility of [labor]" (174–75). True value, a person's worth resides in labor, which is normally obscured behind the veils of money, exchange, inherited wealth ("gold [saved] from the flames") and the false distinction of titles. Labor is the source of value and exchange value: "Labor is still the purchase-money of every thing here" (176).

There remains no need for money or exchange within the settlement at the close of the story. There is now, however, room for virtuous love. The prudent young lovers Katie and Robertson, the "Malthusian couple" of the tale, wait to wed until the propitious moment when it is not only evident that they can support themselves by dint of their labor, but can also receive the approval of the rest of the settlers (186–87). The pair quickly marry and the settlers build them the first sturdy English-style house, garnishing it with "ornamental luxuries" (188). The stable solution to the threat that love and money represent to the health of the social body is one where individual and social interests happily coincide in the formation of a cashless yet prudent household. Prudence tempers desire and the union is satisfactory not only to the individuals but to the community.

The story's conclusion reconciles love and money through the triumph of virtuous love. The marriage signifies the recognition that labor is the true source of value. The reestablishment of trade with the world outside the settlement suggests that the household-based concord between the domestic sphere and the market marks the return to civilization. And civilization is a state more harmonious than that of England. Despite the exploitation of comparative advantages that results in the reversion to a more or less strict sexual division of labor, there is no hierarchy, no economic dependence based on patriarchal property relations or the structure of the market. Rather, the members of the community work according to a natural division of labor: each labors according to his or her ability and is remunerated according to his or her need. *Life*'s utopia is a communist one.

Within a year of the appearance of *Life in the Wilds*, Mrs. Marcet published her own rewrite of *Crusoe*, the allegorical tale "The Three Giants," in *John Hopkins's Notions on Political Economy*. The structure of the collection mirrors the education of the title character, slowly moving from fairy tales and fantastical explanations of the distribution of wealth by the ignorant rural laborer in the beginning of the text to the resigned and sober calculations of the advantages of free trade by the Ricardian convert at the conclusion. At each step of his education in economic reasoning, John is contested by his wife, Dame Hopkins, with appeals to sentiment and common sense.

"The Three Giants" portrays quite a different picture of the structure of relations between race, class, and gender, the relation between family and work, and the question of economic value from that depicted in *Life*. The tale, a Malthusian fantasy, depicts the fate of a shipload of emigrants, all equally poor, fleeing rural England. Marcet includes the standard elements of a Robinsonade, shipwrecking her characters on an isle lush with fruits and vegetables. The isle is uninhabited—there is no racial conflict here—and the settlers bring civilization (manufacturing and commerce) to the land through the exploitation of the division of labor. The title refers to man's ability to advance by working in harness with natural forces, in this case the giants Aquafluens (water power), Ventosus (wind power), and Vaporifer (steam power).

The first year of the story is telescoped so that individual households, each with "a little garden of vegetables," are reestablished at the beginning of the text. The necessity to provide for household needs sets off the chain of events that allow the settlers to advance beyond mere satisfaction at living off the fat of the land. Despite the isle's fertility, Jobson and his large family, the main characters of the piece, struggle to feed themselves until Jobson stumbles upon Aquafluens. Jobson and his neighbors construct a sawmill powered by Aquafluens. He and his family are soon far more prosperous than their neighbors owing to the demand by all households for the floorboards, tables, and chairs that the mill can provide.

The desires generated by the requirements of family economy give rise to economy, understood as a set of barter relations extending beyond the household. The family economy also lies at the heart of the initial formation of ranks between the previously undifferentiated mass of refugees in the tale. Among the neighbors who come to exchange with Jobson are a poor widow and two idle fellows. On the one hand, Jobson and the idlers exemplify the ideal of rewards flowing only to the possessors of capital, the skilled, and the hard working. The logical place in the economic hierarchy of those who have nothing to exchange except their labor is at the bottom. On the other hand, Jobson and the poor woman signify sheer luck, good and bad (the poor woman is poor simply because her husband has died), as a principal determinant in establishing ranks.

Once the division of labor takes hold it reinforces ranks established in the first year of settlement. The barter system remains the method of exchange throughout (indeed, the narrator of "The Three Giants" is a peddler who exchanges the tale for board at the Hopkins's), and ensures that rewards flow to the skillful and lucky. But this division of rewards does not in any way establish a standard, such as money or labor, that would solve, once and for all, the question of economic value. Although "The Three Giants" does not take the extreme position, expressed in *Life in the Wilds,* that gold is useless, Marcet echoes Smith in indicating that money (gold) is too variable a standard to be a reliable indicator of wealth (Marcet 1833).

What is certain is the tale's denigration of the value of household labor.

There is a clear link between time spent on household labor and the inability of women to be deemed or to become full-fledged economic subjects. Dame Hopkins, the sentimental foil to her husband John's education in the principles of political economy, being too busy about her household affairs, "had not heard above half the story." And as she "did but half understand the meaning of the story," the entire household is soon laughing at her ignorance (61–62).

Conclusion

Life in the Wilds posits the absence of money as a means to stabilize desire and property and, by implication, the economy. The Malthusian threat that strong individual bodies represents to the social body is negated through the operation of virtuous love: Katie and Robertson prudently wait and then seek public recognition and approbation of their marriage contract. These stabilizing procedures do not entail deleterious consequences for women's economic agency. Quite the contrary, women's economic dependence recedes despite the reemergence of both a sexual division of labor and private households. Labor may lie at the source of value, but household production is still largely communal at the conclusion of the tale, and the distribution of economic rewards is based solely on need.

Martineau's story idealizes cooperative labor and levels all ranks: all labor is of equal value, including female domestic labor. "The Three Giants," on the other hand, makes apparent the principal role of uncertainty and providential luck (starting with the initial shipwreck) in determining economic value and the division of rewards. Economic value is unstable. What is a certain and stable value in the story is marriage, which appears as an unexamined natural category. The bodily desires central to the Malthusian struggle give vent to two Malthusian solutions in "The Three Giants": the first, emigration; the second, inventive economic activity spurred by the goad of poverty and hunger. The threat of a hungry family is actually a positive incentive in Marcet's utopia—the need for food sets off Jobson's roving and leads to the discoveries and industry that quickly erase the natural checks to population. Rewards flow naturally to the married due to the positive pressure of provisioning, while single men (the feckless laborers) and single women (the widow) at least temporarily suffer the consequences of not belonging to the idealized Malthusian household. Marriage and the family economy, sources of economic value in the tale, entail economic independence for males. And, as in the case of the widow in the peddler's tale and Dame Hopkins, the family economy entails economic dependence and less than full economic subjectivity for women.

Despite their radically different idealizations, the reestablishment of families or households are critical to the both narrative and the lessons of *Life* and "Three Giants." The stories helped usher in Crusoe as the economists' "economic man" in a systematic fashion for the first time in the 1850s (White 1987). Ironically, this character could never have arisen had writers like Martineau and Marcet not domesticated their versions of him through virtuous marriages to "domestic woman." The stories signify the degree to which a conservative construction of women's role as guardians of family, virtue, and national health could nonetheless sanction a visible and active, if still limited, role for women in public policy. They testify to the mutability of taxonomies such as economics, family, gender, race, and class. They testify to the capacity of those categories to surprise us. And they bear witness to the necessity for us to rethink and recombine our categories as we continue the struggle to make ourselves better economic subjects.

Notes

1. Maria Edgeworth, aunt of the marginalist F.Y. Edgeworth, is best known for her collaboration with her father, Richard, on *Essays in Practical Education* and for her stories on the division of labor, "The Cherry Orchard" (1802), and rent, *Castle Rackrent* (1800). She is the sole author of the essay discussed here.

2. In England, Catholic emancipation was legislated in 1829; rural disturbances such as rick-burning and the agitations of Captain Swing unnerved the local gentry at the beginning of the decade; the Reform Bill passed in 1832; and the cholera epidemic of the same year fueled apocalyptic fears. Revolutions in France and Belgium added to the sense that the old order was about to be replaced by the new.

3. This section borrows heavily from Erica Harth, "The Virtue of Love: Lord Hardwicke's Marriage Act," *Cultural Critique* (Spring 1988): 123–54. The citations refer to the column numbers in William Cobbett's partial reconstruction of the parliamentary debate in *The Parliamentary History of England, from the Earliest Period to the Year 1803. Volume XV.* London: Longman, 1813.

4. Elizabeth Langland, in "Nobody's Angels: Domestic Ideology and Middle-Class Women in the Victorian Novel," *PMLA* 107:2 (March 1992): 290–304. Citing Michael Curtin's *Propriety and Position: A Study of Victorian Manners* (New York: Garland, 1987), Langland describes a shift in emphasis from conduct books to etiquette books as a shift in emphasis from "individual standards of moral and civil conduct . . . [covering] topics like 'fortitude,' 'honesty,' and 'fidelity' to etiquette manuals which discuss 'balls,' 'introductions and calls,' 'cuts,' and so on. . . . Thus the [etiquette] manuals apparently served more to consolidate a public image within the middle classes than to facilitate a rise in status for other ranks; they helped construct an identity for a group that might otherwise seem bound together only by Carlyle's 'cash nexus' " (293).

5. She draws on Patrick Colquhoun's *Treatise on the Police of the Metropolis* (1796, 32), a text that mixes proposals on the control of the lower classes with the conventions of travel literature. Colquhoun, a magistrate, wrote treatises on a wide variety of economic subjects including national revenue–raising schemes, indigence, and education for "the labouring people."

6. Cited in Thompson (1984).

3

Female Labor Supply During Early Industrialization

Women's Labor Force Participation in Historical Perspective

Margaret S. Coleman

There exists a unique document from the nineteenth century that has been underutilized for estimating gendered labor supply, the Louis McLane Report of 1833 (McLane). As secretary to the Treasury of the United States, McLane developed a questionnaire that was distributed throughout the Northeast to manufactories of all types. The result for academics today is an unparalleled statistical portrait of labor force involvement in a wide variety of occupations by both men and women throughout the Northeast. An examination of the McLane report (1833) and other nineteenth-century government records indicates that the involvement of women in industrial waged labor was almost as prevalent during the years following the rapid rise of industrialization in the Northeast as it has been during the twentieth century since World War II. This chapter provides strong evidence for the contention that twentieth-century female labor force participation (FLFP) is not a new trend. Rather, it is the latest rise in a cyclical pattern of permanent involvement of women in nonagricultural waged labor. First, to explain women's entry into industrial waged work after 1810, the history of women's contribution to the rural economy of the eighteenth and nineteenth centuries, the social construction of labor, and the changing economic forces of the post–American Revolution United States are examined. Second, for the years 1830 to 1833 in Massachusetts, an FLFP rate of 45 percent is developed for women involved in waged labor outside the agricultural sector. In the conclusion, women's participation in the labor market is described as a long-term cyclical norm representing two-thirds of the time period since industrial expansion began. This permanent involvement by women in waged labor provides a lower boundary for a cyclical pattern of FLFP which describes women's economic roles more realistically than the homemaker model so common in rational choice theoretic work (e.g., Becker 1991). This points to the need for a reevaluation of the role of "woman as homemaker" within the entire economic discipline, not just within those areas of economics labeled as feminist.

Section One: Historical Overview

In this section, first the essential contribution of women's production to rural economies is established. Second, the changing nature of this production and the history of the social construction of labor in the new world are outlined. Finally, the interaction between the definitions of labor and increased industrialization are used as an explanation for the extensive entry of women into waged labor.

Rural Economy

The colonial economy was comprised of interconnected households and communities (Ulrich 1991). Commonly held production resources enabled farms within a geographic area to invest in different kinds of tools, which were shared.[1] Finished products, along with the labor of individuals, were traded within the community (Ryan 1983; Simmler 1990; Blewett 1988). Barter markets in conjunction with individual self-sufficiency supplied the needs of the agrarian community.

Prior to the beginning of widespread manufacturing in the Northeast, the production work of women in agriculture was equal to roughly half the necessary work and production in rural areas (Gutman 1989). While there was crossover between the genders, women tended to be in charge of finished products used by the family and the community such as yarn, cloth, clothing, preserved foods, baked goods, furniture, blankets, and quilts. Women turned the raw products into edible and preserved foods: butter and cheese making; preserving meats by salting or smoking; canning and preserving fruits and vegetables. They also raised animals such as chickens, geese, turkeys, hogs, and cows (Blewett 1988; Ryan 1983; Kessler-Harris 1981; Ulrich 1991; Matthaei 1982; Hymowitz and Weissman 1978; Gutman 1989; Simmler 1990).

Aside from feeding and clothing the household and community, women provided services: teaching, medical care, and dependent care. Children were educated in the home. When the inhabitants of the farm became ill, they were tended at home. If the pregnant woman was fortunate, she was aided by a midwife with experience (one out of thirty pregnant women died in childbirth, Gutman 1989, 111).

Household production during the eighteenth and nineteenth centuries was fundamentally different from household production today within capitalist countries. Women did not simply produce more products for use in the home. Rather, the surplus of women's labor was directly available to them in the form of self-made products for distribution in both the household and the community. Except for a few items that used the skills of both men and women (e.g., shoes), the goods women produced were the staple of the barter markets that provided for the day-to-day needs of the entire community.[2] The result of women's ability to distribute the surplus of their production was increased well-being for both the individual household and the community at large. In summary, women used community tools, such as spinning wheels or smokehouses, to produce goods; owned the product of their own labor; and were in charge of the distribution of that product.

Beginning of Industrialization

When the means of production within the household and rural community began to be controlled by merchants and speculators, household production went through a profound revolution. Both craft (male) and home (female) production became wage work within the home, or in the factory, and those producing commodities no longer controlled the distribution of the surplus from that production. Between the end of the American Revolution and the eve of the Civil War, much of the production in the Northeast went through two stages.[3] First, the work changed from craft or household labor for use and distribution to waged labor within the home (this was generally referred to as "outwork"). Second, work moved from wage work within the home to factory labor as mechanized production crowded out home and craft labor. Simultaneously, barter markets were crowded out by the abundance of cheaper goods produced with new technology. Communities became increasingly involved in wage labor as the need for cash, or any universal medium, increased.[4]

This transition period is one that a few economic historians are beginning to explore (Dublin 1994; Gutman 1989). For example, Blewett (1988) provides a detailed account of the transition of the shoe trade in Lynn, Massachusetts, the site of most domestic production of shoes since the early eighteenth century. After the American Revolution, speculators gained control of the supply of shoe leather, and hence the means of production. By 1810 almost all shoebinding, work traditionally performed by women in family-owned businesses, was performed on an outwork, waged basis as part of large rural distribution networks. The change of the male craftwork on shoes first to waged labor in the home, then to mechanized factory labor, happened at a slower pace than shoebinding, but, by 1860, both lasting (males) and binding (females) had become factory work.

The different types of traditionally female production in rural areas became the first large industries of the capitalist market: yarn and textiles, processed foods, and ready-made clothes (e.g., Gutman 1989; Ryan 1983; Kessler-Harris 1981; Ware 1924). In December 1807, on the eve of the War of 1812, Thomas Jefferson passed the Embargo Act limiting imports (Blewett 1988). In 1808, there were fifteen cotton mills in the United States; by 1809 there were eighty-seven new mills (North 1974; Scoresby 1845). The 1807 embargo also spurred dramatic growth in the shoe industry (Blewett 1988). During the recession following the 1812 war, cotton manufactories and related businesses (bleaching, calico printing) failed in droves (McLane 1833). However, many reopened concurrently with a large variety of new businesses after the passage of stronger tariffs in 1816, 1824, and 1828 (Massachusetts Bureau of Statistics of Labor [MBSL] 1885). Further spurring the growth of industry, "[B]etween 1820 and 1824 Massachusetts authorized $6,840,000 additional corporate capital.... [This] led to the foundation of factory villages such as Lowell, Fall River, Taunton, and Chicopee" (MBSL 1885, 175).

As capital markets expanded, demanding labor in a country with chronic, localized labor shortages, (Carey 1819–28; Lebergott 1964; Katz 1986) a combination of economic, political, and social changes interacted with the traditions governing labor in the colonies to create the climate in which massive numbers of Yankee women migrated into waged labor both within the household and in the explosion of factories.

Social Construction of Labor

Quantities and availability of labor change with definitions that reflect the power relationships and economic needs within the community: gender, age, race, legal standing, and property ownership. One need only compare the World War II picture of Rosie the Riveter, tools in hand, with the 1950s image of a homemaker in a frilly apron (Faludi 1991) to understand how social images influence a woman's decision as to where to supply labor (market or home) and what kind of labor to engage in (gendered jobs). Where an individual stands in relation to the different hierarchies of power in the community determines what types of labor that person engages in.

Certainly gender is a social construct. For example, enslaved women, captured in Africa or born in the United States as slaves, lived, flourished, and bore children as part of their masters' investment under some of the harshest labor conditions in recorded history (Sterling 1984). The lives of rural Yankee women were only marginally less harsh, lived within the confines of an economy where resources were traditionally scarce and where the labor of each individual was vital to the survival of the entire community (Kelso 1922; Morris 1946; Kessler-Harris 1978; Ryan 1983; Gutman 1989). The social framework of the Puritans equated hard work with virtue, and the cultural norms for women's labor were defined by religion. Despite the intensity of their labor, the economic roles of colonial and nineteenth-century women remain a shadow on the records of business and government (Ulrich 1991). Anyone other than those few Caucasian males not laboring under indenture contracts (e.g., women, slaves, Asians, American Indians) was legally prevented from owning property or businesses and directly receiving wages. Hence, there are only the barest documents recording the economic activities of the bulk of the population in the nineteenth century. As Norman Ware (1924) put it in discussing how to approach studying the conditions of the working class, "One may fix attention upon the condition, activities and ideas of the dominant group, or one may attempt to uncover the workings of those that were submerged or being submerged. The annals of the poor are short, ... not because they are uninteresting, but because the poor are inarticulate."

The Colonies: The Beginning of the Social Definitions of Labor for the New Republic

The overriding characteristic of labor in the colonies was lack of freedom. This lack of freedom can be exemplified by the traditions and legal construction of indentured labor, which existed well into the nineteenth century.[5] Most Caucasian labor emigrated with long-term contracts that kept them tied to specific masters for significant portions of their adult lives, especially given the high rate of mortality.[6] On the eve of industrial growth, "of the 6,000 emigrants leaving England between December 11, 1773, and October 30, 1775, approximately 4,000 left from the port of London for the colonies; 87 percent of these went over as indentured servants" (Morris 1946, 315), and "If we exclude the Puritan migration of the 1630s, it is safe to say that not less than one-half, nor more than two-thirds, of all white immigrants to the colonies were indentured servants or redemptioners or convicts" (Abbot E. Smith quoted in Grub 1985, 317).

Once this labor arrived, the legal and social structures served to keep labor captive. Indentures who ran away to live with the Indians as a choice preferable to remaining with European masters were systematically hunted down and publicly hanged (Galenson 1984). Further increasing the ranks of non-free labor was the practice of using indentured servitude as the primary form of punishment for residents in the new world until after 1800. There were almost no jails; rather, indentured servitude was meted out for everything from past-due debts to out-of-wedlock pregnancies to theft to murder (Morris 1946; Kelso 1922; Katz 1986). In short, most labor prior to the American Revolution was either indented or enslaved.

It is within this context of a tradition of non-free labor, along with the expectation that everyone in the community make a productive contribution, that the surge of women into wage labor as a response to changing economic conditions makes sense. There were two economic factors that underlay the change in social construction of labor and dictated the entrance of women into the waged labor force: an increased need for cash in a country suffering from chronic specie shortages and an increased rural debt associated with land shortages in the Northeast.

1. *Specie shortages.* The United States did not have a uniform currency until after the Civil War. The new nation was plagued with cyclical, chronic money shortages beginning with the withdrawal of specie by the English during the American Revolution right up through the beginning of the gold rush in the mid-1850s (Ware 1924; Warren and Pearson 1933). The most common currency was Spanish silver dollars minted in Mexico. Other currencies in use were notes printed by banks, state currencies, old English pounds, and new English pounds (Cole and Smith 1935; Warren and Pearson 1933).

The crowding out of barter markets increased the need within communities for currency. A farmer who could formerly have subsisted for years with little cash, other than that necessary to run the business end of the farm, now needed cash to buy goods that had traditionally been produced by household labor. Mathew Carey (1819–28, 18) notes some of the results of the chronic lack of specie on the Massachusetts economy. Civil unrest following the American Revolution nearly decimated the new federal government: "The scarcity of money is so great, or the difficulty of paying debts has been so common, that riots and combinations have been formed in many places, and the operations of civil government have been suspended. The almost complete withdrawal of specie from the country decimated local economies. The local revolts necessitated the protection of local officials by federal troops until democratic government could be re-established."

Clearly, the farm that could produce a member able to work for cash wages, or store orders, to buy goods in the cash markets, was in a position superior to those farms that could not. One of the reasons quoted over and over for young women engaging in factory labor was the need of the household for the cash her wages brought in (Farley 1850; Scoresby 1845; Kessler-Harris 1981; Ryan 1983).

2. *Increased debt.* In "The Emergence of a Capital Market in Rural Massachusetts, 1730–1838," Rothenberg (1985) found a significant increase in the number of debtors making claims on wills probated in Massachusetts courts, an indication that farmers were accumulating more debt during their lifetime. The increase of rural debt prior to 1800 is also noted by Ryan (1983) and Matthaei (1982). Shammas (1993) found a high incidence of wealth inequality prior to the American Revolution that intensifies throughout the nineteenth century. Kuznets (1965) found an increase in wealth and income inequality following the American Revolution, and his early work was supported by a number of economic historians (Williamson and Lindert 1980). With the evidence at hand, it seems that while the country was expanding west, while cash crops in the South were bringing prosperity to plantation owners, while the sea trade was making wealthy merchants, and while there was growth of industry in the North (North 1974; Atack and Passell 1994; Ryan 1983; Gutman 1989), rural farmers in New England were facing growing debts, in part related to decreased farm size. The practices of splitting farmland equally among sons and providing daughters with land for dowries had greatly reduced farm size by the early 1800s.

The changing economic conditions brought about by growing industrialization throughout the Northeast created new roles in the economy for men and women. At first, relatively fewer men than women moved into factory labor. Those industries that engaged large numbers of men in one location (e.g., mining, metal works, shoemaking) did not begin rapid growth and mechanization until the second half of the nineteenth century. Men had more options than women and spread out over a range of growing occupations such as seafaring (Montgomery 1984), construction of roads and canals (Carey 1833; Gutman 1989), military,[7] and moving west (Gutman 1989). Much of the change in the behavior of nineteenth-century women was predicated on the changes in male employment patterns. Prior to the American Revolution, a woman assumed she would receive a dowry, marry, have children, and continue in the same kinds of production that had been carried on for generations. With the shortage of land, and potential marriage mates moving west, women faced a future that was not defined by the social patterns of past generations.[8]

The answer of women after 1800 to changing social and economic patterns was twofold: they moved into urban areas and factories, and they stopped getting married or postponed marriage to a later age. For example, 13 percent of women born in Massachusetts in the 1830s would never marry (Ryan 1983, 137). Fertility rates declined and an estimated one in five pregnancies terminated in abortion during the mid-nineteenth century (Ryan 1983, 140).

The image often presented of nineteenth-century working women is one of young women employed in mills for a few years before retiring to marriage (Scoresby 1847; Henry Carey 1835, 1847). This simplistic image, in light of the 45.22 percent FLFP estimated in the next section of this chapter, must be untrue. Thousands of women left the farms and populated the urban areas of Boston, New York, and Philadelphia. They became seamstresses, milliners, servants, washerwomen, and prostitutes (Ryan 1983; Gutman 1989; Gilfoyle 1992; Hill 1989; Pease and Pease 1990; Providence First 1837). Almost all urban women engaged in jobs that barely provided enough to keep body and soul together.

Colonial Definitions of Labor Are Transformed to Apply to Factory Work

From the beginnings of the growth of industry in the Northeast, generous compensatory payments were not the primary method used to attract women into wage work. Women earned, on average, between 30 and 40 percent of male income (McLane 1833). Rather than paying women generously for their labor, industrial and government leaders relied on propaganda and the expectation that all members of society must labor.

The large mill towns used lures based in gender ideology. The firms that comprised the mill megacenter in Lowell, Massachusetts, offered a structured work environment that was exclusively aimed at female workers. Housing was monitored by matrons who imposed curfews and restricted visitors. The wages of mill girls were not paid directly in cash; rather, they were deposited on a quarterly basis to accounts held and controlled by the mills. Forced deductions were made out of these wages for housing, church tithes, health and schooling costs, and penalties for lateness or defective production. In some cases, the cash wages of girls were sent back to their households (Ware 1924; Kessler-Harris 1978; Scoresby 1845; Farley 1850; Ryan 1983). In short, the practice of restraining labor by indenture combined with gender biases created new restrictions for women working in the mill towns.

Propaganda released by both government and industry was used to attract and hold women workers. Women were called to labor as a duty; their labor would release men for the more important jobs required to build the new nation. Wage labor for women was presented as a duty to man, God, and government; to have demanded a living wage would have been sacrilegious! "Advocates of governmental aid to manufactures ... felt obliged to echo Hamilton's famous assurance that manufacturing would not attract able-bodied men away from the land ... Philadelphia's first large-scale use of spinning jennies was undertaken by the United Company of Philadelphia for Promoting American Manufactures, founded by patriotic subscriptions in 1775. By the late 1780s it employed 400 women, most of them recruited from the city's poor rolls" (Montgomery 1984, 17).

With the Tench Coxe Report, government took an even more active role in helping factories attract female labor. The entire first section was written to encourage the employment of women in manufacturing. Summarizing some of the argument: mechanization vastly improved the productive capacity of women. National production would be increased by applying the labor of women to machines, hence increasing the wealth of the land. Here is how Coxe (1812, xxiv) describes mill labor: "Women, relieved in a very considerable degree from their former employments, as carders, spinners, and fullers by hand, occasionally turn to the operations of the weaver with improved machinery and instruments, which abridge and soften the labor, while the male weavers employ themselves in superintendence, instruction, superior or other operations, and promote their health by occasional attention to gardening, agriculture and the clearing and improvement of the land." The reality of mill work was described by a different voice in Lowell, Massachusetts: "It makes my feet ache and swell to stand so much, ... The girls generally wear old shoes about their work, ... but they almost all say that when they have worked here a year or two they have to procure shoes of a size or two larger than before they came. The right hand, which is the one used in stopping and starting the loom, becomes larger than the left" (Scoresby 1845, 60).

It was the tedium of the job that led to the increasing difficulties Lowell and the other large mills faced in attracting labor. The pay for mill operatives, while slightly higher than the pay women received in the extensive rural outwork networks (McLane 1833), was not enough to keep women in the mills for any length of time. The living conditions at Lowell, Waltham, and the other large mill towns deteriorated within a decade of their being built (Kessler-Harris 1978). Ware (1924) documents the crowded living conditions and prevalence of illness as a result.

Scoresby (1845) notes that most women in Lowell factories had been recruited from homes more than one hundred miles away, indicating that the large mill towns were looking further and further for laborers. This observation is verified by examining the records of the birth locations of operatives at one of the largest Lowell mills, Hamilton. In 1830, when Hamilton first opened, 82.2 percent of its mill operatives had been born in Massachusetts. By 1835, 41.3 percent of the mill operatives were born in Massachusetts, and the rest were born in surrounding states (Layer 1955, 71). The fact that Hamilton had to cast such a wide net to find employees indicates an endemic problem with the local labor supply, and a reluctance on the part of the company to pay a higher wage as an incentive.[9] The result of these economic and political pressures on women to engage in wage labor is detailed in the next section, which derives an FLFP for Massachusetts, 1830–33.

Section Two: Statistical Estimation of Female Labor Force Participation in Massachusetts, 1830 to 1833

Using the detailed employment records from McLane (1833), data on adults engaged in nonagricultural, productive labor were compiled for several states. Out of 2,461 returns, 1,778 (72 percent) of them were from Massachusetts, and specifically Boston. This numerical advantage was bolstered by the fact that Boston was the only urban area that produced a significant number of returns. In the 1,778 reports used, 82,782 adults were recorded, with 40,121, or 48.5 percent, men and 42,661, or 51.5 percent, women. Race and/or ethnicity was not a category recorded in the McLane report. Massachusetts census records for 1830 reveal that of the total state population, 603,359 were Caucasian, and 7,048, or just over 1 percent, were freed African Americans. The assumption for this estimation of FLFP is going to be that the population is Caucasian. In short, there were numerically more women than men engaged in waged production labor in 1833, as reported in the McLane report by business owners.

This is not a complete picture by any means. The occupations not recorded in the McLane report that engaged large numbers of women during the time under examination were servant, seamstress, teacher, and prostitute. What follows is a separate estimate for each category. From these categories, a summary estimate is arrived at for Massachusetts FLFP circa 1830–33.

1. Servants

The number of servants is derived from an estimate of the number of Massachusetts and Boston households in 1830. Determining the number of households relies on first estimating household size, and is a somewhat complicated task. The variables that must be taken into account are fertility rate, child mortality, life expectancy, and the nature of the extended household. In 1830, there were approximately five to six live births per woman (Gutman 1989; Ryan 1983). Only 70 to 75 percent of these births survived to age fifteen, providing an average of three and a half children per household (Jacobson 1964; Uhlenberg 1978). Households frequently contained adults other than parents. Adulthood began at age fifteen or sixteen, so that even with a low life expectancy of forty-five (Jacobson 1964), there could well have been adult children and/or grandparents in the same household. The average age of marriage rose during the first half of the nineteenth century, leaving those young women who did not move to urban areas in the parental household for a longer period of time (Ryan 1983). Taking all these factors into account, an average New England household might have had two and a half children under fifteen, one child over fifteen, one elderly person or unmarried spinster, and two adult parents, making an estimated average household size six and a half persons. This results in 92,824 Massachusetts households.

There were 150,000 female domestics in the United States in 1830, and Lebergott (1964) estimates that one in eight and a half households used servants. The use of servants, though, was not uniform. Ryan (1983) and Dublin (1994) note that the use of servants in urban areas was much higher than in rural areas. Dublin (1994) finds that one in three Boston households used servants around mid-century. He also notes that the number of servants was roughly double the manufacturing population in Boston. With all of this in mind, the method of estimating the number of servants was to: (a) double the working female population of Boston, compute how many domestics that implied per household when assigned to one-third of the Boston households; and (b) compute the average number of domestics per household in the city, then multiply that by one in eight and a half households for rural Massachusetts. The final result of this procedure was that 26,357 women worked as domestics during the early 1830s in Massachusetts (the step-by-step calculations are listed in the Appendix to this chapter).

2. Seamstresses

Another occupation employing large groups of women workers was that of seamstress, most of whom labored on piecework in the home (Gutman 1989; Dublin 1994). Mathew Carey (1830) notes that not only did women in urban areas sew for private clients but a large portion of seamstresses were employed by the government in making clothes for the armed forces.

Table 3.1
Seamstress Employment Estimates for Four Cities

City	Population	Percentage of Population	Number of Seamstresses
New York	202,589	40	4,800
Philadelphia	161,410	32	3,840
Baltimore	80,625	16	1,920
Boston	61,392	12	1,440
Total Population	506,016,100		

Source: Lee and Lalli (1967).

In 1833, Carey estimated that there were about 12,000 women seamstresses in Boston, New York, Philadelphia, and Baltimore. Establishing the share of the combined urban population in each city and distributing the seamstresses in equal proportions produced the estimates of the number of seamstresses per city listed in Table 3.1. The 1,440 seamstresses estimated for Boston are 6.8 percent of the 21,075 adult women in Boston circa 1830. Applying the same ratio of seamstresses to the adult female population, a statewide estimate of 13,000 seamstresses was arrived at.

3. Teaching

Teachers were not a large proportion of women workers during the nineteenth century. Dublin (1994) notes that in the 1850s, more than two decades after public primary schools were well established in Boston (Ferdinand 1992), less than 3 percent of women workers were teachers. Boston during the period 1833–39 employed about fifty women teachers per year (Boston City Council Records 1834–39). In 1830 there were 21,075 women between the ages of fifteen and sixty-nine (Lee and Lalli 1967), making teachers 0.0024 percent of the female population. There were 191,106 females aged fifteen to sixty-nine statewide; 0.0024 percent of the state population results in an estimate of 459 women teachers in the State of Massachusetts.

4. Prostitution

All major port cities in the United States were home to large numbers of women who engaged in sex for sale. For example, up to 49 percent of women wage workers in New York City in the 1830s may have engaged in prostitution full- or part-time and/or temporarily to cover industrial layoffs, or inadequate wages, or both (Gilfoyle 1992, 61). Hill (1989) estimates that between 5 and 10 percent of the total female population of New York was involved in prostitution as a full-time occupation during the antebellum years. The pattern of prostitution in Boston seems to have been similar to that of New York City. Pease and Pease (1990) estimate a steady level of about 2,000 full-time prostitutes plying their trade in Boston between the years 1820 and 1850.

For the purposes of estimating FLFP, consideration of part-time and/or temporary prostitution requires too many assumptions about women holding more than one job. Therefore, what follows is an estimation of full-time prostitution. In 1830, Boston contained 21,708 women aged ten to forty-nine.[10] If the Pease and Pease (1990) estimate is correct, then about 9.2 percent of women in this age range were full-time prostitutes; a number that falls within the range of full-time prostitutes estimated by Hill (1989) for New York City during the same time period.

Outside of Boston there are no available records of the number of prostitutes. It is likely that in most seaport towns there was at least one brothel. Larger towns off the coast, like Springfield and Worcester, already growing manufacturing sites, certainly must have also contained a trade in sex for sale. There is some indication of venereal diseases showing up in the medical records of mill girls in the model factory towns like Lowell, though the existence of sex for sale was hotly denied by local authorities, and there are no records of prostitution (Ware 1924). It is unlikely that prostitution flourished at the same rate in the small towns and rural areas off the coastline of Massachusetts as it did in Boston and the seaports (Gilfoyle 1992). Given the lack of evidence as to the extent of prostitution in areas outside urban centers and ports, it would be impossible to make a statewide estimate of prostitution in the same manner as for teachers, servants, or seamstresses. Hence, for use in the FLFP, the estimate of Pease and Pease (1990) is doubled to reflect 4,000 prostitutes statewide.

Adding up all the women wage workers who can be clearly estimated or documented for Massachusetts in Table 3.2, as a portion of the adult female population of 191,226, 45.22 percent of all adult women in Massachusetts can be said to have been engaged in nonagricultural waged labor during the 1830s. This is probably a conservative estimate. For instance, a smaller household size would have produced larger estimates in the servant category.

This is a very extensive FLFP, especially in the light of twentieth-century labor force patterns. Except during the peak years of war production, the labor force participation of women in the twentieth century did not rise

Table 3.2

Estimate of FLFP in Massachusetts and Boston, 1833

Occupation	Number
Manufacturing	42,661
Servants	26,357
Seamstresses	13,000
Prostitutes	4,000
Teachers	459
Total	86,447

Source: Data from author's calculations. See text for methods and sources.

above 40 percent until after 1955 (Shank 1988). During the time period of this study, 90 percent of the population still resided in rural areas and received its support from agriculture. As shown in the previous section, the labor of women was central to the survival and well-being of households and communities in agricultural areas. Such a high nonfarm, waged labor force participation rate can only mean that there was a great demand for the waged labor of women.

Another conclusion that can be drawn from this high FLFP is that women engaged in waged labor at all ages and regardless of marital status. While the mills of Lowell hired primarily young, unmarried women, the smaller mills that peppered the entire countryside employed not only young girls, but widows and married women as well (McLane 1833). Dublin (1994) and Blewett (1988) show that 40–75 percent of rural households in New England were engaged in outwork production of cloth, shoes, palm hats, or straw braid; all occupations engaged in primarily by women. The two outwork occupations of palm/straw weaving and shoebinding employed 56.3 percent of all women noted in McLane (1833). Put another way, less than 44 percent of the over 42,000 women listed in McLane (1833) worked for wages outside of the home, the rest worked for wages within their households.

This points to three new conclusions about women's wage work in the nineteenth century. One, most women engaged in waged work for significant portions of their lives. Two, women's waged work occurred regardless of marital status or age. Three, while the move of production out of the home pushed a significant number of women into factory production, many more women reacted to the changing nature of production by combining waged work with their traditional reproductive responsibilities in the home.

It was the combination of social and economic pressures that created the high FLFP estimated for 1830s Massachusetts. Instead of women applying their labor to the capital investment of the household in the form of a loom and distaff, women split their labor between wage labor and all the other forms of household production for which they were responsible. Single women went into factories full-time or populated growing urban areas. Married women performed manufacturing wage work at home in conjunction with their household responsibilities (Dublin 1994; Blewett 1988; Ryan 1983; Carey 1830, 1833; Gutman 1989; Providence First 1837).

Conclusion: The Cyclical Pattern of FLFP

An examination of FLFP in waged work since industrialization began in earnest in 1809 shows that the most recent increase in FLFP is one upswing in a long-term cyclical pattern. Further, there is a constant floor of women engaged in wage labor below which the cyclical FLFP does not go. While in some time periods a majority of women have concentrated on unpaid household labor, a historical perspective shows that these periods of female non-involvement in waged work are not the norm. During the following wars, women assumed primary responsibility for production: the War of 1812, the Civil War, World War I, and World War II. Prior to the Civil War, women were a majority of both servants and the manufacturing workforce in the United States (Ryan 1983; Gutman 1989; MBSL 1885). From the beginning of industrial expansion in the United States in 1809, to the present, 1996, there are 187 years. The 1812 War, antebellum, and Civil War years (72 years); the two world wars (10 years); and the years since 1955, which represent twentieth-century increases in FLFP (41 years) add up to 123 years. This leaves only 64 years in the last 187 (one-third) during which a majority or near-majority of women were not involved in waged labor.

Reliable statistics on women's wage work would probably make FLFP even higher than that estimated for the nineteenth century, and higher than that recorded in the twentieth. There has been a generalized undercounting of women in the labor market since the beginning of census taking by the United States. During the nineteenth century, women's wage labor was dramatically undercounted for four primary reasons:

1. Prior to 1850, married women were not legally entitled to receive their own wages (Ryan 1983; Friedman-Goldstein 1989). Wages for work performed by married women were paid to husbands (Dublin 1994; Blewett 1988); and wages for work performed by single women were occasionally sent to fathers (Kessler-Harris 1978). Hence, there

are many discrepancies in wage records between the individual receiving payment and the individual performing the labor.
2. Frequently, women performed labor in rural communities that would have been paid had that labor been performed by a man.
3. Women's labor was not systematically recorded in the federal census until after 1860.[11]
4. Women tended to be involved in gray market activities and in paid service industries, which, as an extension of traditional female labor in the home, were seen as not worth counting; prostitution, elder/child care, nursing, seamstress work, and bleaching and laundry are all examples.

In the twentieth century, this undercounting of females in waged labor continues. There is still an official blind eye to the same gray market activities mentioned for the nineteenth century, even though the superficial form of those gray market activities may have changed somewhat. For example, instead of laboring over hand sewing in the home, thousands of women, primarily Asian and Latina, labor in illegal garment factories.

In a *CBS Evening News* report on sweat shops (6:30 P.M. EST, June 11, 1996), economic correspondent Ray Brady interviewed Labor Secretary Robert Reich. Reich estimated that more than half of sewing and garment cutting in the United States takes place in illegal sweat shops. The size of gray market industries is such that they can no longer be considered insignificant in a statistical analysis of the labor market.

In the twentieth century, women still tend to combine wage labor and household responsibilities by performing both within the home. Undocumented day-care centers, elder care, microindustries, and piece-rate-in-the-home all hide the involvement of women in waged labor. The continued existence of conflictive social norms as to whether or not women should focus their energy on self-support (poor women) or homemaking (middle/upper-class women) continues to force women to combine them. This makes the separation of waged labor from production for self-use in the home a difficult and tedious task for economists.

While the economy and society of the United States have become far more complicated in the twentieth century than when the Industrial Revolution began in 1809, the patterns governing labor supply, established in the early nineteenth century, can still be seen. The gendered nature of labor continues as a strong factor defining the kind of labor men and women engage in. Government and private industry still benefit from mutually developing policies that guide the "choices" of women in deciding to provide labor for wages.

The three patterns of women's engagement in waged labor established in the nineteenth century have continued into the twentieth:

1. Most women engage in waged labor.
2. Women engage in waged work regardless of age or marital status.
3. Women's work tends to be locational so that they might combine their reproductive responsibilities in the home with the economic need for cash wages.[12]

It seems clear that the pattern of female involvement in waged labor is a cyclical one that does not fall below some minimum number of women who are always engaged in waged work. Once women's involvement in waged work is seen as a long-term, permanent part of the functioning of our economy, then it is apparent that traditional assessments of our economy need to be reevaluated. For example, the discussions on policy issues that affect primarily women's lives, such as quality child or elder care, take on a new structure. The need for institutions that perform the caring and reproductive work normally assigned to women regardless of their involvement in waged labor moves from the arena of temporary arrangements to the fulfillment of long-term or permanent needs of society.

Notes

1. The Tench Coxe Report is Volume 4 of the 1810 census. Coxe was commissioned by Albert Gallatin, secretary of the Treasury, to create a report that was used to support bids for tariffs for manufactured products in Congress. The report contains a wealth of information on different industries throughout the United States and makes careful note of commonly held production resources in rural counties. MBSL (1885) notes both the sharing of equipment and the wearing of homespun by all but the wealthy.

2. Men also produced finished goods, but other than shoe bottoms, these goods tended to be used in capital construction and in the growth of agricultural produce, e.g., glass, metal and wooden tools, stills. The primary area of home production men made a contribution to was the beating and softening of flax, which was then spun into yarn by women (Kessler-Harris 1978). There is an indication that the gendered nature of weaving changed in different areas of the country, with weavers in Philadelphia being primarily men (Ware 1924). However, in New England, most weaving was performed by women (McLane 1833).

3. Different types of production went through these two stages at different times. For example, in Massachusetts weaving was almost completely automated by the 1830s, ending cloth weaving as outwork (Dublin 1994). Shoebinding continued as waged outwork until after 1850 when sewing of leather uppers was automated and brought into factories (Blewett 1988).

4. The payment of both male and female labor in a combination of store orders and cash was deemed preferable to all cash payments by factory owners. On the one hand, the laborer was able to buy goods on the cash market, on the other, labor was held

captive because the medium with which they purchased the necessities of life was not transferable to other locations. Some of the earliest organizing issues for labor were demands for all cash wages (Blewett 1988; Ware 1924).

5. The last indentures came off the books following the Civil War in Philadelphia (Morris 1946).

6. Morris (1946) estimates that 50 percent of the white population arrived in the new world as indentured labor. Examining the passenger lists of ships does not give the whole picture as many ships were sent only with either convict labor or indentures and did not legally have to register their passenger lists in London.

Galenson (1984) finds that indentured servants were about 75 percent of the white population.

Grub (1985) disputes the high rate of indenture found by earlier historians. His findings do not justify his overall conclusion, though. In the shipping records he presents, passenger lists contained 44.8 to 74.4 percent indentured servants, falling well within earlier estimates. What recommends his work are the gender, marital status, and age breakdowns he provides of those arriving as passengers. Women, single persons of both genders, and young people were more likely to become indentured servants than married couples and older adult males.

Length of indenture contract varied with gender, age, and circumstance. Generally, terms ranged from four to ten years, with children indentured until aged twenty-one. Since life expectancy was about forty years, this was half a lifetime. Convicts were generally indented for life (Morris 1946).

7. Soldiers traditionally provided domestic enforcement. Urban areas in the north were fraught with riots on a regular basis (Headley 1970; Carey 1970; Boston City Council Records, 1835–39). Soldiers were also used in the ongoing campaign to push Native American peoples off the East Coast (Brown 1970; Gutman 1989).

8. For descriptions of the changing expectations of women in the nineteenth century, see Ryan (1983; 1990), Hymowitz and Weissman (1978).

9. Within a few years of opening, the mills began to be plagued by labor strife. Dublin (1991) notes that the patriarchal rules that put women into close contact in the monitored boarding houses probably had a great deal to do with the women in Lowell organizing earlier and with more success than in other mill towns where living conditions were worse. Ware (1924) notes this phenomenon as well. He attributes this to the need of the working class to maintain a portion of their lives separate from their employers.

10. Gilfoyle (1992) and Hill (1989) both note the prevalence of child prostitution during the nineteenth century. They attribute this to a number of causes. First, there was no age of consent for sex or marriage. Second, the belief of the time was that sex with a virgin cured venereal disease. Therefore, young girls were much in demand.

11. Early census takers did acknowledge the labor of women in the mills, but did not accurately count it. Even in the 1810 census, which exhorted women to supply waged labor, the labor of those women is not recorded in the statistical portion.

12. Ivy Pinchbeck (1930) was the earliest economist to examine the close connection between women's work and location.

Appendix

The formula for determining the number of servants in Boston and Massachusetts, circa 1830, can be expressed algebraically as:

$$(2FW/3)/H = X;$$
$$X(H/8.5) = D;$$
$$X + D = D';$$

where FW = female workers in Boston; H = households; X = domestics per household in Boston; D = domestics in rural areas; D' = total estimate of domestics.

Following this procedure:

1. Of the 42,661 women wage workers in the McLane report, 2,953 of them were listed as waged workers in Boston, making an estimated [2,953 × 2] = 5,906 women working as domestics.
2. Assuming six and a half persons per household, out of 61,392 persons, there were roughly 9,445 households in Boston. One-third would be 2,833 servant-using homes. Dividing 5,906 by 2,833, there were an estimated 2.0847 servants per household.
3. In rural Massachusetts, dividing 541,967 persons by six and a half produces 83,380 households. Divided by eight and a half, this yields 9,810 households using servants. Multiplying this by 2.0847 yields 20,451 servants.
4. Adding the rural estimate of 20,451 to the urban estimate of 5,906, the final estimate is that 26,357 women worked as domestics during the early 1830s in Massachusetts.

4

Gender, Sexuality, and Sexual Orientation

All in the Feminist Family?

M.V. Lee Badgett

During a lively discussion of the economic relationships between women and men within families at the first IAFFE conference in 1992, I reminded my fellow participants that not all families are based on a heterosexual married couple. In addition to single-parent families, lesbians and gay men also form families that do not conform to the traditional male–female marital model. Kathryn Larson expanded on this point later in the conference in discussing the near complete invisibility of lesbian couples and households within economic theory and in empirical research on women and families.

Although neither of our comments generated much discussion at the time, their modest impact became apparent in other ways. In particular, in more than one subsequent presentation of a model of family economic behavior that weekend, the presenters specifically noted that their models could be applied to any kind of family, whether heterosexual or homosexual. While I welcomed the greater acknowledgment of lesbian and gay families, I have remained skeptical of the idea that economic models developed to explain the behavior of heterosexual families can be simply transferred to explain lesbian and gay families.

At the time of the conference, I had hoped that this initial acknowledgment was a harbinger of more inclusive feminist economic models to come. My intense interest in these questions is undoubtedly related to the fact that, as a lesbian, I must deal with these issues in a personal way every day. And as a feminist, I see the questions raised by considering sexual orientation as pointing to a need to rethink much economic and feminist thought on many topics. But in the two years since that conference, only a few economists—most of us self-identified feminists—appear to have made efforts to consider seriously whether existing theories are good explanations of the economic lives of lesbian, gay, and bisexual people, or to contemplate the broader implications of sexuality for economic theorizing.[1]

In the meantime, many economists who are feminists have continued to collectively and self-consciously identify our work as having some common feminist thread, even though we may come from different economic methodological perspectives. For example, Marianne Ferber and Julie Nelson (1993, 9) support the practice of many feminist economists and social scientists of using gender rather than biological sex as the primary analytical category to understand women's experiences, where "gender is the *social meaning* given to biological differences between the sexes." Simply adding gender as an additional analytical category, however, risks universalizing "women," forgetting the very different experiences of women of different racial, ethnic, and class backgrounds and of different sexual orientations. Rhonda Williams (1993) warns of this universalizing tendency in some recent definitions of feminist economics, which ignore important racial differences among women. Nancy Folbre suggests that "the real contribution of feminist theory lies in its efforts to reconceptualize the relationship between different forms of social inequality, rather than simply to empower women" (1994, 268). Folbre analyzes social reproduction in the context of many different dimensions of collective action where groups (defined by gender, age, sexual orientation, race, class, and/or nation) act within "structures of constraint," or "sets of asset distributions, rules, norms, and preferences that empower given social groups" (51). All of this is not to say that gender as an analytical category and feminism as a way of using that category to understand and break down the suppression of women have no use. But to understand and facilitate change in the material circumstances of women requires a nuanced analysis incorporating the "divided loyalties and competing interests" (cf. Folbre 1994) of different groups of women and men.

In the next section of this essay, I argue that a focus on gender (and the use of gender-based family models) is, first of all, inadequate for the development of the economics of sexuality (broadly defined) because of important differences between "gender" and "sexuality" as analytical categories. Also, without separate attention to sexual orientation, which I use to refer to the aspect of sexuality based on the gender of one's sex partners, the experiences of lesbians as women and gay men as men may remain invisible even within a feminist economic model.[2] Later in the chapter, I will demonstrate the extent of this invisibility by analyzing examples from prominent economists who study gender and families, with a particular emphasis on the work of Gary Becker. Becker has explicitly used his family model to "explain" some aspects of gay people's family lives, making him one of the few economists to acknowledge the existence of such families (Larson 1992). Barbara Bergmann's work, while feminist, reflects economists' general inattention to possible differences in the concerns, interests, and behaviors of lesbian, gay, and bisexual people. As I will show, the gender-centered models of Becker and most other economists are seriously inadequate once the existence of sexual orientation as an issue is acknowledged.

Making lesbian, gay, and bisexual people visible within economic theory requires more than forcing them into standard economic conceptions of family based on gender differences alone. I will argue that lesbian, gay, and bisexual people do not emulate the heterosexual marriage model when creating interpersonal relationships characterized by love, commitment, sacrifice, and interdependence, in other words, in creating what we might commonly think of as a "family." One consequence of the academic homogenization of families is that economists tend to overlook the important legal, political, and cultural differences that shape the economic position and behavior of families formed by lesbian, gay, and bisexual people. Acknowledging this common limitation of economic modeling should encourage us to open up our research on families to consider how variations in sexual orientation might direct us to rethink the influence of gender norms and family legal institutions on economic behavior.

Recently I have seen firsthand another consequence of homogenizing lesbian and gay families. While feminists—both heterosexual and homosexual—have been busy theorizing about the family, lesbian, gay, and bisexual activists have been successfully organizing and lobbying for new legally and socially recognized forms of family relationships, often right under our academic noses in colleges and universities across the United States. These newly recognized family relationships, commonly called "domestic partnerships," represent an important step forward for gay people, both socially and materially. However, the structure and implementation of these new relationships are generally quite conservative, being modeled on a property-based heterosexual marriage ignoring potentially powerful feminist principles and underpinnings. Using the domestic partner movement in colleges and universities as a case study, I argue that the relatively conservative outcomes are at least partly the result of a failure of collective action in the form of heterosexual "free riding" on the efforts of the lesbian, gay, and bisexual activists. This active rewriting of family definition and policy presents an important opportunity for feminists of all sexual orientations to affect what a "family" means and does.

Gender, Sexuality, and Sexual Orientation

Why should feminist economists think about sexual orientation? How should feminist economists think about sexual orientation? One possible answer is that issues of gender and of sexuality are not just intertwined, but inseparable. In that case, a focus on gender-based economic theories will provide the essential tools for understanding sexuality, making issues related to sexual orientation a subfield of feminist economics. This would be a useful integration if sexuality explains a large part of gender oppression, and if gender oppression is at the root of oppression against lesbian, gay, and bisexual people. I will argue, however, that gender and sexuality constitute two separate analytical axes, and that simple gender-based economic models seriously misinterpret or implicitly omit the lives of lesbian, gay, and bisexual people.

To the extent that women's economic choices and well-being are limited by or structured around reproduction, the economic effects of gender and sexuality are closely connected. Even economists with empirically flawed and incomplete theories recognize some relationship between sexuality and gender. Richard Posner's (1992) rational choice model of sexuality, for example, traces family organizational forms back to biologically determined differences between the sexes, mainly in terms of sex drive and reproductive roles.[3] (See Robert Anderson 1993 for a critique of Posner's analysis and his use of questionable empirical information.) Outside of a family and reproductive context, sexuality has an important influence on women's labor market opportunities and experiences: both sexual harassment and employers' assumptions about women's likely fertility decisions have limited women's job opportunities.

Further, sexuality has an important influence on the social and legal treatment of individuals of differing sexual orientations. In one important article, for instance, Adrienne Rich (1983, 191) addresses the interactions between sexuality and gender in explaining the status of lesbians and heterosexual women: "But whatever its origins, when we look hard and clearly at the extent and elaboration of measures designed to keep women within a male sexual purlieu, it becomes an inescapable question whether the issue we have to address as feminists is not simple 'gender inequality,' nor the domination of culture by males, nor mere 'taboos against homosexuality,' but the enforcement of heterosexuality for women as a means of assuring male right of physical, economical, and emotional access." Similarly, a gender-based analysis that considers sexual orientation would be essential to understanding the often troubled political and social relationships between lesbians and gay men.

One very concrete example of the connection between sexuality and gender is the argument that discrimination against lesbians and gay men is simply a form of gender discrimination: lesbians face discrimination because they love women instead of men, and gay men face discrimination because they love men instead of women. Using this interpretation to frame employment discrimination against gay men and lesbians as an illegal practice under Title VII has been unsuccessful, however (*Harvard Law Review* Editors 1991, 68–70). Judges have generally turned the sex discrimination argument around, pointing out that lesbians and gay men are treated in the same way, so no gender discrimination exists.[4] A plausible but as yet untried variant of this gender-based legal strategy argues that employment discrimination against lesbians and gay men is rooted in their violation of traditional gender roles, particularly those related to reproduction (*Harvard Law Review* Editors 1991, 17–18 and 70–71). A gender-based analysis was successful in one recent and potentially significant marriage case, however. The Hawaii Supreme Court ruled that marriage laws forbidding same-sex marriages violate the state's constitutional prohibition of sex discrimination. A lower court must now decide whether a compelling state interest exists for such a violation (Homer 1994). Even with the possibility of one significant victory, the overall lack of success of this legal strategy has helped to make acquiring explicit protections against sexual orientation discrimination a priority of the lesbian and gay civil rights movement.

Although the failure of a particular legal strategy does not negate the possibility of a gender-based analysis of sexual orientation, the crucial question remains: Can the study of sexuality be made equivalent to or be subsumed by the study of gender? Noted literary critic Eve Kosofsky Sedgwick argues persuasively that sexuality should constitute a separate analytical axis because many aspects of sexuality do not overlap with gender:

> An objection to this analogy [of sexuality with race or class as an analytic axis] might be that gender is *definitionally* built into determinations of sexuality, in a way that neither of them is definitionally intertwined with, for instance, determinations of class or race. It is certainly true that without a concept of gender there could be, quite simply, no concept of homo- or heterosexuality. But many other dimensions of sexual choice (auto- or alloerotic, within or between generations, species, etc.) have no such distinctive, explicit definition connection with gender; indeed, some dimensions of sexuality might be tied, not to gender, but *instead* to differences or similarities of race or class. (Sedgwick 1990, 31; emphasis in the original)

According to this view, sexuality is too complex to be explained adequately with a simple gendered analysis. Bisexuals' sexuality cannot be defined simply by the gender of their sex partners, for instance (see Steven

Seidman 1993 on challenges to gender-based sexual identities). And as Sedgwick notes, the race or class of a sex partner might be more important than gender for some people, suggesting that an analysis of sexuality must include interactions with many potentially eroticized characteristics.

Considering sexual orientation in particular, Sedgwick then argues that even when gender is a *necessary* component of the analysis (as in Rich's argument, for example), gender analysis is not *sufficient*. Sedgwick suggests that gender analysis is inherently incapable of revealing the subtle underpinnings of the differential status and treatment of gay people: "The ultimate definitional appeal in any gender-based analysis must necessarily be to the diacritical frontier between different genders. This gives heterosocial and heterosexual relations a conceptual privilege of incalculable consequence. . . . It is unrealistic to expect a close, textured analysis of same-sex relations through an optic calibrated in the first place to the coarser stigmata of gender difference" (31–32). For economists, this point implies that attempts to graft models of heterosexual families onto families formed by lesbian, gay, and bisexual people will perpetuate heterosexist assumptions about the appropriate form of families and will neither explain nor transform the lives of lesbian, gay, and bisexual people's families. (While some might argue that no existing economic theory provides a "close, textured analysis" of opposite-sex relations, many economists have sought, and continue to seek, a better model.)

Examples of the failure of a gendered economic analysis to explain the behavior and economic situations of lesbians and gay men are easy to find in the work of both feminist and nonfeminist economists. Sometimes the failures are particularly egregious. Economic models of fertility, for example, generally ignore how sperm and egg actually connect. Economists clearly consider the mode of conception to be obvious, given the implicit assumption that all families contain a man and a woman. Even when economists are more specific, heterosexual blinders often lead to incorrect conclusions: "Indeed, their [men's and women's] times are *complements in sexual enjoyment,* the production of children, and possibly other commodities produced by the household. Complementarity implies that households with men and women are more efficient than households with only one sex, but because *both sexes are required to produce certain commodities* complementarity reduces the sexual division of labor in the allocation of time and investments" (Becker 1991, 39; emphasis added).

Even assuming that Becker means making babies rather than making love when he refers to the production of "certain commodities," his reasoning curiously ignores the fact that sperm—not the physical presence of a man in a household—is the necessary complementary good for lesbians seeking to conceive, and sperm is available in various forms and from many different sources, e.g., friends or sperm banks. As anthropologist Kath Weston points out in her study of lesbian and gay families, "New reproductive technologies have collided with ideologies that picture a child as the 'natural' product of the union of a woman and a man in an act of sexual intercourse that gives expression to contrasting gender identities" (Weston 1991, 169–70).

But neoclassical economists are not the only ones to universalize and privilege the male–female-based family. Some feminist economists, in their attacks on neoclassical models' assumptions and policy implications, have criticized those models while continuing to locate the roots of women's unequal economic position within the gender dynamics of a heterosexual family structure: "One way to achieve equity between the sexes—very possibly the only way—would be for women and men to take similar economic roles. By social custom husbands and wives would do the same amount of family-care work and devote the same time and energy to paid employment" (Bergmann 1986, 266). Indeed, the very concept of "the sexual division of labor"—the focus of many feminist economists—is rooted in a division *between* the sexes, that is, it assumes a male–female distinction within the family. Although Bergmann's perspective might advance heterosexual women's status, the invisibility of same-sex couples (and of individuals not in a couple) within feminist economists' ideas of "a family" leads to an incomplete political agenda. Even though an improvement in heterosexual women's economic position is likely to improve lesbians' economic position relative to both heterosexual and gay men, lesbians and bisexual women (and gay and bisexual men) might still face a labor market disadvantage because of their sexual orientation, just as women of color will still face race and ethnicity discrimination (see Badgett 1995). A "feminist" policy agenda based on the male–female couple will not address the legal, social, and economic disadvantages of gay families' households, and such an agenda risks perpetuating important inequities.

Learning about All Families from Lesbian, Gay, and Bisexual People's Families

Some might argue that since lesbian couples and gay male couples often appear similar to heterosexual couples—each implying a relationship between two people characterized by long-term commitment, emotional and physical intimacy, and economic interdependence—existing economic models of families (whether based on maximizing a single family utility function or on bargaining within the family) can still be used to explain some aspects of lesbian and gay household members' behavior. Those models of household production and distribution, it might be argued, do not necessarily require a male–female couple, even though they have been historically developed out of concern for heterosexual families.

Certainly many lesbian, gay, and bisexual people form a relationship with one person of the same sex in a way that seems comfortingly similar to heterosexual married couples.[5] But too little representative or detailed analysis of lesbian and gay families exists to make me comfortable with any sweeping generalizations. For instance, in her study of lesbian and gay male kinship (structures that she calls "families we choose"), Weston (1991, 109) finds that "in the Bay Area, families we choose resembled networks in the sense that they could cross household lines, and both were based on ties that radiated outward from individuals like spokes on a wheel. However, gay families differed from networks to the extent that they quite consciously incorporated symbolic demonstrations of love, shared history, material or emotional assistance, and other signs of enduring solidarity. Although many gay families included friends, not just any friend would do." Economists' forcing such complex family structures into a narrow heterosexual tradition simply reproduces the problems associated with equating gender and sexual orientation as categories of analysis, and in particular makes invisible the distinct experiences of lesbian, gay, and bisexual people and their families.

On a more theoretical level, a lively political debate continues among lesbian, gay, and bisexual people about the nature and form of relationships. Some writers advocate the right of same-sex couples to marry (e.g., Stoddard 1989) and see such marriages as desirable (e.g., Mohr 1994). Others warn that marriage would undermine "the affirmation of gay identity and culture; and the validation of many forms of relationships" (Ettelbrick 1989). Ruthann Robson (1994) argues for resisting even the idea of "family," warning that lesbians should not enter into the "redefining the family" debate. Robson worries that even liberal redefinitions of "family" will inevitably result in the application of traditional heterosexual forms, assumptions, and legal regulations to lesbian relationships, destroying the diversity and complexity of these relationships. She argues for resistance to the category of "family" and for a thorough reconceptualization of categories of relationships between individuals: "Thus, rather than lesbians requesting inclusion into the privileged legal category of 'family,' what if lesbians advocated the abolition of benefits based on family status, the reconsideration of what constitute 'benefits,' or even the abolition of the category 'family' itself?" (Robson 1994, 992).

Of course, one might argue that lesbians (and gay men and bisexuals) are not the only people whose complex relationships are delegitimized and disadvantaged by existing legal definitions of family relationships. In the same way, the standard economic model of "a family" privileges one increasingly uncommon form and ignores many other forms of family organization. Feminist anthropologists and sociologists have studied the diversity of family forms in the United States that result from "women's resistance to and negotiation of the structures that subordinate them" (Thorne 1992, 7). While not rejecting the entire category of "family," Jane Collier et al. (1992) view "The Family, not as a concrete institution designed to fulfill universal human needs, but as an ideological construct associated with the modern state." They provide some useful guidance for theorizing about families: "What we can begin to ask is what we *want* our families to do. Then, distinguishing our hopes from what we have, we can begin to analyze the social forces that enhance or undermine the realization of the kinds of human bonds we need" (34).

While the task of reconceptualizing "family" from a broad feminist perspective is certainly a large and daunting one, feminist economists moving beyond a narrow critique of existing family models to new conceptualizations have several possible starting points. Expanding the economic theory of the family should involve *analyzing* that which is normally *taken as given* in economic models, that is, the range of functions performed by families, the legally and culturally sanctioned idea of what constitutes a family, and the roles of individuals within the family. In this project, variation in the sexual orientations of individuals collected into something called "a family" or household provides a way to study the impact of legal and social institutions and norms on the formation and economics of all families, not just heterosexual ones. Thus, rather than dealing with sexual orientation by either squeezing one form of gay family (the same-sex couple) into the heterosexual model or by developing an entirely separate model of gay families, feminist economists could contribute to the development of a theory explaining the existence and dynamics of *many* kinds of family structures.

Sketching out a few examples illustrates the usefulness of this approach. Take, for instance, a question of central concern to feminist economists: Is the sexual division of labor a product of rational choice or a product of gender norms about appropriate work for men and women? The neoclassical model of the family's allocation of time starts with the household maximizing one aggregate utility function by combining time and market goods in the production of commodities for consumption. An efficient household (of any size and regardless of gender composition) allocates its members' time between market and nonmarket production based on their comparative advantage in one or the other, leading to specialization by most or all household members (Becker 1991, 3–6). For heterosexual couples, biological differences and wage discrimination give a comparative advantage to women in nonmarket work and to men in market work, leading to the observed sexual division of labor. Specialization leads to dependence on other household members, giving rise to the institution of marriage for male–female couples, defined by Becker as "a written, oral, or customary long-term contract between a man and a woman to produce children, food, and other commodities in a common household" (1991, 43), and reinforcing the existing division of labor.

Would we expect rational lesbian, gay, and bisexual people and their families to specialize in the same way? Becker argues that same-sex households cannot take advantage of what he (inaccurately) cites as complementarities exclusive to opposite-sex couples (producing children and sexual enjoyment). In Becker's model, the absence both of those complementarities and of within-couple gender wage differentials should reduce specialization within same-sex couples. Given differences in education, upbringing, and tastes, however, it seems likely that gay individuals' marginal products in home and market production vary, making comparative advantage of potential equal relevance for same-sex households. (Also, some gay people's families and households might include men *and* women and possibly people of differing sexual orientations.) Becker's model therefore implies that specialization would also be efficient in lesbian, gay, and bisexual people's families when the individuals share the same physical households.

Other factors normally taken as given in economic models suggest that gendered patterns of specialization would be much rarer among lesbian or gay households. The first factor is the impact of gender norms on the division of labor. Sociologists Philip Blumstein and Pepper Schwartz (1983, 14) argue that comparisons of heterosexual couples (both married and unmarried) and gay couples constitute a natural experiment for studying gender roles: "By contrasting homosexual couples with both types of heterosexual couples, we can see how relationships function when there are no male/female differences to contend with. By comparing gay men to lesbians, we explore differences in male and female contributions to relationships." Within same-sex couples or households, a strictly gendered division of labor is simply not possible. Further, as Letitia Anne Peplau (1991) points out, research in other social sciences reveals that same-sex couples typically reject gendered roles. In their study of a nonrandom sample of couples, Blumstein and Schwartz discovered relatively little market–nonmarket specialization within lesbians and gay male couples, and they found that respondents' personal values were a major influence on the market labor supply of both individuals in same-sex couples, most of whom believed that both partners should engage in market work (127–31). And while such comparisons have focused on couples, similar questions could be asked of larger households.

The second factor that might be expected to decrease the extent of specialization in gay couples is that the legal and social institutions supporting heterosexual couples and families are not accessible to gay people's families. For example, legal marriage is limited to heterosexual couples, making people in homosexual couples legal strangers to each other (Robson 1992), a distinction absent from Becker's analysis. The absence of legal marriage increases uncertainty about pooling assets and income, since the division of assets would not be governed by the rules applicable in the case of marital divorce. Gay couples and their lawyers have created some imperfect substitutes for marriage, including contracts regarding mutual support and division of property, wills, and the assignation of power of attorney (*Harvard Law Review* Editors 1991). However, the transaction costs of such substitute arrangements are higher than those of marriage, so all couples may not have such agreements. Further, such contracts are sometimes ruled unenforceable (Rubenstein 1993, 439). Families of adults extending beyond a couple have no options for establishing a legally recognized set of family relationships.[6]

Tax policies and the widespread practice of tying employment benefits to marriage (supported by tax policy) also have differential consequences for specialization in gay families. The federal income tax system still includes a marriage penalty for couples whose incomes are similar and therefore reinforces traditional divisions of labor, with men doing market work and women doing (untaxed) nonmarket work. With the option of marriage closed off, same-sex couples (and larger lesbian, gay, and/or bisexual households) will not have this tax incentive for such specialization. Employment-based health care (and other) benefits for employees, their legal spouses, and their children also encourage market work by all lesbian, gay, and bisexual people. Because employers rarely extend family benefits to the partners (and in some cases the children) of lesbian and gay employees, specialization in nonmarket work would likely carry the additional consequence of no benefits for gay partners.[7]

Thus, analyzing the impact of differences in legal and social norms and institutions for gay families provides new research strategies for understanding the division of labor within households generally, and the sexual division of labor in heterosexual households in particular. Kathryn Larson suggests that heterosexual couples will also have an alternative model for the division of household work from studies of gay families (Larson 1992, 252).

In addition to the household division of labor, economic models of the family also attempt to explain fertility and the demand for children. Becker (1991, 330) and many others assume that lesbians and gay men are not likely to have children.[8] Two surveys, one a random sample of the United States (Briggs 1994) and the other a random sample of U.S. voters (Badgett 1994a), both showed that lesbians are just as likely as heterosexual women to have children in their homes, although gay men are much less likely than heterosexual men to have children. But even if lesbians and gay men have fewer children, this difference is unlikely to be simply the result of a lower demand for children. Lesbian, gay, and bisexual people who want to raise children face institutional and legal constraints that few heterosexuals need to consider (see *Harvard Law Review* Editors 1991, 119–50). Some states prohibit adoption or foster care by gay people. A biological parent (such as a former spouse) or other relative may successfully challenge a lesbian or gay parent's right to child custody. The relationship between biological parents and nonbiological co-parents is ill-defined and subject to legal challenge. Some state laws restrict lesbians' access to reproductive technologies. Given these conditions, gay families could have the same "demand curve" for children as heterosexual couples but have fewer children (either biological or adoptive) because they face a far higher price of conceiving or adopting and raising children.

Children are also important in the context of another subject of family models—the stability of marriage and relationships. Becker argues that "investment in children" is the main form of "marital-specific" capital for heterosexual couples, an investment that partially determines the likelihood of divorce. Becker cites one study of a nonrandom sample that showed homosexual couples were less stable than married couples (Becker 1991, 330), and he attributes to this lesser stability the gay couples' lower number of children, less stark division of labor, and fewer investments in relationship-specific capital. These characteristics, in his opinion, reduce the stability of marriages and thus his circular logic leads to self-fulfilling prophecies.[9] However, he again fails to recognize the role of underlying legal and social institutions that treat heterosexual and homosexual couples differently and may account for all of any difference in stability.[10] Regarding larger household configurations, Becker argues that the possibility of shirking and the loss of individual privacy reduce the stability of those arrangements, again without reference to the lack of legal ties that might encourage more permanent bonds (1991, 48–53).

Because it ignores the impact of strong social norms related to the division of labor as well as exclusionary institutions (and their historical development), the neoclassical model of family decision making is left open to justifiable criticism from feminists. Furthermore, feminists could develop a more damaging empirical challenge to Becker's model (and similar models) by using comparisons among families differentiated by the sexual orientations of their adult members. Such a feminist research agenda would serve dual purposes: learning more about an understudied group of people as well as furthering our understanding of how *all* families work. Both goals will be increasingly important as policymakers are compelled to respond to changing family structures and to the rapidly developing political efforts of lesbian, gay, and bisexual people.

Political Lessons from Lesbian and Gay Families Are Opportunities for Feminists

Just as consideration of sexual orientation could lead to an expansion of feminist economic theory, the experiences and successes of lesbian, gay, and bisexual activists demonstrate that changes in public policy and employment practices related to the family are possible. The movement to recognize "domestic partners" (or "spousal equivalents") shows that new legal family structures *can* be created to respond to changing family concepts and needs. At the same time, though, the domestic partner issue reveals the power of tradition to mold and limit debate. The resulting domestic partner policies are often relatively conservative reforms that do not include all of the diverse family structures of either gay or heterosexual people. As I will argue, without more active involvement of heterosexual feminists, the material gains will mainly go to some gay people—still a positive outcome, of course—but we feminists will have missed an opportunity for more direct shaping of family policy.

This historic movement to create new legally and socially recognized relationships is found in many places. Denmark and Sweden have created an alternative form of marriage for same-sex couples. Some municipalities and employers in the United States also recognize committed same-sex relationships for purposes ranging from hospital visitation rights to employment benefits (Gossett 1994).

Institutions of higher education are a rapidly growing source of domestic partner benefits for employees. Since 1992, for instance, over twenty-five colleges and universities have agreed to cover domestic partners of employees and their children in employer-provided health care plans (Badgett 1994b). Other campuses extend more limited benefits to partners of employees. As my own university took up the domestic partner issue in spring 1994, I conducted a study of colleges and universities with domestic partner policies and of other campuses engaged in active discussion of those policies. The study revealed some important patterns in the development of domestic partner policies that should concern feminists, whether heterosexual, bisexual, or homosexual.[11]

As on my own campus, the collective action of lesbian, gay, and bisexual employees has been the motivating force behind the consideration and adoption of domestic partner policies at most universities. Whether working through layers of campus bureaucracy, lobbying high-level officials, or taking their employers to court, lesbian and gay employees have diligently progressed through the basics of collective action: collecting information, strategizing paths, calling in favors, marshaling allies, and educating co-workers. According to all of the interviews conducted during the study, heterosexual allies played important roles, although those vocal allies were rarely heterosexuals with domestic partners, as will be discussed below.

What was the underlying motive of the activists? As with other gay political struggles, some gay civil rights activists see the domestic partnership effort as a step toward the equal treatment of lesbians and gay men with heterosexuals. In this view, basing benefits on legal marriage blatantly discriminates against gay people, who cannot marry. Domestic partnerships, then, are an interim step on the way to larger goals, such as legalization of same-sex marriage. As noted earlier, however, other activists (call this the "liberation" perspective) seek not the right to participate in the institution of marriage, but an expansion of the options for validating relationships (Ettelbrick 1989). In the view of this camp, tying employment benefits to marriage discriminates against all unmarried couples, and domestic partnerships constitute an alternative to marriage that should be open to *all* couples, straight or gay. In practice, many groups started off advocating the extension of domestic partner recognition to both same-sex and opposite-sex couples. But out of the twenty-five schools studied, only five offered benefits to opposite-sex partners (Badgett 1994b).

Limiting eligibility to same-sex partners resulted in part from administrators' resistance to the higher costs of including heterosexual domestic partners. The leadership of lesbian and gay employees and the "free riding" of heterosexual employees with domestic partners may have also influenced the limitation of eligibility to same-sex partners. Unmarried heterosexual couples do not appear to have developed a self-conscious identity or sense of community on the campuses studied—perhaps the cause of their low participation in most organizing efforts. In contrast, lesbian, gay, and bisexual faculty and staff often organize to deal with diverse issues, including campus safety, curricular changes, social events, research seminars, and campus political issues. Partnered heterosexuals may also fear homophobic reactions to their advocacy of an issue so closely associated with gay people. Gay activists often reveal their (stigmatized) sexual orientation in the course of lobbying, either directly or through the assumptions of co-workers, often risking their careers in the effort; but a sense of solidarity and community may reduce gay employees' apprehension or reluctance. At the campuses in the study, the greatest collective involvement from heterosexuals with unmarried partners came at the end of the process, in the form of complaints about an announced domestic partner policy for same-sex couples only.

Other elements of the domestic partner policies studied reveal a fundamentally traditional modeling on heterosexual marriage. For instance, the formal definition and eligibility standards are usually based on an idealized vision of marriage, with time requirements (to establish commitment), shared assets and debts, and a joint residence. Although none of those elements are required for legal marriage, they are nevertheless identified as characterizing a "real" marriage. In two cases (Dartmouth and Smith Colleges), partners must even attest that they would marry if legally allowed to do so.

During this rare time of active rewriting of the most basic element of family—defining relationships between adults—the underlying traditionalism and the limits of current collective action should serve as a warning to feminists interested in family matters. In the lesbian and gay staff and faculty group at my own campus, for example, theory has influenced practice: heterosexual domestic partners would most likely have been dropped from our political goal (and probably from the official proposal under consideration by our university) without the persuasive efforts of myself and other self-identified feminists, who were committed to the general principle of equitable treatment for employees regardless of marital status.

Many universities, however, are likely to remain resistant to counting opposite-sex partners as domestic partners, even with active efforts from heterosexual feminists, since such inclusion could increase the cost of the policy. But feminists of all sexual orientations can learn from and contribute to these efforts in important ways, starting with posing some important questions for active consideration: What functions does marriage serve that should be preserved and extended to other family formations? Why should two adults in a couple receive privileges that two single individuals would not receive? What impact should children have on the legal status of their parents? This moment in the development of domestic partner policies and debate seems particularly ripe for opening up these broader issues in a way that could lead to meaningful advances in the status and economic position of all women and their families.

Toward an Economics Incorporating Sexual Orientation

Some scholars have already begun to consider sexuality and sexual orientation in the context of economic theory and policy. Folbre's (1994) framework for understanding how individual and collective interests shape economic behavior provides the most comprehensive vision of how gender and sexuality fit together along with race, class, age, nationality, and other identities. Because economics has lagged significantly behind other social sciences attending to both sexuality and sexual orientation, even less ambitious undertakings addressing sexual orientation may make important contributions, both to academia and to lesbian, gay, and bisexual people more generally. Although gender and sexuality might constitute separate analytical axes, they are complementary and interdependent rather than mutually exclusive. My hope is that feminist economists will be inspired by the opportunities for fruitful inquiry that an economic analysis of sexual orientation will provide, influencing the economics profession, economic theory, and public policy.

Notes

This chapter is reprinted from M.V. Lee Badgett, "Gender, Sexuality, and Sexual Orientation: All in the Feminist Family?" *Feminist Economics* 1, no. 1 (spring 1995): 121–39, with the permission of Routledge.

1. For a review of the early offerings, see M.V. Lee Badgett and Rhonda M. Williams (1992).

2. Terminology is contested terrain in discussions of sexuality. In general, I use "sexual orientation" to distinguish between heterosexual, homosexual, and bisexual people. Because a long history of using "gay" to refer to both lesbians and gay men perpetuated the invisibility of lesbians, and because bisexual people often share a common cause, history, and culture with lesbians and gay men, I collect nonheterosexual people under the "lesbian, gay, and bisexual" umbrella whenever practical. No blanket term has achieved widespread acceptance ("queer" currently tends to provoke readers of all sexual orientations), so I will occasionally lump all three groups into the term "gay," with the understanding that this refers to all three groups unless I specifically refer to "gay men."

3. Posner's ambitious project is weakened by his taking as exogenous important gender-related factors, a reminder of the important interactions between gender and sexuality:

> Much of the variance among different eras, cultures, social classes, races, and the sexes themselves in behavior, attitudes, customs, and laws concerning such aspects of sexuality ... can be explained, and the changes in them predicted, by references to the handful of variables that the theory identifies as likely to be significant. The principal variables are the occupational profile of women and ... women's economic independence, plus urbanization, income, the sex ratio, and scientific and technological advances relating to the control of fertility and to the care of mothers and infants.

4. *DeSantis v. Pacific Telephone & Telegraph Co.*, 608 F. 2d 327 (9th Cir. 1979).

5. The scope of this paper prevents going into detail about the similarities and differences of same-sex and opposite-sex *couples*. For first-person accounts of ceremonies and commitments of lesbians and gay men, see Sherman (1992). For more comparisons of the division of labor, etc., between gay couples and heterosexual married and unmarried couples, see Blumstein and Schwartz (1983); Larson (1992); and Kurdek (1993).

6. In California, larger nontraditional families are allowed to register as private associations, but those registrations have no practical value as yet (Rubenstein 1993, 442–43).

7. Also, these social and economic institutions will influence any specialization that occurs, resulting in perhaps unexpected patterns. For instance, Phyllis Burke describes her family's decision that she would stay home to care for her young son while her partner, who was the biological and, therefore, legal mother of their child, returned to her job to provide health insurance for herself and the child. Because Burke was not a legal parent at the time, her employer's health insurance would not have covered their son (Burke 1993, 31).

8. The surveys do not ask what the legal relationship is to the child. Also, at least some of lesbians' children may have been conceived while one of the mothers was in a heterosexual relationship.

9. Becker and Posner offer two other reasons more intrinsically related to homosexuality that would reduce the stability of gay relationships. Without documenting his claims, Becker suggests that high search costs result in poorer matches (Becker 1991, 330). But from another perspective, high search costs would also reduce the gains from "divorce" to search for another mate, increasing the stability of couples (Larson 1992, 254). Posner argues that "the male taste for variety in sexual partners makes the prospects for sexual fidelity worse in a homosexual than in a heterosexual marriage" (Posner 1992, 306), an effect that would destabilize gay male couples but not lesbian couples, of course. Anderson counters this conclusion with an alternative prediction that such tastes "could lead to an understanding about allowable infidelity that would make the relationship *more* stable than that of a couple whose members disagree on the desirability of variety" (Anderson 1993, 197).

10. Becker also likens gay couples to heterosexual trial marriages when he points out that the lower legal costs of ending relationships might reduce stability, but he fails to mention the difference in the ability to marry in the first place.

11. Of the twenty-five colleges or universities that offered (or planned to offer) health care benefits to domestic partners as of April 1994, I was able through personal and professional networks to contact and interview activists closely involved in the approval process at twelve of those campuses. I also interviewed activists at three campuses that do not yet have such policies. In addition to the interviews, I collected documents (official forms, press releases, new articles, etc.) from most of the twenty-five campuses. More details of the study are available in Badgett (1994b or 1994c).

5

A Structural Connection Among Race, Gender, Class

Marx's Political Economy Without the Subject

Teresa Brennan

Most radical papers today begin and end with one or two paragraphs lamenting the fact that the author has been unable to take account of race or gender or class, and that the author recognizes how important it is that such work be done. Well, this author recognizes it too, but wants to claim that a value theory without the subject/object distinction will enable us to make connections between race, gender, and class that go beyond goodwill, or the desire for these various forms of exploitation to have something in common.

What is a value theory without the subject/object distinction? It is an interpretation of Marx's labor theory of value that begins by criticizing Marx's assumption that in all modes of production, across all historical periods, production is organized by the opposition between a subject (the laborer) and an object (technology and the means of production). In the first part of this chapter, I will briefly sketch this argument, before turning to its implications for race, gender, and class in Part 2.

The environmental implications of the argument in this chapter are developed in Brennan (1996).

The Labor Theory of Value Without the Subject/Object Distinction

What Marx did, and the other nineteenth-century political economists did not do, was to stress the "twofold" nature of a commodity (Marx 1954, 54). A commodity, as Marx defined it, is always produced for exchange, and has exchange value. But it also and always has use value; there can be no use value without nature, or natural substance. Even Marx, despite his much touted admiration for industrialization, stressed that nature is the source of all use value.

Moreover, because of Marx's emphasis on the twofold nature of a commodity, the labor theory of value can become a theory with considerable explanatory force in relation to the exploitation of the environment. It becomes this in that, without the subject/object distinction, the theory reveals that the essential contradiction in production is between the reproduction time of natural energy and the time or speed of exchange for profit. Marx himself saw this basic contradiction in terms of labor power and technology, where labor power alone adds value, but where value will necessarily be diminished as more is spent on technology. Technology adds no value in itself, but more has to be spent on it in order for capital to produce in the fastest time possible, and thus compete. Understanding of this contradiction has been limited due to the centrality of the subject/object distinction in Marx's thought. Because of that centrality, he singled out labor for special treatment. I will briefly sketch his analysis before discussing how it can be reworked without the subject/object distinction, as Marx understood it.

I mentioned that nature and technology alike are seen by Marx as "the object." Together they constitute the means of production, which Marx defines as the "objective factors," while he defines the "subjective factor" as labor power (Marx 1954, 179). For Marx himself, surplus value, or profit, is made possible because of the difference between what the subjective and objective factors add in production. The subjective factor, or the subject, labor power, adds value while the objective factor, or the object, nature and technology, does not. This is because the subject, labor power, is variable in its capacity for adding value, while the object is constant. Marx formalizes the difference between them by terming the subjective factor "variable capital" and the objective factors "constant capital." Variable capital is variable because it adds more than it costs in the production process. It does this because it adds more, within a given time in production, than the time it takes to reproduce labor power overall. Marx dwells at length on labor power's ability to add more than it costs. But it comes down to this: labor power is living energy. Labor power, as Marx said quite precisely, is energy transferred to "a human organism by means of nourishing matter" (Marx 1954, 207 *n*1). Its livingness distinguishes it from constant capital (nature and technology), which is ostensibly dead. Its value accordingly is precisely constant. Being ostensibly "dead," nature and technology can give no more than they cost.

Despite all this, the profit maker will spend more on constant than on variable capital. This is so for the following reason. In order to compete, to get more products onto the market in the shortest possible time, greater amounts have to be spent on constant capital and less on variable capital. More will have to be spent on constant capital as improved technologies make for faster production: in other words, to stay in the race, profit makers have to produce and distribute commodities in the fastest possible time. Thus they have to spend more on constant capital, on technologies and the natural resources that feed them. At the same time, they spend less on variable capital, because the more sophisticated the technology (as a rule, and there are, of course, exceptions) the less labor intensive the industry. In short, while technological expenditure enables profit makers to compete more effectively in the short term, it leads, according to Marx, to a "tendency of the rate of profit to fall" in the long term (Marx 1967). In assuming that there is such a tendency, Marx assumed that profit depends on the difference a living subject makes to a dead object.

Both theoretically and politically, this subject/object distinction is the wrong place to begin. In fact, and obviously enough now, it is not only labor or human subjects that live and add energy; it is also nature, although it was easy enough to forget this, to objectify nature, when it was abundantly there to be taken for granted, as it was at Marx's time of writing. But if nature or certain natural forces are shown to have an energetic property in common with labor power, and I will try to show this, Marx's "essential contradiction," between time and technology, has more explanatory power. Nature is the source of all value, and ultimately of all energy, but the inherent dynamic of capital is to diminish this value and this energy in favor of time and technology. Not only this, but from a standpoint in which time and speed become central, a structural connection among gender, race, and class becomes evident.

For Marx himself, energy can only be added by "living labor" (Marx 1973, 362); all other constituents of production are supposedly lifeless. As far as the behavior of capital is concerned, their livingness is irrelevant. But this does not mean that it is irrelevant to the inner workings of production, or to a value theory that is not based on the subject/object distinction. It is important to remember that Marx, in discovering what he thought was the source of capitalist profit, also showed how capital loses consciousness of that source (Marx 1954, 76 ff.); as an oblique result, more is spent on constant capital, less on the variable capital that adds value. This source was so obscured that part of it remained hidden even from Marx.

As labor power is precisely energy, even "tension," (Marx 1954, 583), meaning an energetic force, it has everything in common with other natural forces, capable of realizing energy as humans can. These sources are also produced and replenished by the transfer of "nourishing matter." Labor power even has a potential affinity with natural substances that are inanimate as well as animate, insofar as these can be made into sources of energy.

Once labor power is treated as a source of energy, one form of all natural sources of energy, and once the opposition between subjective and objective factors is replaced by one between living nature and the commodified dead, then value theory's logic can be extended. We can keep the logic that led Marx to break capital down into two components: constant and variable capital. We can even say that variable capital is the source of surplus value, while constant capital is not. We can deduce, too, that the greater the outlay on constant as opposed to variable capital in production, the less the surplus value extracted. We can even deduce, with Marx, that the imperative to produce more in the shortest possible time will lead to a greater outlay on constant capital.

The difference from Marx lies in this: I assume that *all natural sources of energy entering production should be treated as variable capital and sources of surplus value*. I assume, too, that to an extent, these sources, including labor power, can stand in for or be replaced by one another. If another natural substance can supply what labor supplies, that natural substance also counts as variable capital. Moreover, because substances can stand in for one another as variable capital, *there is no real check on the speed with which variable capital can be used up. The only check is whether a particular form of variable capital, a particular natural substance can be replaced.* If it cannot, its reproduction has to be guaranteed, that is to say, taken into account, by capital.

Does this mean that any natural force or source of energy will do the same profit-making job that labor power does? Only under certain circumstances, and with many qualifications. How extensively one energy source will be replaced by another depends on what I will term the law of substitution. It is necessary to explain this law before the speeding up of production time, and its disjointedness with natural time, can become apparent.

According to the law of substitution, capital will, all other things being equal, take the cheapest form of energy adequate to sustaining production of a particular commodity at the prevailing level of competition. Many of these energy forms will be refined; they will be—from one to many times—removed from their natural state. But this does not mean that they cease to be valuable. They only cease to be this when their capacity for adding energy is exhausted. Up to this point, their value may be increased as other forms of energy (including labor power) are mixed into them, although this mixing can also diminish energy sources overall, especially when their reproduction time is discounted. We will see that the reproduction time of other natural substances aside from labor power will be discounted whenever possible; labor power is the only source of energy whose reproduction time capital *has* to pay for—as a rule.

But our immediate concern is with qualifying "natural sources and forces." Some substances are more ready forms of energy and add more energy than others. In everyday thinking, the extent of the energy they have or add is precisely what makes them valuable. And this cuts both ways. *If labor power can stand in for another energy source more cheaply and more effectively, it will be the source chosen.* Nonetheless, the points remain that: (i) at the level of substance, the material energetic level, the common denominator is energy, not labor power; and (ii) all energy sources, including labor power, vary in what they cost compared to what they add. At the same time, the critical distinction Marx drew between labor and labor power is amplified massively in the case of other natural sources and forces. Marx's critical point was that *labor* added more in production than the reproduction cost of the commodity *labor power,* although capital did not cheat: it paid for labor power at its value. Other natural forces and sources also add more than their reproduction costs, but capital (and for that matter state socialism) *does* cheat in relation to other natural forces; it does not pay for them at their value. The law of substitution can offset trends toward the immiseration of the working class, to the extent that other energy sources can stand in effectively for labor. I say "to the extent" because while the immiseration of the working class did not occur in the capitalist heartlands in the manner Marx predicted, it has occurred in the global context.

There have been arguments among Marxists as to whether the nonoccurrence (yet) of the immiseration of the working class in the capitalist heartlands can be explained by imperialism. There is a general consensus (cf. Renner 1978) that the rise of the new and vast middle class in the advanced West requires more explanation than that provided by the labor theory of value as it stands. However, by this reworking of value theory, the relative benefits of the working and middle classes could be explained by the exploitation of nature.

The effects of the law of substitution here are similar to those wrought by imperialism, and to the creation of a labor aristocracy (Hobsbawm

1964). When Lenin, following Marx and Engels, argued that a labor aristocracy, a richer segment of the working class, could be created through the exploitation of other sections of that class, nationally and internationally, they were drawing attention to how the rate of surplus value extraction of one portion of the labor market could be less in one place if it were higher elsewhere. We can now see how a similar "benefit" to portions of the labor market can be effected through increasing the rate of surplus value extraction of other natural entities and things. If coal or wood or oil provide energy that labor power would otherwise provide, if they add value in the same way, and if they can be exploited more ruthlessly, then labor power can "benefit." Labor power can be better off when wood, coal, and so forth receive less than they need to reproduce, in that cheaper substitutes increase GNP. As a rule, the reproduction time of natural substances is not factored into capital's costs; as I said, frequently this reproduction time is not paid for at all, let alone paid for at its value. However, this means, as we shall see, that all aspects of the production process, including the reproduction of labor power, have to be speeded up. And labor power, whose reproduction time has to be taken into account, unlike that of many other natural forces, cannot on the face of it be speeded up. It is exactly here that we will locate the structural intersection of race, class, and gender.

The question of the reproduction of natural sources returns us to time. Capital does not pay for the reproduction time of natural substances in order to make a profit. It is at this point that a value theory without the subject/object distinction reveals that capital's basic contradiction is between the time of natural reproduction and technology. By this theory, for a particular capital to stay in the race, it has to speed up the materialization of energy, the value added by natural substances in production, and so speed up the rate of surplus value extraction. While this speeding-up diminishes overall use value in the long term, it is compelling in the short term. It leads to speedier profit via speedier production. But this speedier production is out of joint with the time of natural production.

Consider here Marx's concept of "socially necessary labor time." This is based on the average amount of time required to produce a given object at a given level of technology. Now the average amount of time a tomato plant takes to produce a tomato can in fact be calculated with some precision. The real point is that the plant's technology *appears or appeared* to be fixed. One of the main historical limitations affecting the author of *Capital* was the assumption that the reproductive time of natural substances cannot be speeded up; that is, the tomato plant's inner workings cannot be regulated or controlled. It is historically plain that this is not so, and that capital has indeed found social ways of speeding up various forms of natural reproduction.

The speeding up of the natural products takes place by regulating their conditions of production. This cannot be done with human labor power (yet), which is why labor power becomes the odd element in this reworking of value theory. But as capitalism cuts back the supply of natural substances, it not only diminishes the energy, or "nourishing matter" labor power relies upon, it also diminishes the conditions for other natural sources of energy to regenerate as well. Natural reproduction time is seriously out of joint. How this is played out in total terms should be reflected in the crisis of capital, in its "long waves" and "laws of motion." In sum, what Marx saw clearly and before all was the inherent contradiction in capital as a mode of production. He saw it in terms of labor and technology, or variable and constant capital, as he defined it, where the former, to keep pace, had to expand at the expense of the energy input of labor. The contradiction is recapitulated in this account, although its terms of reference have changed. Or rather, its terms of reference have been stripped of their phenomenal forms, so that the contradiction emerges as what it is: essentially one between the substantial energy of nature—the source of value—and the artificial speed of production.

Two forms of time are at issue: the generational time of natural reproduction; and speed, the artificial time of short-term profit. It is clear that generational time suffers because capital tends inevitably to speed up the production of all commodities, including naturally formed or agricultural ones. While there are countervailing tendencies in agriculture, and in the very existence of labor power, and in scarce or apparently irreplaceable sources, the speed imperative will override them wherever possible.

A Structural Connection Among Race, Gender, and Class

The disjunction of time and space, as analyzed in Part 1 of this chapter is one key to how the exploitation of race, gender, class, and nature are connected. One caveat before continuing: The connections among race, gender, class, and nature discussed here are made solely at the economic level. Specifically, the connection between race and the other forms of exploitation analyzed below is limited to neocolonial situations and the imperative to migrate in search of work. The people in these situations are usually racially or ethnically stigmatized, although which groups are stigmatized in this way varies cross-culturally and historically, a fact which shows that the intensity of racism is seriously affected by economic factors. At the same time, one cannot reduce racism to the economic level, if for no other reason than that yesterday's economically inflected racism drags into the stereotypes of tomorrow. Nor can the analysis of gendered exploitation be reduced to the economic level. But the significance of making the economic connections remains: it provides grounds for resistance and critique of the forces in power that extend beyond a neoliberal sympathy.

The focus on the implications of this revised value theory for sexual and neocolonial exploitation is sharpened by attending to the state in the first instance. We need to talk about the state first because the state joins with capital in regulating time and space. The momentum of capital alone is insufficient to account for the power of agency, the "invisible hand," in the centralizing process of modernity. Centralization is inextricably tied to the state, which provides the "general conditions of production." The more the emphasis shifts to portability and acquisition, and the more by implication it shifts to expansion, the more the issues of territorial control and transportation, one of those vague "conditions of production" become salient.

To extend centralization, and territorial domination, in which more territories are answerable and/or geared to the same center, one needs means of transportation in the first instance, and for domination, means for war. Spatial control and spatial expansion are the conditions of the invisible hand extending its grasp; in a sense they also are the state.

The state is part of the infrastructure of distribution, the outer sphere of consumption and exchange, all of which are not peripheral but central in this revised value theory. Not only does the state lay the grounds for and regulate key variables in the speed of acquisition (through transportation, energy services, and other forms of extension), but together with capital it also regulates the law of substitution outlined in Part 1 of this chapter. For example, whether oil can substitute for labor power in the production of certain commodities will depend on means of transportation, treaties governing import, and so on.

While the costs of establishing centralized state control may not be of particular significance to use value overall in themselves, they are nonetheless paid for out of that use value, and consume it in the same way that capital does. This homology is, or was, striking in the recent stage of capital's development—state-monopoly capitalism, so-called because the mutually supporting interests of both parties seemed so great as to beggar separate description. But however unwillingly it did so, the state provided the spatio-temporal conditions of production from the beginning.[1]

As we will see in a moment, however, while all states feed on time to some extent, they vary in the efficiency and extent to which they do so, and in the constraints that their various cultures and histories impose upon them. This variation is reflected in the uneven demise of state power, and of states, for that matter. The demise suggests that while the nation-state was one form in which the "conditions of production" were laid down, it may not be the only form that will sustain them.

Crucial here is the idea that standards of efficiency in denying time are set globally. It was a global economic pressure in the 1980s that made nations "curtail state spending and interventions. Whatever the differences in partisan outcomes, all governments have been pressed in the same direction."[2] But, while this economic direction may be a global trend, not all states are affected equally. While any form of state will embody the spatial dynamic to the extent that it has an apparatus of centralized control, some states embody it in a purer form than others. Indeed, some states are constrained by other imperatives that make them manifestly inefficient when it comes to speeding up the sacrifice of time. Specific genealogies and specific traditions intersect with the totalizing spatial process. The collapse of Eastern Europe can be explained by the conflict between a form of state, and the dynamic whereby space replaces time, and the related desire for instant gratification.

Critically, we have to bear in mind the different roles various states play in providing and regulating general conditions where space replaces time. Marx's analysis of how some states aid accumulation and expansion better than others (Marx 1954, 751) is appropriate here as an exemplar of how the modern state can be evaluated, albeit by different criteria. Some states are far better suited than others to the law of speed, and where the state fails to adjust its form to this law, or attempts to countermand it, there will be gigantic temporal hiccups. The form of centralized state that naturally works in harmony with the process of acquisition, and thence distribution, is a state with minimal checks on the abolition of the linear time of reproduction in relation to labor power, and in relation to the environment.

This last point returns us to the reasons for blockages in the Eastern bloc. State communism, insofar as it did attempt some minimal redistribution of wealth to labor power (which means to its reproduction cost), imposed a temporal constraint on a system designed to eliminate it; for any system of centralized consumption must work to increasing speed in relation to space rather than time, and this is a concomitant not only of competitive acquisition but of centralization. If a state has to introduce some guaranteed measure of distributive justice, this inevitably leads to hiccups if not major obstructions: distributive justice, as we shall see in a moment, is a temporal constraint that can be offset where labor power is imported, but it remains a temporal constraint when it is honored. It sits ill where the elimination of time, and instant gratification, is the end-goal of the game. It sits ill in a centralized capitalist mode of production, the system where queues could signal the end of an era.

The question of distributive justice and temporal constraints will be plainer after we have discussed reproduction, which bears on women and neocolonialism. The key is the intersection of space and time. More narrowly, it is in how this intersection, itself established by speed, brings in the sphere of reproduction, especially of labor power. For while my argument displaces labor power from the absolute center of value theory in terms of production, it also shifts the emphasis to labor power's reproduction, as it shifts it to that of nature overall. To a limited extent, this shift was foreshadowed in debates about women's reproductive labor, which drew attention to the importance of this sphere's *indirect* contribution to surplus value. But this debate foundered because it kept within the classical categories.³ The shift to reproduction in this argument is structural. Reproduction of nature overall becomes the hidden ground of value and exploitation; capital drastically enhances its profit because it does not pay for reproduction at its temporal value, unless it has no option under the law of substitution.

From the perspective outlined above, the reproduction of labor is the perpetually odd element out in production. Labor power is the odd element because the socially necessary labor time required to reproduce it is fixed in part by nature. It is fixed insofar as socially necessary labor time includes the reproduction of children and thus the next generation of labor power. While the time necessary for the reproduction of nature, even of animals, can be short-circuited, that of labor power cannot on the face of it be speeded up. Which means such reproduction is potentially out of step with capital's consumption-for-production, in which all things have to move faster and faster.

Now, as the imperative to speed up other living entities and substances is so evident—in everything from soil poisoned with fertility drugs to wingless chickens and legless cows, animals tailormade to producing flesh at the expense of their own ability to reproduce—human labor power's apparent exemption from the same speedy imperative becomes significant. But, always in the event that no other natural substance can provide what labor power provides (the law of substitution), the apparently impossible end of speeding up the generational reproduction of labor power can be accomplished in various ways. It can be accomplished by keeping the cost of that reproduction down in relation to the other elements entering production. However, if this means is ineffective in a given situation, where the labor required exceeds the short-term supply, then one is left with the apparently impossible alternative of speeding up the generational reproduction of labor power so that it keeps pace with the other elements entering into production.

In fact, speeding up the reproduction of labor power is not impossible, and this is plain once we turn to the alternative means by which human labor power can be reproduced. In referring to "alternative means" of reproducing labor power, I am not invoking the panoply of science fiction and high-tech, of cyborgs and genetic engineering, although the proliferation of fantasies concerning the former and investment in the latter is not irrelevant. In part, it is perhaps a symptomatic recognition of an underlying quest to find a fast-moving replacement for humans, capable of two of their most distinctive functions: portability and the capacity to take direction. For that matter, all the carry-on over artificial intelligence has more obvious purpose and point, if capital seeks a tame direction-taker. And of course, such docile will-less things already exist, in the form of computers, which altogether lack the "imaginative capacity for design" in executing commands. But the computerized component in constant capital expenditure, and the ambition it encapsulates, is not the immediate question. The alternative means of reproducing labor power I have in mind at the moment is what I will term the lateral reproduction of labor power, meaning the migrations of workers.

What I want to propose here is that the lateral reproduction of labor power will increase when the linear reproduction falls behind the imperative to speed up in other ways, and/or when linear reproduction becomes too costly. At the same time, I want to propose that such increases work in tandem with an imperative to keep the cost of the generational reproduction of labor power down, in lieu of the ability to speed it up. These propositions could be tested readily enough, keeping the law of substitution in mind. And insofar as they encapsulate the law of substitution, it should follow that where the lateral reproduction of labor power is prohibited for some reason, the generational cost of reproducing labor power will be forced down.

Clearly, these processes involve international labor flows as well as national labor supplies and national legislation affecting the cost of reproducing the next generation. All these are regulated by the state. And it should follow that a good welfare state will either be "inefficient" or have ready access to guest workers; a state without this access will "speed up" generational reproduction by keeping its cost down. The condition of an efficient and just welfare state is either that it is self-contained enough to keep to economies of scale, and/or that its natural resources make it rich provided they can be exploited fast enough (but substantially rich in the long run anyway). We can note here that the former Soviet Union was restricted when it came to importing labor power. The production of surplus value in a country that disregards a welfare state is enhanced anyway, of course, but enhanced either by speed or natural substance and energy: the United States is amazingly rich in natural substance, while Japan is leading the field of speed (which may bring the United States, rich through substance, into more economic conflict with Japan, rich through speed).

To return to reproduction as such, we are left with the question as to why people have children at all in these speedy times. In feudal and petty-bourgeois modes of production, the interests of social reproduction and the interests of parents coincide. In the capitalist mode of production (CMP), they do not coincide automatically, which means that the overall interests of social reproduction are not guaranteed; they are not in the necessary self-interest of either sex. The striking facts of the increase in single mothers and decline in fathered families may evince this conflict with self-interest for men (cf. Elliot 1991). But we are unable to explain women's persistence in having children in terms of self-interest, especially as the middleman is progressively cut out. We can only explain this, and explain the behavior of men who want children by (at least in part) their resistance to the economic logic of self-interest, and their persisting sense of generational time. There are arguments that adduce that an economic self-interest factor is working for women who have children and receive a state benefit *when other economic options are few or virtually nonexistent.* But the sheer poverty of this condition makes such self-interest unlikely; it is more probable that the state's forcing down of the costs of linear reproduction relies on and exploits women's sense of generational time.

What is clear is that the interests of social reproduction overall are best served by keeping the costs of the linear and lateral reproduction of the labor force to a minimum. This means that two groups are likely to be impoverished: single women and/or women who are positioned low on the class hierarchy; and the vastly heterogeneous peoples from whom a lateral supply of labor power can be drawn. If there is a structural connection among gender, race, and the residual category of class, I suggest that this is it. In other words, the structural connection lies in their exploitation for social reproduction, for keeping the cost of labor power down.

The heterogeneous peoples who supply the migrating labor force are far more likely to be those who are racially and ethnically stigmatized. Balibar and Wallerstein sum up:

> Racism operationally has taken the form of what might be called the "ethnicization" of the work force.... But while the pattern of ethnicization has been constant, the details have varied from place to place and time to time, according to what part of the human genetic and social pools were located in a particular time and place and what the hierarchical needs of the economy were at that time and place. This kind of system—racism constant in form and in venom ... allows one to expand or contract the numbers available in any particular space-time zone for the lowest paid, least rewarding economic roles. (Balibar and Wallerstein 1991, 33–34)

There is more incentive to migrate where there is unemployment or bare subsistence employment in the home country, and/or where there is overpopulation relative to job supply. The international interests of reproduction by the nations of advanced capital would seem to be well-served by overpopulation in the neocolonialist countries, both in terms of a greater willingness on the part of the latter's populations to migrate, and in terms of greater competition for jobs within those countries. Significantly, it is usually men who migrate or move in search of work, while women with children remain fixed in place. This repeats a pattern evident in capital's seventeenth-century genesis, and in the nonmetropolitan countries where capital's advent is relatively recent. As discussed, this pattern goes hand in hand with a major alteration in scale. It is not only the division between town and country that is affected here; it is also the household, as the site of production. Household production, or petty commodity production, as Marx and Engels termed it, accorded women a very different and generally better economic place. Their productive labor was not geographically divorced from their situation as mothers. The significance of household production for women has been relatively neglected in Marxist debates about whether petty commodity production is a precapitalist form or an ongoing form of capitalism. The idea that it may be a form opposed to it was proposed by Clarke (1919), but her remarkable thesis was not developed, although Shiva (1988) has argued a similar case.

But the immediate concern lies elsewhere. Apart from indicating that the production of migrating men and single mothers is endemic to and a condition of capitalization, this pattern also reinforces the notion that these two groups have a great deal in common. They have in common their exploitation for social reproduction, even though their short-term interests are opposed. Or to say the same thing differently, they stand opposed in that one group advances lateral reproduction, the other linear reproduction. The tragedy is that the source of this opposition is not recognized by many who suffer under it, just as their common cause with exploited nature is also overlooked.

Notes

1. The periodization of capital is contentious, when it comes to the third stage. Mandel (1975) ties the idea of state monopoly capitalism to Comintern strategy and prefers to see the present era as an accentuation of that of monopoly capital. Mandel insists that "The era of late capitalism is not a new epoch of capitalist development. It is merely a further development of the imperialist, monopoly-capitalist epoch. By implication, the characteristics of the imperialist epoch enumerated by Lenin thus remain fully valid for late capitalism" (1975, 10). See also Baran and Sweezy (1966) and Poulantzas (1975). In one respect, the periodization of the various "stages of capitalism" in Marxist theory is incomplete because it does not recognize that the establishment of the modern state is integral to the historical process whereby space takes the place of time. The existing periodization moves from competitive capitalism (first stage) to monopoly capi-

talism (second stage) to state monopoly capitalism, otherwise known as late capitalism (third stage). The third stage reveals the spatial imperative in all its munching glory: its speedy circulation and its ever expanding reach cut off the roots of reproductive time. But this imperative is greeted as if it were a novelty introduced by capital alone.

2. Even more strongly: "governments no longer possess the autonomy to pursue independent macroeconomic strategies effectively, even if they were to seek to do so" (Garrett and Lange 1991, 543). Moreover, it is argued that today state power should not be measured in terms of military force but economic capability (Rosecrance 1986; Nye 1989; Jervis 1991) and, at the same time, that government's domain of economic efficacy is now shared with many international organizations (e.g., the IMF) (Cox 1987; Shaw 1991; Hall, Held and McGrew 1992).

3. See, for example, Dalla Costa (1973), Delphy (1977), Gardiner (1975), and Harrison (1973) for arguments to the effect that women's household labor contributed to surplus value—as labor that was not paid for by capital but that nonetheless contributed to the worker's capacity to realize surplus value. By contrast, Humphries (1977) and Brennan (1977) argued that the wife's household labor contributed to the workers' side in class struggle, because it was in capital's interest not to pay for two people (plus children) with one wage and that capital would seek where possible to force both wife and husband into the labor market.

6

Class, Gender, and Culture

A Discussion of Marxism, Feminism, and Postmodernism

Ann Davis

In the development of recent feminist thought, conceptualization of the economic role of women remains elusive. Among early contributions, the exchange of women was seen as a structural element of all societies (Rubin 1975) and the foundation of solidarity among disparate kinship groups. For Hartmann (1981), gender systems and the economy are separate institutions, connected in a "partnership" between "patriarchy" and capitalism. For example, she outlines the ways in which patriarchy modified capitalism, such as with the exclusion of women and children from the wage labor force in the early years of industrialization (19–25). This analysis gave rise to the term "dual systems theory," for the way in which patriarchy and capitalism remained conceptually distinct systems (Benería and Roldán 1987, 10–11; Pateman 1988, 38, 133–35; Fine 1992, 36–39; Nicholson 1986, 40–41). Lerner (1986) sees gender as the foundation of power relations, and integrally related to class. She writes: "For women, class is mediated through their sexual ties to a man. It is through the man that women have access to or are denied access to the means of production and to resources. It is through their sexual behavior that they gain access to class. 'Respectable women' gain access to class through their fathers and husbands, but breaking the sexual rules can at once declass them" (Lerner 1986, 215).

Marxist concepts have been suggestive for some feminist formulations. For example, in an early discussion of the still-hyphenated Marxist-Feminism, Petchesky (1979) stated that "reproduction and kinship are themselves integrally related to the social relations of production and the state," (377) and "control over the means of reproduction is indeed a class issue" (382). More recent work by feminist theorists, such as MacKinnon (1989) and Pateman (1988), explicitly builds on Marxian concepts, including "consciousness" and "objectification" for MacKinnon and "property in the person" for Pateman. Even a critic of meta-narratives like the postmodern thinker Michel Foucault discusses sexuality in terms of the large aggregates of class, such as the bourgeoisie and the aristocracy (1978, 124). He depicts "sex as a political issue" (145), and an "indispensable element in the development of capitalism" (140–41). "The 'conventional' family came to be regarded, sometime around the eighteen-thirties, as an indispensable instrument of political control and economic representation for the subjugation of the urban proletariat . . ." (Foucault 1978, 122). Yet recent contributions by feminists trained in the Marxian tradition, such as Folbre (1994) and Barrett (1991), question whether Marxist concepts like "value" and "class" are compatible with a feminist and postmodern analysis.

This chapter will argue that rigid dichotomies in Marx's thought can be overcome with the contributions of feminist method (Di Stefano 1991). For example, the split between the "material" base and the ideological "superstructure" can be integrated with a view of economic actors, including women, as "embodied," material beings who also conform to (and resist) images and norms of proper behavior that are formulated in historically variable ideology and culture. The idea that there are "separate spheres"— the domestic, which is women's realm, and the market, which is a male preserve—can be replaced by an institutional perspective that reveals the formation of separate spheres as a historical phenomenon (Nicholson 1986; Polanyi 1944) that is integrally related to the formation of the wage labor force and the concentration of production in capitalist firms. Even as the economy apparently "structures" behavior in market settings, economics is itself an ideology and an institution, historically situated, subject to critical methods and textual critique. Rather than seeing economics as "determining" other spheres, economic institutions are the product of unique historical agents acting to resolve tensions and divisions in their own lives, just like other institutions. In this light, "domestic ideology," that apparently most noneconomic of subjects of feminist historians, can be seen as an "economic" variable with important implications for the determination of "class," "work," and the expansion of "value."

This chapter will suggest an integration of the insights of Marxist and feminist thought into a coherent method for a comprehensive analysis of gender relations. The argument will proceed first by drawing upon Marx's formulation of economic forces, highlighting which "imperatives" are heavily structured within the economic institutions of capitalism and which vary historically. Second, the role of domestic ideology in the formation of the working class is discussed, drawing upon recent contributions of women's historians. Third, the historical variation of domestic ideology by economic periods is illustrated. Fourth, the implications for methodology in the analysis of gender are explored.

Marx's Methodology

Materialism

The ambiguity of Marx's method has left him open to charges of economic determinism (Nicholson 1986). At the same time, he provides the example of the critique of political economy that faults "vulgar" economists for lack of sufficient historicity. Bordo (1987, 117) states that Marx is "the single most important philosophical figure in the development of modern historicism, with his emphasis on the historical nature of all human activity and thought.... It was Marx who turned the tables on the Enlightenment, encouraging suspicion of all ideas that claim to represent universal, fundamental, 'inherent,' or 'natural' features of reality." Further, Marx is vulnerable for the relative absence of attention to the institutions of the family and gender, although references can be found in his writings (see, for example, Marx 1978, 156–57). On the other hand, one strength of his approach to the theory of wages is its explicit basis in the costs of reproduction of the labor force on both a daily and generational basis, a glaring omission in mainstream economics.

There has been a long-standing critique of Marx's value theory by feminists as omitting reference to women's contribution to the household (see summaries of the domestic labor debate in Fine 1992; Seccombe 1993; Folbre 1982). They argue that women's work in the household is more important than implied by Marx's label of "unproductive." Yet production of "value" and profit in a capitalist system is not the only standard of merit, especially when understood from a historical point of view. It is argued here that the role of the household can be highlighted by Marx's value circuits, with a slight modification. Further, Marx's focus on analyzing value-creating activities in the capitalist system is an accurate rendition of *that system,* even if not necessarily characteristic of other past or conceivable economic systems in other periods of history. The feminist critique of Marx can be more appropriately aimed at the capitalist system itself. In fact, Marx's *critique* of political economy provides the tools with which to see beyond that system to other possible economic and social arrangements.

Circuits

Marx's abstract circuits of money and commodities provide a conceptual scheme for understanding the systemic requirements of the reproduction of capital. By contrast, his own analysis of concrete historical institutions also illustrates the historical character of many aspects of that system.

To begin his initial analysis of commodities in *Capital,* Volume 1, Chapter 1, Marx identifies two characteristics, use value and exchange value. Use value is related to the concrete physical characteristics of a commodity, by which pleasure or particular effects can be obtained—a qualitative, incommensurate aspect. Use value, or the utility from objects of consumption, can be observed in many different economic systems. On the other hand, exchange value expresses a common element among many different physical commodities, as long as they are present in proper proportion. Exchange value is abstract and quantitative, and is unique to capitalism.

Labor power is similarly characterized by two aspects: use value, the unique skill appropriate in a given context, and exchange value, the amount of general abstract human labor power that is expended, usually measured in units of time. The fact that abstract human labor takes on the appearance of the "value" of commodities is unique to capitalism.

Similarly, there are two circuits that represent the circulation of commodities and the expansion of capital. One circuit illustrates the institution of wage labor, by which workers sell themselves as commodities for a wage (Marx 1967, Ch. 3, Section 2, v. 1). This circuit is represented as

$$Clp - M - Cwg \qquad (1)$$

where Clp is the value of the worker as the commodity labor power, M is the amount of the money wage, and Cwg is the value of the wage goods purchased with the money wage. For the worker, the circuit is an exchange of equivalent values by which the means of subsistence are obtained.

Marx's second circuit, which illustrates the expansion of capital, is

$$M - Clp - M' \qquad (2)$$

where M is an amount of money initially invested by the firm, Clp represents the value of (materials and) labor inputs that are purchased as commodities in the market, and M' is the expanded amount of money for which the finished products are sold. The expansion of value, whereby M' is greater than M, is based on the capitalist's ability to purchase labor power as a commodity for a wage (Marx 1967, Chs. 4 and 5, and pp. 193–94, v. 1).

This wage, based on the costs of the worker's reproduction, is less than the value that is produced by that labor in the workplace, embodied in the commodity, which can then be sold for M'.

A third circuit reflecting the role of the household can complement these first two circuits mentioned earlier as developed by Marx. This third circuit is necessary for the completion of the other two, even if it is not visible in the circulation of commodities (1) or the expansion of value (2). This third circuit is the reproduction of the labor force on a daily (and generational) basis, as follows,

$$L - L' - L \qquad (3)$$

where L is the "capacity for labour" (Marx 1967, v. 1, 171–73) at the beginning of the working day, L' is the diminished workers' value after a day's work, and L is the potential value of the worker restored with rest, recognition, and recreation (as well as procreation, education, and training). This circuit also represents the contradiction of the special commodity labor power, which is a person (L), but also an "object" for sale and "consumed" by the capitalist at the workplace (L').

This third circuit is invisible since it takes place in two private spheres, the firm and the household, where different forms of "consumption" take place: "The consumption of labour-power is completed, as in the case of every other commodity, outside the limits of the market or of the sphere of circulation" (Marx 1967, 176). The consumption of labor power takes place in the private sphere of the capitalist workplace, along with the "productive" consumption of equipment and materials. The restoration of labor power takes place in the private household, facilitated by the consumption of home-produced use values and wage goods.

The institutional context for the restoration of the commodity labor power, from L' back to L, is not specified in the abstract circuits. Marx himself mentions variations such as workers' barracks and agricultural gangs of women in *Capital*. Historically, the restoration of labor power has included households with servants, borders, or apprentices; orphanages; as well as proper middle-class homes with a yard guarded by the "angel in the house."

The role of women is also not necessarily confined to the private home. For example, Marx describes how the use of machinery enables the employment of less-skilled women and children in the factory, and disturbs the work of women in the household:

> Compulsory work for the capitalist usurped the place, not only of children's play, but also of free labour at home within moderate limits for the support of

the family.... We see how capital, for the purposes of its self-expansion, has usurped the labour necessary in the home of the family.... (Marx 1967, 394–95)

The authority in the household is typically male, but is also affected by institutional change. When describing factory legislation, Marx mentions the initial political resistance to any incursion into the traditional family, "patria potestas ... parental authority ..." (489).

The Economics of the Cult of Domesticity

It is clear that the capitalist system requires a commodity—"labor power"—that is owned by the person, "free" for sale in the labor market, whose reproduction takes place in a private sphere separate from the workplace. The particular form of the private household staffed by a female "wife" is a historical development, as is the definition of the working class as male.

Hartmann provides some insight into this development, explaining the exclusion of women from the wage labor force. For example, in Hartmann's discussion, it is "patriarchy" and capitalism that have a "partnership."

> While the problem of cheap competition [from women and children] could have been solved by organizing the wage earning women and youths, the problem of disrupted family life could not be. Men reserved union protection for men and argued for protective labor laws for women and children.... Men sought to keep high wage jobs for themselves and to raise male wages generally.... [A] "family wage" system gradually came to be the norm for stable working class families at the end of the nineteenth century.... (Hartmann 1981, 21)

"The family wage cemented the partnership between patriarchy and capital," writes Hartmann (1981, 25). What Hartmann's discussion of "patriarchy" omits is that the exclusion of women from the labor force and the formulation of the "domestic ideal" was as much the work of women as men, and was integral to the formation of the bourgeoisie as a class, distinct from the aristocracy and the working class. This complex story is now much more clear due to recent contributions from women's history and feminist theory involving the agency of women on both sides of the debate on the "woman question."

Why did domestic ideology arise at the same time as capitalism? This question has been raised by recent scholars of this period (see Davidoff 1995, 8–9). It is argued here that such ideological developments like the domestic ideology are an integral part of the class relations, rather than some separate "superstructure" distinct from a "material" base. Just as domestic arrangements are part of the reproduction of the labor force, as in circuit (3) earlier, so also are the cultural forces that serve to discipline behavior in nonproduction spheres. This cultural "discipline," in a Foucaultian sense, while not part of the capitalist workplace per se, is still part of the social arrangements that permit the system to operate.

Mary Poovey (1988) views domestic ideology and gender constructs as central to legitimating market relations:

> One of the functions of the opposition between the private, feminized sphere and the masculine sphere of work outside the home was to mitigate the effects of the alienation of market relations. . . . The illusion that freedom and autonomy existed for the man within the home therefore depended on the illusion that within the home no one was alienated—and this depended on believing that the woman desired to be only what the man wanted her to be. . . . Only as long as her domestic labor was rhetorically distinguished from paid labor could the illusion persist that there *were* separate spheres, that there *was* an antidote to the alienation of the marketplace, and that men *were* fundamentally different from women. . . . (Poovey 1988, 77–78; emphasis in original)

Leonore Davidoff (1995) maintains that the shift of "morality" onto the family, and even onto women's bodies, occurs as religion is separated from the economy, and as the "amoral" market becomes dominant (pp. 9, 11, 235, 244, 253; see also Valenze 1995, 143; Taylor 1983, 126–27). Separate spheres serves both as an explanation of women's powerlessness and as an ideology that constructed this powerlessness.

The emergence of a wage labor force in England occurred in a cultural context in which traditional religious norms stressed the inferiority of women and the sinfulness of sex, based on the Bible (Pagels 1988) as well as the literary canon and political economy (Valenze 1995). Women were not able to control their own property and were considered to be the legal property of their husbands (Staves 1990; Shanley 1989). Evangelical preachers recruited middle-class women such as Hanna More and her sister to missionary work among the rural poor (Kowaleski-Wallace 1991). This work included training in proper norms of dress, behavior, and sexuality. In reaction to the French Revolution, there was a new stress on Evangelicalism (Hall 1970, 1992; Taylor 1983) as a means of avoiding similar widespread disruption in England.

In other words, in a patriarchal cultural context, some women in the emerging middle class took the opportunity to develop leadership positions by means of the extension and elaboration of dress, moral, and behavioral codes for women of other classes, even while other middle-class women applied the rhetoric of rights to their own "liberation." These codes became embedded in administrative bureaucracies for implementation of the Poor Law of 1834 (Poovey 1995), for example, allocating material and behavioral rewards to enforce such norms.

This formation of distinct classes was integrally and contemporaneously involved with gender (Clark 1995; Rose 1992). The definition of "the working class" at one time included women and the entire community, for Owenites and Chartists in the 1820s and 1830s in the United Kingdom. Labor struggles gradually led to the acceptance of norms of domesticity for women and a narrowing of the definition of working class to men, in order to gain broad support for Parliamentary campaigns after workplace-based strikes had failed to adequately restrict the labor supply (Clark 1995). The appeal to the ideal of domesticity gave working-class males a claim to "respectability" and a common rhetorical strategy to gain cross-class allies for Parliamentary struggles for limitation of the working day, protection for women and children, and male suffrage. The course of "class struggle" was affected by the rhetorical strategies of the working class with respect to the "proper role for women," enabling them to restrict the supply of labor and to protect their wages.

In the context of laissez-faire political economy, which denied the legitimacy of any regulation of the workplace; male suffrage, which was still subject to a property qualification; and a working day still as long as ten hours, the compromise strategy of excluding women from the labor force is more understandable. If not propertied, working-class men could at least aspire to middle-class norms of decency as a claim to suffrage, based on behavior. Appeals for working-class male suffrage were defensible on moral (if not economic) grounds when they could claim obeisance to the same norms of sexual decency (actually a "double standard"; Poovey 1988, 79) as were grounded in the Old Testament. This moral protection of women was presumably impossible as long as women were independently employed in the labor force (although, in actuality, women's work continued to be necessary to supplement working-class male wages). In the context of continual pregnancies, domestic drudgery, and long working days, some women also supported this compromise. Working-class men and women could aspire to "leisure" and "privacy" in the home, designed along middle-class models (Taylor 1983, 262–64, 272–75). In the context of intense class struggle and a highly oppressive workplace, the formation of the separate sphere of the private family can be seen as a refuge for women and children (Humphries 1977a, 1977b; Seccombe 1993, 34–35, 116–17).

A similar development of norms of domesticity took place in the United States (Kerber 1980; Cott 1972, 1977). In the nineteenth-century United States, such literary women as Sarah Hale and Catherine Beecher gained access to professional positions as writers and editors, ironically by using the norms of domesticity as their discourse (Sklar 1973; Okker 1995). The emerging magazine and book publishing industries gave them an outlet for literary talents, and aspiring middle-class women became a "leisured" audience with time in the home for reading. The sentimental ideal led to what Ann Douglas called the "feminization" of American popular culture.

In the early-twentieth-century United States, women philanthropists and social workers such as Jane Addams and Florence Kelley also gained political power and professional privilege by advocating for the benefit of women in the lower classes, but at the behavioral cost of imposed norms appropriate for the middle class (Koven and Michel 1993; L. Gordon 1994; Sklar 1995).

While women of the middle class were often active in the articulation and dissemination of the domestic ideal, there were also peers who challenged this ideology. For example, Mary Wollstonecraft was an eighteenth-century English contemporary of Hannah More, arguing that the "rights of man" should be applied equally to women (Valenze 1995; Kowaleski-Wallace 1991). Alice Paul organized the Women's Party and pushed for equal rights for women in the early-twentieth-century United States while other women's advocates lobbied for protective legislation and *against* equal rights (Sklar 1991). In the late twentieth century, Phyllis Schlafly organized for traditional norms, challenging the appeal to a resurgent feminism led by Betty Friedan and Gloria Steinem (S.J. Douglas 1994).

Periodization

To support the argument that gender roles and domestic ideology are historically variable, one must demonstrate changing relationships of class and gender within different historical periods. Some scholars have proposed such periods (Seccombe 1992, 1993; Fine 1992; Fraad, Resnick, and Wolff 1994; L. Gordon 1996) with no clear consensus yet emerging as to methodology and criteria for differentiating one period from another.

For example, Fine differentiates periods primarily by economic criteria (116–17). The first period of early industrialization in which women are present in the wage labor force is characterized by absolute surplus value, the strategy of producing surplus by extending the number of workers (laissez-faire capitalism). The second phase is characterized by relative surplus value, whereby surplus is expanded by increasing productivity (monopoly capitalism). For this strategy to be effective, the labor force is constricted, withdrawing the labor of women and children in particular (134–40). The third stage, state monopoly capitalism, involves the expanding role of the state in the reproduction of the labor force, and increasing women's labor force participation (although at times Fine locates this phenomenon in the second stage, p. 133). In the third stage women also are more present in the labor force to finance the growing "family consumer economy" (143).

Seccombe (1993) examines such factors as the age of first marriage (the "nuptiality valve"), fertility rates (the "demographic transition"), and shifting wage norms. For example, in early industrialization, a joint family wage is paid for family members who are collectively working as a team, often on a subcontracting basis. Subsequently, the "family wage" is paid to the *individual* male head of household; this is presumed sufficient to support a "nonworking" wife and children. Similar to Fine, Seccombe associates both the removal of women from "productive" work as well as the decline in the birthrate with the shift of production regimes from absolute to relative surplus value (182).

Foucault (1978) identifies periods by the diffusion of particular "technologies of control" like "schooling, ... housing, public hygiene, institutions of relief and insurance, the general medicalization of the population ... an entire administrative and technical machinery [which] made it possible to safely import the deployment of sexuality into the exploited class" (126) from its origin within the bourgeoisie (120). At still other points, he refers to the changing nature of the discipline required in the labor force, as more developed capitalism does not require "the same violent and physical constraints" for the exploitation of wage labor as in the nineteenth century (114).

The hypothesis here is that cultural norms for women vary by distinct periods and serve as a useful barometer to changes in the role women play in the economy. Building on the Social Structure of Accumulation (SSA) approach, an institutional Marxist framework (Gordon, Edwards, and Reich 1982), the following discussion emphasizes domestic ideology as occupying a central place among the normalizing institutions that facilitate periods of economic expansion.

Contrary to the recent contribution by O'Hara (1995) to the SSA literature, the approach here examines both concrete forms of housework and social meanings in a time perspective long enough to identify structural similarities and variations in the institution of the household in the capitalist economy. Rather than rely exclusively on what seems "functional for capital" (97–105), this approach also identifies the contribution of unique historical agents in concrete, historically verifiable contexts, and the struggles among conflicting norms and people in a given period. Rather than seeing a dualistic opposition between the market and social institutions (93), drawing on Polanyi's work, this approach sees the "economic" and the "social" as integrally related institutions. Rather than seeing "private capital" as having "no control over household labor" (105–6), this approach sees social norms and ideologies as central to the integrity of both social and economic institutions. At the end of his discussion, O'Hara mentions alternate forms of the household, but without a concrete historical understanding of the development of those forms, there is less comprehensive understanding of the process of change.

There have been a variety of ideologies in different periods that circumscribe women's behavior, norms, and identities, from the cult of the true woman of 1830 to 1890 (Crow 1971; Cott 1977; Welter 1966), to motherhood in the early 1900s (Fine 1992; Aries 1962; Katz 1986), to the consumer in the 1950s (Cowan 1983; Ewen 1976), and sexuality in the late twentieth century (Goffman 1976; Baty 1995; S.J. Douglas 1994; Ehrenreich 1983). Enforcement institutions have included the medical establishment (Showalter 1985), women's magazines and other media (Okker 1995), educational institutions, and legal mandates. Although women participate in and shape these norms (Smith-Rosenberg 1985), their voices are joined by others, often with superior institutional resources, which shape their responses and constrain their feasible strategies. At times, ambitious women seize the leadership in defining and articulating these norms, as a way of gaining power in their own lives, even by contributions that constrain the lives of other women (Sklar 1973).

In fact, there seems to be a coincidence between major shifts in the social construction of gender and substantive economic dislocations. For example, from 1830 to 1890, the formation of the industrial male labor force was reinforced by the "cult of the true woman" in the home, an "angel in the house" and moral guardian. From 1890 to the 1930s, with radical movements in the United States and Europe and the Russian Revolution, the "flappers" and newly educated women leaders in the settlement house movement were "Red-baited" in their efforts at social reform and international peace movements (Lemons 1973; Sklar 1995). The construction of the abnormal category of "lesbian" also served to constrain the easy familiarity of independent, educated women (Smith-Rosenberg 1985; Simmons 1991). Mothers' pensions were preferred to poorhouses because of the newly discovered need to keep women home to raise their own children in the early twentieth century (Katz 1986; Fine 1992, 135–38).

The post–World War II period, with its macroeconomic concerns with underconsumption and defense conversion, was also characterized by McCarthyism, marriage bars (Goldin 1990), consumerism (Ewen 1996; Cowan 1983), and sex, as in the transformation of Norma Jean Baker from "Rosie the Riveter" to glamorous screen idol Marilyn Monroe (Baty 1995). Certainly, the auto/oil/housing/consumer finance/advertising complex associated with suburbanization has propelled the postwar economy into the present period.

The explicit public visibility of sexuality and the more relaxed norms of sexual behavior in the postwar period seem a distinct reversal of the apparent "repression" and seclusion of sexuality in the Victorian ideal. With the nude centerfolds of *Playboy,* first published in 1953, and *Sex and the Single Girl* by Helen Gurley Brown published in 1962, followed by a reworking of *Cosmopolitan* magazine under her editorship, premarital sex was openly celebrated and incorporated into advertising campaigns and popular culture (S.J. Douglas 1994; Ehrenreich 1983). While the Victorian norms were focused on disciplining behavior both at home and at the workplace of the newly differentiated classes, the focus of twentieth-century codes may have been more related to norms of consumption. In an economy saturated with material goods and concerned with lack of effective demand after the world wars, the use of sexual imagery was designed to associate infinite bliss with consumer products, as part of a renewed sales effort. In the twentieth century, classes were more differentiated by conspicuous consumption of highly differentiated products than by behavior.

Yet the ubiquitous visual images of (largely female) sexuality present in late-twentieth-century popular and commercial culture may require even more control of the "body" than in the Victorian period, especially since norms of virtue are now more widely diffused through all classes, and "technologies of control" are more fully developed. With the increasing presence of women in the labor force, and public presentation of women as sexual objects, the control of the body at work requires more skill and discipline, as sexual harassment cases show. Contemporary norms of beauty combine thinness and fitness, indicating discipline, with voluptuousness, indicating comfort and complete gratification of desires. Norms for the contemporary female require accomplishment of both at once, leading to role conflicts and new forms of female disease, such as anorexia (Fraad, Resnick, and Wolff 1994; Bordo 1993), and health hazards from breast implants.

The images of the chaste angel in the nineteenth century and the sexy housewife/working girl in the twentieth seem like opposites in many ways, primarily with respect to protected versus overtly displayed sexuality. Yet both images accomplish some similar "functions." Both provide highly differentiated roles for women, which serve to separate their behavioral norms or areas of activity from those of men. Both norms serve to silence women, the first with respect to the rigid separation of spheres, the latter with respect to the objectification of women's bodies (MacKinnon 1989). Both maintain the household as normatively "empty" of the production of use values, left for the exclusive preserve of capitalist firms (Boris 1994). Both reinforce the market and the separate importance of the cash nexus, either in terms of the expectation that men will provide for women in the nineteenth-century "family wage," or in terms of the twentieth-century "commodity ensemble" of appropriate status and conspicuous consumption by which even the single man can purchase sexual access (Ehrenreich 1983).

Women's political activism has often been shaped by reactions to these ideologies. Early movements for women's control of property were coincident with the separation of the domestic sphere and drew upon the rhetoric of Enlightenment "rights of man" (Staves 1990; Shanley 1989; Poovey 1988). Women were active in abolition, temperance, moral reform, and Evangelical awakenings, and later for suffrage (Crow 1971; M. Ryan 1981; Sklar and Dublin 1991; Smith-Rosenberg 1985; Walkowitz 1980), drawing upon the special role of women as protectors of morality to address public concerns and conditions. Later, the "maternalism" of women's social welfare reform movements in the early twentieth century was shaped by women's identities as "mothers" (Koven and Michel 1993). The bourgeois feminism of Betty Friedan's *Feminine Mystique* was in reaction to the consumerism of postwar suburbs. The prolife movement of the later twentieth century can be seen as a reaction to the ideology of (hetero)sexual liberation of the 1960s (Luker 1984). While women have been active in opposing the definitions of themselves imposed from male-oriented perspectives, each of these reaction movements has itself been partial, and divided from the others.

Contemporary Ideological Formulations

As in the 1890s, 1920s, and 1950s, the capitalist economy in the 1990s can also be understood to be in the midst of a major structural transformation. During the most recent period of capitalist development since the mid-1970s, productivity growth in advanced countries has been stagnating, newly industrializing countries have become more competitive, and hypermobile capital has intensified international competition. The advanced capitalist countries have begun to reduce the provisions of their welfare states, seen as too costly and hampering "flexibility" in this new climate, as well as to attack unionization and erode institutional provisions of job security. The growing inequality of wealth and income is wider than it has been since World War II (Holmes 1996). As in the earlier periods, a resurgence of laissez-faire economic ideology is coupled with a reinforcement of norms of the traditional male control of women in the household (Ehrenreich 1983, 155–56). This coupling of free market ideology and "family values" is not accidental, but related to the ideological male/female poles of the class relations of the commodity "labor power."

As an example of the use of gender and class ideology to legitimate economic policy, consider the Republican "Contract with America," continuing themes from the "Reagan revolution" of the 1980s. In the 1994 election campaign, "welfare" called to mind promiscuous inner-city black women who sponged off of tax-paying middle-class white men and their moral, church-going wives. This characterization helped de-legitimate any role of government in the economy and drew attention away from tax cuts for the rich and growing inequality and job insecurity for everyone else (Krugman 1990; Harrison and Bluestone 1988; Wolff 1995). The appeal to "family values" is a thinly veiled critique of middle-class women who work, and a bid to reinstate the man as the sole household head, at the same time that poor women are considered lazy if they do not work. Working-class men are encouraged to aspire to become rich capitalist entrepreneurs, the true "creators of wealth," whose taxes and burdens the contract's authors will happily remove in order to buy an identification with the ultimate symbols of manhood—control of money, other men, and women. "The social power [of money] becomes the private power of private persons . . . the social wealth of its owner" (Marx 1967, 132–33). As contemporary commentator Barbara Ehrenreich paraphrases the *Playboy* philosophy, "the issue was money: Men made it; women wanted it" (Ehrenreich 1983, 46).

Unlike the female leaders of the Women's Christian Temperance Union in the nineteenth century, the most prominent leaders of the Christian moralists in the 1990s are men who have media and/or political ambitions, including Pat Robertson, and Ralph Reed of the Christian Coalition (DeParle 1996). As in the antisuffrage (Bendroth 1993) and anti-ERA (Ehrenreich 1983) backlash, religious conservatives form a powerful block of highly motivated activists, supporting "family values" and opposing abortion, using religious norms to reinforce women's "proper place." Twenty-three percent of registered Republicans currently identify with the religious right, and it dominates the party in eighteen states. Religious conservatives have been the base of the coalition that brought Republican victories for Reagan and Bush, and established the party dominance nationwide (DeParle 1996). According to Reed, the Christian Coalition now has 1.7 million members in 2,000 local chapters, and is the "best organized constituency in American politics" (Lemann 1996).

By blaming women's uncontrolled sexuality, and by hampering any independence from marriage (with reductions in welfare as well as restriction on abortions and roll-backs in affirmative action), voters have been willing to acquiesce to the elimination of "entitlements" in the "welfare reform" bill of 1996. The symbolic nature of the welfare issue is highlighted by the fact that a program comprising only 1 percent of the federal budget continues to be a major issue in presidential campaigns (Cushman 1995). The focus is on reducing illegitimacy by punitive measures, when there is evidence that the rise in illegitimacy is in fact caused by a decline in the marriage rate due to economic insecurity rather than an increase in the birthrate due to more promiscuity (Wilson and Neckerman 1986; Lind 1996; Luker 1996).

The focus on wealthy (white) males as progenitors of the system is as completely inverted as the impression that "money can reproduce" as self-expanding value. Completely masked in the circuits of money and commodities are the roles of household and wage labor in the expansion of value, and the role of the state in stabilizing and undergirding the capitalist economy. With some variation along a common theme, the current ascendancy of the right wing in other advanced capitalist countries provides an indication of how capitalist-class interests can be advanced by exploiting gender, race, and class divisions and identifications, in this case in the interests of reducing the tax burden on profits, lowering the floor under wages, reinforcing the discipline of the market on (male) labor, reinforcing male control of female sexuality, harnessing sexuality to reproduction of workers and consumers (as in "sex sells" [Goffman 1976]).

The abstract equality that women may have achieved in the workplace is now offset by reassertion of the ideological power of the concrete institutional norms of their subordinate role in the home. The coupling of these two strategies in the contemporary period again suggests that the presence of women in the home, at least ideologically, helps to manage the contradictory effects of the market hegemony. This ideological elaboration of gender norms is a necessary accompaniment to "economic" policies, in order to manage the contradictory roles of men and women in the capitalist system.

As in the eighteenth and nineteenth centuries, the debate about welfare in contemporary United States can be seen as using gender to police and maintain class boundaries. The dual image of women in Christian tradition is divided by class. Middle-class "traditionalists" are dedicated homemakers and mothers, the daughters of the Victorian "angels in the house." By contrast, welfare mothers are descendants of Eve the temptress, whose body represents sexuality and lack of control and discipline. The legitimacy of social provision is denied, since appropriate needs are contained either in the market or the household. Self-respecting men are employed; and proper, deserving women are supported by them. The needs of legitimate children of the bourgeoisie are met in these private households. The children of single women are illegitimate, and so must be disciplined by the market and by Christian morality, enforced by "welfare reform" and the coercive power of the state. As in the Contagious Disease Acts in England in the mid-nineteenth century (Walkowitz 1980, 3–4, 71, 246, 251), contemporary welfare reform has justified an enormous expansion of state surveillance power into the lives of private (low-income) individuals (Pear 1996), ironically by those adhering to laissez-faire ideology.

The contemporary popularity of such domestic experts as Martha Stewart attests to the continuing appeal and sway of norms of domesticity. Stewart's "empire" includes a five-year-old magazine with a circulation of 1.5 million; a cable TV show; a dozen books on gardening, cooking, life style, and home decorating; a mail-order business; a nationally syndicated newspaper column; and (formerly) a weekly slot on the *Today* show, among other achievements (Talbot 1996). Despite flux and challenge, the resilience of the domestic ideology signifies its importance in managing the contradictory roles of the commodity "labor power" (a countervailing tendency noted in Kessler-Harris and Sacks as well (1987, 78).

Implications for Methodology

In conclusion, I would like to draw attention to several implications of this argument for methodology.

The "Economy" as "Structure"

The separate spheres of the economy and the household, by which gender and class appear to be "dual systems," are historical constructs, although now appearing as "natural" in modern market economies (Nicholson 1988). The extreme polarities that developed in gender roles with the emergence of the wage labor force can be understood by using Marx's concept of the contradictions in the commodity "labor power," which both is and is not a "commodity." The concrete role of women in the household reflects the polar opposite of concrete relations among men in the workplace. As the male worker is normatively an "object" that mechanically obeys rational rules at work, the ideal female in the household embodies humanity, emotion, morality (in the nineteenth century), and sexuality (in the twentieth). This polarity of gender roles was developed in the Victorian era in England, coincident with the ascendance of the capitalist labor market. This duality is integrated over time in the circuit of the working day, which includes both work and recreation at home (circuit (3) on page 96). This unity of disparate roles is maintained with difficulty, and is supported with ideological norms, which change over time in response to conflicts and challenges from people who resist the direction of their lives by the abstract principles of the expansion of capital.

Feminist economists have struggled to characterize women's labor and its value to the capitalist system by cataloging its specific attributes. Undeniably, essential concrete use values are created and shared in the household, including sexual services, bearing and raising children, housework, shopping, and family and community relationships. They have focused on such issues as whether domestic labor produces value, and whether women are also exploited in the home (Folbre 1982, 1994).

The approach here would shift that focus to a broader understanding of the role of the household and gender. For example, additional dimensions include the historical specificity of the private sphere, varying forms of control, ideological underpinnings, and symbolic meanings, all of which change across historical periods with economic transformations. In addition to the importance of counting the hours of labor worked in the household, also important are the socially constructed, qualitative meanings attached to this work. For example, although working-class women historically performed very demanding physical labor in cooking, cleaning, and child rearing (Seccombe 1993, 46), the housewife is just as "essential" in upper-class homes with servants, or in modern economies in which much of her work has now been commodified. The "objectified," symbolic value of the CEO's wife is just as important in his home and in social settings as are the women in sex-segregated jobs, such as the CEO's secretary in his office. Women themselves serve as class markers (Davidoff 1995, 252–55), their bodies representing, and their activities policing, class boundaries. The control of women by internalized institutional norms in capitalist economies assumes a distinct, particular form, warping and restricting opportunities for personal development (Gilman 1966) just as palpably as the female circumcision practiced in parts of Africa, although less overt and physically debilitating.

Social Structures of Accumulation

This understanding of the role of women in capitalism goes beyond enumerating the concrete types of work actually performed in or related to the household. It examines the images that are widely "known" to describe women's labor (Barrett 1988) and the methods by which these norms are spread, accepted, internalized, and enforced. This particular form of the control of women and their sexuality is posited as an integral part of the "class relation" of the commodity "labor power." Consequently, the norms and ideologies by which their behavior is circumscribed are just as fundamental to understanding the economy in a given period as is a detailed analysis of the labor process, that method of control of labor in the workplace that occupies a prominent place in *Capital*. Just as an entire body of work has examined the concrete institutional detail of managing the labor process in the face of alienated working conditions (Edwards 1979; Gordon, Edwards, and Reich 1982; Burawoy 1979; Shaiken 1984), so there is also developing a body of work that analyzes the norms and practices of women in the household and in the labor force in relation to the developments of the capitalist economy (M. Ryan 1981; Rose 1992; Clark 1995; Valenze 1995; Poovey 1988, 1995; Kowaleski-Wallace 1991).

A further implication is that such methodological approaches as the Social Structure of Accumulation (SSA) should also include attention to domestic ideology and the forms of the household. Given the centrality of the household for labor supply, labor discipline, and consumption, arguably this factor is appropriate to be included among the "core institutions" of the SSA (Kotz 1994b, 65–67; O'Hara 1995). In fact, the relative stability of domestic ideology may provide the underlying cohesion that allows other aspects of the SSA to vary and develop historically.

The above discussion suggests that there are dominant images of women in certain periods. For example, in the nineteenth century, the middle-class ideal is the chaste moral angel in the house, helping to legitimate the amoral market economy and the formation of the wage labor force; in the twentieth century, the image of the sexy housewife/supermom helps prop up domesticity in the face of increasing women's labor force participation. Each image is gradually subject to a dynamic "expansionary logic" (Bowles and Gintis 1986, 29–32), which may then jeopardize the institutional bounds of capitalism. For example, in the early twentieth century, the increasingly educated maternalist moralist activists dared to challenge the legitimation of the First World War, privatized child care, and even monogamy, followed by a Red- and lesbian-baiting backlash. In the late twentieth century, women's equal rights demands are being extended to equal wages, occupational integration, and the legitimation of gay marriage, amounting to a fundamental challenge to the "sexual contract" (Pateman 1988) and combated in turn by a national coalition of business and the Christian Right. Each challenge is met with attempts to reformulate a more powerful domestic ideology with the associated sanctions, engaging both men and women in a variety of class and institutional settings. Times of transition are characterized by dramatically opposing gender norms and justifications, as at present.

Ideology and Culture as "Transitional Space"

Just as humans are characterized by both mental activity and embodiment, an interaction of psyche and soma, so also culture represents the interaction of material processes of production with imaginative texts from history and myth (Flax 1990). The focus on culture, such as the ideology of domesticity, is not separate from material forces, and provides a way to move beyond such dichotomies as the material and ideal, subject and object, base and superstructure. "The capacity to play and the process of symbolization associated with it eventually expand 'into creative living and into the whole cultural life of man.' . . . Culture arises out of that . . . [transitional] space [in which] each relatively healthy individual carries on the lifelong process of creatively managing the strain of reconciling inner and outer realities" (Flax 1990, 119–20). A "turn to culture" (Barrett and Phillips 1992) does not necessarily require a renunciation of attention to material and production relations. Abstract economic forces come into play in a systematic fashion once the market economy becomes dominant. The "symbolization and representation—the field of culture" (Barrett and Phillips 1992, 204) of these economic forces are still part of the larger class relations. For this latter enterprise, Marx's (critique of) value categories and historical methods of analysis are still provocative. A deeper understanding of the integration of class and gender can only enrich the analysis of the historical interconnections between culture and the economy, without necessarily assuming that one determines the other (Fraad, Resnick, and Wolff 1994; Nicholson 1986). The integration of class and gender that is symbolized in culture helps to mediate what are seemingly separate spheres, in dynamic interplay with the "economic."

Agency

Under the influence of postmodern thought, which eschews "meta-narratives" and economic determinism, there is a certain hesitation among contemporary scholars to discuss the economy as having a distinct structural dimension. Yet it is clear that economic constructs such as "money" and "property" are heavily circumscribed by elaborated codes of meaning and behavior, enforced by law and the authority of the state. The "economy" has clear and distinct "rules of the game," although always changing in the particulars. Yet it is also clear, from the contribution of feminist theory, that it is important to pay attention to the actions and choices of individual agents.

Marx's distinction between abstract and concrete can help to mediate this apparent dilemma. The value circuits of money and commodities can help to identify the rules and requirements of the abstract self-expansion of capital. At the same time, the concrete struggles of historic agents, even women on opposing sides of an issue within the ongoing process of class struggle, influence the course of the economy within those relatively wide structural conditions. Women's historians aid us immeasurably in this task by allowing us to study the character and context of those who articulated and disseminated the domestic ideology, for example, as well as those who organized and lobbied against it.

The analysis of both dimensions, the abstract as well as the concrete, enables us to gain a fuller understanding of the dynamics of the economy, as well as the historical agents who were actively involved in the construction of the norms and institutions that continue to condition our lives as well as to channel abstract economic forces.

Part II

Engendering Production

The Social Construction of Low-Wage Labor Markets

7

Comparable Worth in a Restructuring Economy

Discourse and Counter-Discourse

Ellen Mutari and Deborah M. Figart

The U.S. economy of the 1980s and 1990s is in transition. While the basic contours of the market-based economic system remain unchanged, the rules of the game that seemed to apply during the postwar period are in flux. Among political economists, a number of frameworks have been proposed to analyze economic restructuring in industrialized countries: most prominently, social structures of accumulation (SSA) and regulation theory. These analyses focus on the institutional and technical conditions underpinning, and eventually undermining, long waves of accumulation. While political economists have devoted substantial attention to the political and economic institutional arrangements fostering long waves of accumulation, the linkages between gender relations and accumulation during specific economic regimes have been undertheorized. To the extent that gender is analyzed within this restructuring literature, women's increased labor force participation as a demographic, supply phenomenon is analytically separated from structural changes within production. In contrast, Bakker (1996) advocates viewing "gender as an interactive category of analysis in a complete account of the transforming global order." Thus, gender interacts with class, race, ethnicity, sexuality, and nationality in specific historical contexts (Bakker 1996, 8–9; see also Mitter 1986).

Politically, contemporary economic restructuring has been associated with the rise of conservative governments in the United States and other Western nations. Although taking different forms in different national contexts, the state's revised mission has been "to subordinate social policy to the needs of labour market flexibility and/or to the constraints of international competition" (Jessop 1994, 24; see also Howell 1992). In the United States, this has taken the form of supply-side policies to cut spending on social programs, reduce taxes, and deregulate business. Throughout the 1980s, this delegitimation of the state in domestic affairs was accompanied by tremendous military expansion and the acceleration of cold war ideology (Bernstein 1994). Similarly, European governments, especially the United Kingdom, have pursued deregulation and privatization as a central policy objective, along with the dismantling of European welfare states (Howell 1992; Faux 1995a, 1995b). As articulated in *Beware the U.S. Model,* published by the Economic Policy Institute: "The choice is between the hard-edged Social Darwinism of Thatcher and Reagan and a softer version represented by the neoliberalism of Clinton and Delors. Scratch the surface of either strand of the U.S. version of the model and you find anemic job growth and plummeting wages for the majority of workers" (Faux 1995a, xi).

Viewing economic restructuring through the lens of gender analysis can redirect our attention to neglected dimensions of social and institutional transformation. First, feminist contributions to political economy have noted that the postwar economic order was constructed upon a specific set of gender relations. Specifically, the relative prosperity of white male workers in core industries rested on the family wage ideology and married white women's unpaid household labor (McDowell 1991; Williams 1994; O'Hara 1995; Bakker 1996; Brodie 1996; Jenson 1996; Cameron 1996). Economic policy was predicated upon the hypothesized stability of this gender order, a nuclear family supported by a male breadwinner. Second, feminization of wage labor has been posited as a managerial response to declining profit margins (see, for example, Jenson, Hagen, and Reddy 1988; Bakker 1996). The dynamic tension between the family wage ideology and the process of feminization has implications for the future of the pay equity movement.

The postwar order has perpetuated the systematic undervaluation of work done by women and people of color. Pay equity activists assert that this undervaluation is reflected in market and organizational wages; the remedy is to pay jobs according to the skill, effort, responsibility, and working conditions required rather than the gender or race of incumbents. The 1980s had begun as a period of optimism for pay equity advocates and a period of concern for antagonists. The favorable 1981 Supreme Court Decision in *County of Washington, Oregon v. Gunther* sparked a wave of pay equity litigation, initiatives, and activism (McCann 1994).[1] Numerous public sector jurisdictions in the United States and Canada reformed their classification systems via feminist utilization of job evaluation, yet transmitting these models to private, profit-seeking sector employers proved more difficult.[2] Subsequent court decisions were less auspicious, and pay equity slipped down the agenda of those labor unions without significant public sector membership.

In the United States, the organized opposition to pay equity has found sustenance in the emerging political economy of liberalization and deregulation. Business organizations, long opposed to comparable worth, find newly elected conservative politicians increasingly receptive to arguments against comparable worth and other labor market regulations. Pay equity opponents maintain that raising wages in female-dominated occupations would result in "economy-wide turmoil" (Rhoads 1993b, 38). By the end of the decade of the eighties, business interests, in the words of pay equity adversary Rhoads (1993b), "pretty much enjoyed a respite" from demands for pay equity as the women's movement turned greater attention to reproductive freedom, family leave, sexual harassment, and other issues.

The focus of this chapter is the relationship between changes in the political economy and shifts in gender relations. This research was motivated by our interest in how to revive the pay equity movement in the United States, given the problems posed by contemporary economic and political transformations. The discourse against comparable worth reform is analyzed in order to reveal opponents' assumptions about women's work and women's wages. Following the analytical approach of Nancy Fraser and Linda Gordon (1994, 311) in examining welfare reform debates, "we seek to contextualize discursive shifts in relation to broad institutional and social-structural shifts, and we welcome normative political reflection."

In the following section, we argue that contemporary economic restructuring cannot be understood without considering the gendered basis of managerial strategies for alleviating the crisis in profitability. These managerial strategies have consequences for the movement to improve women's economic status, which we explore through discourse analysis in two sections. First, we focus on how the ideological commitment to labor market flexibility is used to discredit pay equity reform. Second, we contend that gender ideologies represent one potential site of contradiction for the conservative offensive. This cultural confusion about gender roles presents opportunities for alternative visions. As David Gordon (1994b, 302) notes, "The global economy is up for grabs, not locked in some new and immutable order." Feminist, labor, and other progressive movements are challenging the gendered basis of economic restructuring by linking pay equity to a redefinition of gender roles and a broad living wage movement. The goal is new, shared prosperity, accessible to a diversity of family forms.

Economic Restructuring and Gender

Attempting to overcome spurious divisions between macroeconomic and microeconomic analysis, political economists have developed historically based accounts of the relationship between macroeconomic stability and the institutional organization of production. We find that these accounts, primarily developed under the rubric of the social structure of accumulation (SSA) and regulation approaches, provide a useful context for viewing stability and change in gender relations. Yet neither school provides a completely satisfactory account of contemporary restructuring, in part because of the gender-blindness of each analysis.[3] Therefore, the discussion that follows is a broad synthesis of literature from both schools, focusing especially on the U.S. experience.[4] This is followed by a presentation of some feminist contributions to the analysis of contemporary restructuring.

Gordon, Edwards, and Reich (1982), in their original formulation of SSA theory, suggest that each wave or regime is marked by three periods: (1) exploration (when stagnation prompts experimentation with alternative structural arrangements); (2) consolidation (when one set of institutional arrangements becomes hegemonic); and (3) decay (when a new period of prolonged stagnation or crisis develops). Because of its evocative imagery, we utilize the term Fordism, borrowed from the regulation school founded by Aglietta (1979), to describe the institutional bases of the postwar wave of accumulation. Fordism is typically defined as having two components: an economic regime founded on mass production for mass consumption and a political regime or mode of regulation founded on the Keynesian welfare state. Within the SSA framework, the parallel concepts are the (limited) capital–labor accord and the capital(ist)–citizen accord. U.S. economic hegemony, "Pax Americana," which reduced intercapitalist rivalries, is a further dimension in SSA theory.

Depictions of the stability of the Fordist regime focus on the concept of a "virtuous circle" that enabled Keynesian policies to flourish in the United States during the postwar period. That is, growth in worker productivity and in employment went hand in hand, permitting increased consumption with stable prices. The key to this process was the domestic market for manufactured goods; if employers shared the benefits of increased productivity with workers in core industries—through wage increases, fiscal policy, or welfare state provisions—the resultant increase in demand would fuel profits (see Appelbaum 1995). Of course, this arrangement primarily bestowed the prosperity of the Pax Americana upon white males in core industries within manufacturing, although there was positive spillover for other groups (Albelda and Tilly 1994; Badgett and Williams 1994; O'Hara 1995). Economies enter periods of restructuring when sustained crises generate "major structural changes in the organization of work and the structure of labor markets" (Gordon, Edwards, and Reich 1982, 2). Under both the SSA and regulation frameworks, the period since the early 1970s is viewed as a period of relative stagnation among Western industrialized nations due to a mismatch between current institutional structures and the new phase of economic development (Bernstein and Adler 1994). Within the more materialist regulation theory these contradictions originated within the accumulation process itself, while SSA has taken a more eclectic approach to the institutional sources of collapse. Nevertheless, SSA theorists distinguish their analysis from neo/post-Keynesian underconsumptionist approaches by emphasizing that the crisis originated in class conflict, which generates a profit squeeze (see, for example, Weisskopf 1994).[5] Both theories agree that globalization is central to contemporary economic restructuring, although they disagree as to whether globalization is the cause of or the cure for economic insecurity.[6]

Feminists have drawn attention to the existence of a stable, but not immutable, gender order that impacts upon macroeconomic stability (see Bruegel and Perrons 1995). One pillar of the gender order is the family wage. Though its roots can be traced to nineteenth-century industrialization, the family wage was most extensively institutionalized during the postwar period: "Within this paradigm, adult men were seen as the primary workers, single or otherwise husbandless women and young people comprised a secondary labour force, and women were expected to withdraw from the paid labour force upon marriage" (Cameron 1996, 55). This hegemonic system of gender relations during the postwar period has been extensively critiqued in early writings by feminist economists and sociologists; however, as McDowell (1991) attests, many feminist analyses do not recognize the historical contingency of this system.

While much of the postwar economic expansion was founded upon industrial sectors where traditionally male, unionized jobs earning a so-called family wage predominated, economic restructuring has placed feminized sectors at the core of postindustrial economies. Standing (1989) introduced the concept of "global feminization through flexible labor," presenting a unified analysis of trends in both developing and industrialized countries. Feminization is the direct result of employer strategy to decrease wages and increase control over external and internal labor markets. Mitter (1986) emphasizes that feminization strategies rely on women's marginalization within the labor movement as well as gendered assumptions regarding women's docility and domesticity.[7]

On an empirical level, feminization refers to women's rising share of the labor force brought about by their increased labor force participation along with male workers' displacement from manufacturing jobs. In a cross-country study, Ça atay and Özler (1995) find that women's share of the labor force exhibits a U-shaped pattern over the course of development; the rising portion of the pattern has been intensified by contemporary macroeconomic policies and export-oriented growth. Although the 1920s mark the historical turning point in U.S. women's labor force participation rates, as white married women increased their labor force attachment, this process intensified during the 1970s and 1980s (Kessler-Harris 1982; Goldin 1990).

Standing defines feminization broadly, encompassing structural changes in employment as well as quantitative changes in employment shares by gender. His global process of feminization entails three aspects: (1) direct substitution of women for men within jobs; (2) the expansion of traditionally female-intensive employment sectors; and (3) the expansion of forms of employment associated with women, such as part-time, temporary/contingent, and informal work (see also Jenson, Hagen, and Reddy 1988; Bakker 1996; Jenson 1996). Standing emphasizes that deregulation and flexible employment strategies foster "the types of work, labor relations, income, and insecurity associated with 'women's work' " (1077). Because they do not have the characteristics of male breadwinner jobs, these jobs are gendered female. Thus, Armstrong (1996) refers to the process of feminization as a harmonizing down since men's and women's employment prospects are increasingly similar (see also McDowell 1991).

Feminization, along with deindustrialization, has undermined the masculine ideal of the male breadwinner without establishing a clear replacement. Fiona Williams (1994, 57–58) argues that such shifts in gender relations should not be viewed as a passive outcome of economic change, but the result of women's own agency and struggles over gender relations. Critiquing standard accounts of economic restructuring, she notes, "rarely is the power of explanation or the power of agency granted to gender, 'race' or any social relation other than class" (57). The emergence of new concepts of masculinity and femininity is a contentious terrain with an indeterminate outcome that feminists can hope to influence. The comparable worth movement, which attempts to extend the family wage to traditionally female jobs, can be viewed as one dimension of such efforts to develop a new gender order. Therefore, it is illuminating to analyze the economic and cultural arguments raised in opposition to such efforts.

Pay Equity and Flexibility

As the hegemony of Keynesian demand-oriented theory among economists and policymakers diminished, a rejuvenation of laissez-faire social Darwinism seeped into this intellectual vacuum. The *market* once again became the "central category of economic discourse" (Block 1990, 46; see also Faux 1995a). The word most closely associated with the reassertion of the market and optimistic visions of the postindustrial economy is *flexibility,* which is ideologically linked to the concept of competitiveness in an era of heightened international competition. If the hallmark of the Fordist era was mass production and consumption, the emerging era has been labeled a period of flexible accumulation (Brown 1991, 1091; see also Harvey 1991). The term flexibility is used by different authors to signify various aspects of institutional arrangements (see McDowell 1991; Gilbert, Burrows, and Pollert 1992). Our focus is on flexibility in employment relations rather than flexible specialization as indicated by product differentiation.

Labor market flexibility has been depicted as a crucial dimension of this process in order to permit firms to adapt to changing markets. Public policy was redirected to increase flexibility and eliminate rigidities so as to facilitate the smooth operation of markets, especially labor markets. "Increasingly, public debate has come to hinge, not on what kind of society we are or want to be, but on what the needs of the economy are. Hence, a broad range of social policies are now debated almost entirely in terms of how they fit in with the imperatives of the market" (Block 1990, 3). Sam Rosenberg (1991) contends that the drive for labor market flexibility takes three forms: wage flexibility, employment or numerical flexibility, and functional flexibility. The first two reassert the central role of supply and demand forces in external labor markets, signaling a return to classical notions of free market equilibrium. Greater wage flexibility is pursued through labor market deregulation, such as implicitly or explicitly lowering minimum wage standards, and through concession bargaining. Employers' increased use of part-time, temporary, and contingent workers, as well as subcontractors and homeworkers, is part of their strategies to increase employment flexibility. Functional flexibility focuses on introducing flexibility within internal labor markets. This internal flexibility reduces the traditional power of workers in unionized, core sectors through flexible job descriptions and assignments. Functional flexibility may also be accompanied by a reduction in job mobility and union-developed career ladders within firms (see Standing 1989).

Gender adds a new perspective on this analysis of flexibility. Each of these three forms of flexibility are gendered. Wage flexibility undermines the family wage for male workers; more and more jobs pay "a woman's wage" (see Kessler-Harris 1990). Employment flexibility is frequently accomplished by increased use of part-time and temporary workers, largely women. Internal flexibility transforms working conditions in male-dominated, core industries to resemble women's "secondary" employment—vague job descriptions with few prospects for promotion.

Brodsky (1994) traces the shift in the meaning of labor market flexibility as advocated by the Organization for Economic Cooperation and Development (OECD) over the past thirty years. During the 1980s, Europe's relatively higher unemployment rates ("Eurosclerosis") were used by the OECD as a basis for positing the United States as a model of labor market flexibility; deregulation to promote flexibility in external labor markets was the central policy objective, along with dismantling of European welfare states.[8] As the U.S. economy became increasingly troubled in the early 1990s, new strategies for economic restructuring were promoted by the OECD and others. Flexibility for the 1990s was redirected toward internal, or functional, flexibility, although attacks on social welfare programs and labor market regulations continued.

This gendered basis of economic restructuring has made pay equity directly contradictory to contemporary accumulation strategies based on external and internal flexibility. Popular discourse against pay equity, as expressed in the United States by business lobby organizations, their funded researchers, and Republican officials, warns of the dangers of tampering with labor markets (see Greenwood 1984; Steinberg 1986; Bergmann 1989a; and Peterson 1992). As articulated in a publication sponsored by the Cato Institute, a libertarian public policy research organization in Washington, D.C.: "Most proponents of comparable worth argue that it is not an alternative to the market, that it is like other correctives to the market that have been instituted by government in recent years. I contend that this is false. Comparable worth . . . cannot be grafted onto the market. Rather, the market and comparable worth emanate from two entirely different normative assumptions about individual action" (Paul 1989, 116).

Not surprisingly, the cornerstone of opponents' arguments has centered on flexible wage-setting. Specifically, pay equity is argued to interfere with the ability of market forces to adapt and respond to changing economic conditions: "What has characterized capitalist economies since the Industrial Revolution is precisely the options that workers have, the fluidity of labor markets, and the ever-changing possibilities the market creates" (Paul 1989, 113). Steven Rhoads, a professor of government who writes for both academic and business audiences, sums up this position: "Well-functioning market economies use rising wages to ameliorate shortages of labor in an occupation or at a particular location, and use static or falling wages to reduce surpluses by encouraging worker exit and discouraging entry. Comparable worth does not allow this flexibility" (Rhoads 1993b, 40).

This defense of the market mechanism rests on the explicit assumptions of value theory in neoclassical economics. Comparable worth advocates are accused of the economic heresy of a "fair" or "just" price—a theory held by classical economists such as Adam Smith, but abandoned by neoclassical theorists (see Hildebrand 1980, 83; O'Neill 1984a, 177–78; Thomas 1985, 2; U.S. Office of Personnel Management 1987, 37).[9] For example: "Flawed from its inception in the notion that jobs have objective value, comparable worth compounds its initial error by calling for job evaluations freed from market constraints. This sets the supporters adrift in a sea of subjectivity. Since they cannot eliminate values, they seek to replace the values of millions of free individuals expressed every day in the marketplace with the values of job-evaluation experts imbued with feminist ideology. And a misguided feminism at that" (Paul 1989, 57).

Although this free-market argument has a long history, it has gained new credibility with the return to laissez-faire. Advocacy of labor market flexibility rests on the assertion that government regulation of wages introduces rigidities. Conservative discourse utilizes antistate rhetoric. Pay equity and other forms of employment regulation are depicted as barriers to competitiveness. Despite the focus of the pay equity movement on a decentralized strategy implemented at the establishment level, opponents testifying before the U.S. Commission on Civil Rights and at a conference sponsored by Phyllis Schlafly's Eagle Forum Education and Legal Defense Fund continually raised the specter of centrally administered wage boards, saying, for example: "Perhaps the most pernicious aspect of the comparable worth theory is that it would establish a governmental agency as the final arbiter of wages" (Northrup 1984, 98); and "In spite of assurances to the contrary, a central system of government-dictated wages appears to be the inescapable long-range consequence of the currently advocated step process" (Berger 1984, 70).

Reflecting the "consensus" that an unregulated economy represents a model of external flexibility, the relative success of the United States has been trumpeted. In the following passage, Rhoads makes a broadscale comparison between the United States and Australia: "The economic costs of comparable worth are likely to be enormous. Since Australia began its centralized wage-fixing system in 1913, its per-capita income has fallen from highest in the world to 13th, 30 percent behind the United States. Many economists think Australia's inflexible wage system explains much of this deterioration, and all the major Australian political parties now favor more decentralized, market-driven wages as a way to improve efficiency and growth" (Rhoads 1993b, 41). Thus, the cost of pay equity reform, increasingly depicted as a threat to profitability, is receiving increased attention (Rhoads 1993a, 1993c).

Yet the emergence of supply-side economic theory has added a new dimension to the neoclassical defense of markets. George Hildebrand, writing for the Equal Employment Advisory Council (the Orwellian-named, employer-funded, antiregulation organization), reflects the supply-side concern with regulation's impact on productivity:

> Turning to the broader issues, what we actually face, as a latent and so far unrecognized element in this new proposal for wage regulation, is yet another large-scale regulatory intervention into the private sector.... In addition, it has at last begun to be recognized that the overall productivity of labor and capital has been slowing in its annual gains for over a decade, and now, ominously, has turned negative. Unless this tendency can be turned around quickly and strongly, there can be no hope for the continued broad improvements in real per capita incomes, including real wages, that we have enjoyed for so long. In the presence of this very real threat to national well-being, therefore, productivity rather than controversial notions of wage justice should dominate our attention. (Hildebrand 1980, 104–7)

Economist Wendy Lee Gramm (1994) presents supply-side policies as a feminist agenda, maintaining that women share in the losses wrought by pay equity and other forms of government regulation: "Women's advocates should support free and competitive international markets, lower capital-gains taxes, lower income taxes and fewer burdensome government regulations. And they should oppose government-imposed solutions like quotas, comparable worth, or socialized medicine, because these measures promote economic inefficiency, increase employer costs and decrease the demand for labor."

The pursuit of productivity underlies the newer calls for functional, in addition to external, flexibility. However, functional flexibility presents a moving target for the technocratic versions of pay equity strategy, which were most successful in the public sector during the 1980s; if workers are not assigned fixed responsibilities, formal job evaluation becomes more difficult (Bakker 1991). In a restructuring political economy, with the state under attack as diverting resources from the market, and corporate strategies emphasizing lower labor costs and functional flexibility, pay equity strategies may themselves need "restructuring." Pay equity, broadly understood as addressing inequities in low-wage jobs and occupations and as drawing upon the notion of the undervaluation of women's work, can be pursued through a variety of means. These alternative mobilizations are discussed further in the final section of this chapter.

Pay Equity and Gender Relations

The rise and fall of family wage ideology illustrates the institution and unraveling of Fordism's gender order. Focusing on the development of a family wage policy at Ford Motor Company, Martha May (1982) suggests that the family wage ideology contained two elements. The relationship between these two components is crucial to understanding contentious debates over the historical meaning of political and economic struggles to achieve the family wage. First, the family wage represented a demand for subsistence and survival for working-class families. Second, it was based on and reinforced emerging social relations that posited separate spheres for men and women. Thus, the controversy over the family wage has centered on whether it was a unified working-class strategy or a means by which male workers gained privileges at the expense of working women while capitalists maintained women's low wages. It has been a lightening rod for debates over the relationship between class and gender struggles.

Rather than reflecting the primacy of class, gender, or race conflict, the family wage embodies the complexity and interaction of these social forces in both production and reproduction. Sonya Rose (1992) argues that the rhetoric of the family wage was founded on definitions of masculinity as wage-earning and femininity as homemaking, which indicate that gender was fundamental to the construction of class relations in the nineteenth century. Her analysis emphasizes that the family wage operated primarily at the level of ideology and was achievable for only a small segment of the working class. May (1982) concurs, noting that many working-class families, especially African American families, were excluded from this idealized family structure. Thus, even in times of relative stability, several models of gender relations coexist within the overall system, differentiated by race, ethnicity, class, sexuality, or age.

Contemporary feminization illustrates the complexity of cultural interactions between gender, class, and race. Because the gender order was unevenly developed and contained elements that disempowered women, the relationship of women and people of color to the "loss" of postwar prosperity is more ambiguous than that of men. Viewed optimistically, contemporary restructuring has led to the demise of the ideology of women's domesticity and working women's increased economic autonomy (Hartmann 1987; Kessler-Harris and Sacks 1987). Yet it has also intensified the hardships faced by women of color, whose communities have been devastated by urban decay and cutbacks in social services (Zinn 1987). Badgett and Williams (1994) find empirical evidence that white women working outside the home, more than black workers of either gender, are improving their employment status as a result of economic restructuring. McDowell (1991) emphasizes the intensification of class differences between women reaping the gains of lower barriers to managerial and professional jobs and working-class women in part-time, contingent, and undervalued jobs.

The discourse against pay equity also exemplifies the contemporary tension and confusion over gender relations in transition. On the one hand, a gender order of male breadwinner, female homemaker is assumed. Based on this presumption, opponents put forth the traditional argument that women choose female-dominated jobs in order to balance work and family responsibilities. At congressional hearings on pay equity for federal workers, Phyllis Schlafly, president of Eagle Forum, summarizes this position:

> The pay gap between men and women is not due to discrimination. It is due primarily to the fact that men and women get married. . . . Most married men are motivated to work harder in the labor force to provide for their families. Most married women are motivated to spend more effort on the daily care and nurturing of their children. That's why most women choose occupations which allow repeated entry and exit from the labor force, part-time work or shorter hours, transfer to another city in order to accompany their husbands, and which have pleasanter and less risky work environments. Comparable worth is an attempt to force employers, taxpayers and consumers to pay women as though they had not made those career choices. (Schlafly 1985, 267)

In this framework, women's lower wages are explained by "crowding" (an excess supply of workers driving down wages) and intermittent labor force participation, which generates less on-the-job experience: "[F]amily commitments and a variety of feminine traits affecting job preference may always leave women somewhat less mobile in the labor market than men" (Rabkin 1984, 190).

Some writers attempt to display their neutrality by not overtly advocating this gender division of labor. Instead, the division of labor is portrayed as a social, but not economic, question: "Regardless of one's views of these traditions, they are factors that must be considered separate from discrimination by employers. For example, women as a group, to a greater extent than men, have traditionally assumed the primary role for child-raising responsibilities" (Williams and Kessler 1984, 20). In a book entitled *Equal Pay for UNequal Work* published by the Eagle Forum, one commentator takes the most extreme position, affirming that "the main trouble with the feminist diagnosis of the economic division of labor is its disregard of biology" (Levin 1984, 130). He continues, "Any cultural universal as the sexual division of labor suggests a non-social, biological cause, and indeed it is as certain as anything in science can be that men and women do differ in the abilities and, more importantly, the motivations, they bring to paid labor and everything else." On the other hand, some opponents argue that younger women's priorities are changing and they are increasingly breaking down barriers to higher-paid occupations (O'Neill 1984a, 1994; Brody 1984; Roback 1986; Paul 1989). At the same hearings in which Schlafly defends the existence of dual spheres, June O'Neill maintains that social roles are changing. After citing statistics on women's rising share of medical degrees, she proclaims: "These changes are taking place because of fundamental changes in women's role in the economy and in the family—changes that themselves reflect a response to rising wage rates as well as changing social attitudes. Pay set according to comparable worth would distort wage signals, inducing inappropriate supply responses and unemployment.... If women have been discouraged by society or barred by employers from entering certain occupations, the appropriate response is to remove the barriers, not try to repeal supply and demand" (O'Neill 1984b, 264). Jennifer Roback, a self-described "skeptical feminist," argues that comparable worth inappropriately glorifies stereotypical female jobs rather than encouraging women to enter nontraditional fields. She declares "It is similar to arguing that blacks are segregated into shining shoes and scrubbing floors, so that raising the wages of those jobs is the only fair thing to do" (1986, 43).[10]

There is a cognitive dissonance to these arguments, as conservatives grapple with the impact of feminization and feminism on gender relations. This dualistic analysis of women's roles—the continuance of the full-time homemaker versus the emergence of a new generation of married career women—enables pay equity's antagonists to pit groups of women against each other. Asserting that the labor market merely reflects women's supply-side decisions to value family over career, some opponents claim pay equity harms married women and the structure of the nuclear family: "Thus, the income redistributed by comparable worth theory would flow mainly to single women and to families without young children.... We doubt that a convincing case could be made that such a redistribution of real income would be beneficial to the nation as a whole" (Nelson, Opton, and Wilson 1980, 399).

The explicit assumptions behind this analysis are that married women do not work and that single women do not need to earn a breadwinner's wage. However, there is no clear consensus on *which* women are harmed by pay equity. Paul (1989, 123) asserts that pay equity harms women entrepreneurs: "One group of women who would be harmed if comparable worth artificially inflated entry-level salaries are women entrepreneurs, especially those in the process of creating new businesses, since these start-up companies are quite labor intensive." In fact, Paul finds few women who would actually benefit from pay equity, echoing the common pronouncement that raising the legislated minimum wage would create unemployment: "However, to women reentering the labor market after a marriage has broken up, to women just out of high school, to newly arrived immigrants, and to those with little skill, the freedom to take the clerical, factory, and sales jobs is the difference between having a chance to better themselves or being condemned to dependency. Comparable worth, by artificially raising the wages of such jobs, would restrict the number of such positions and make the lot of the poorest and least skilled women that much worse" (Paul 1989, 124).

These attempts to fragment women's interests are indicative of a broader right-wing strategy in the United States. Specific groups of women have been direct targets of conservative political rhetoric, fueling race and class divisions between women. For example, in discussions of welfare reform, women on welfare are portrayed with racist imagery. "Career women" in managerial and professional jobs are demonized as sexual predators and/or negligent mothers in popular culture. Much of this rhetoric provides misty reminiscences about the postwar gender order. The irony of this cultural onslaught for the pay equity movement is the relative invisibility of working-class women and the reality of their work and family lives in this discourse. In the final section of this chapter, we argue that progressives need to seize upon this vacuum in proposing alternative strategies.

Strategic Implications of Feminization

Jane Jenson (1996, 92) asserts that "it is only by understanding the extent to which a new set of gendered employment relations is at the heart of the restructured economies that we can begin to comprehend the restructuring, as well as any space available within it for generating equality." Global feminization in interaction with an active feminist movement has begun to unravel one of the institutional pillars of postwar accumulation—the family wage supporting the ideology of separate spheres. Flexible employment, with wages and working conditions that are culturally gendered as female, is being promulgated as the solution to restoring profitability. Unfortunately, the prospect offered is jobs that permit neither women nor men of the working class the possibility of supporting families on an individual's earnings. The challenge is to resist these aspects of economic restructuring without hearkening back to the "good old days" of postwar gender relations and the male breadwinner ideology. Pay equity attempts to extend the concept of a breadwinner wage to female-dominated occupations just as the family wage for men is disappearing, undermined by the deindustrialization process. Unfortunately, this has generated resistance to pay equity among potential allies (see Figart and Kahn 1997). Therefore, it is still a low priority on many progressive agendas. Progressive strategies need to be reformulated to embrace gender and race analysis. Further, economic issues need to be central to revitalizing a feminist movement in the United States that has been preoccupied with the single-issue politics of reproductive freedom, as articulated by Burk and Hartmann (1996).

In a sense, activists need to present a "counter-discourse," as part of a social movement for economic security. The discourse of pay equity's conservative opponents has illustrated many of the cultural preoccupations of U.S. society in the 1990s. The relative weakness of the left has led to a revival of promarket ideology in the wake of Keynesian economics and the welfare state. Further, a cultural confusion over gender emanates from the right. We believe the latter represents an opportunity for feminist and other social activists.

With the recent change in leadership in the U.S. labor movement, the prospects for bringing marginalized workers into the heart of a new labor strategy has improved. The new language of a "living wage" is evidence of emerging efforts to raise wages, including those for predominantly female and disproportionately minority jobs and occupations. Three developments can be construed as aspects of this living wage movement. First, raising the legislated minimum wage has become a priority issue at federal and state levels. Advocates point out that the real value of the minimum wage has declined to well below the level needed to support a family (Geoghegan 1996; Rubin et al. 1996). Since six out of every ten minimum wage workers are women, this policy is one way of addressing women's overrepresentation in low-paid jobs (Figart and Lapidus 1995). Second, progressive critiques of welfare reform mandating paid employment argue that work paying poverty-level wages cannot substitute for public assistance; antipoverty policies must include labor market reforms such as pay equity and increasing the minimum wage (Rutten 1991; Figart and Lapidus 1995; Kuttner 1995). Finally, over thirty municipalities have considered legislation requiring companies receiving "corporate welfare" (tax rebates, supplier contracts, etc.) to pay workers a "living wage" well above the federal minimum. Such initiatives have already been adopted by Baltimore (Maryland) and Santa Clara County (California) (Garza 1996; Tyson 1996; Uchitelle 1996). These efforts de-gender the concept of the family wage, and the movement becomes one to ensure that all workers can support their families, embracing a diversity of family forms. Decentralized, creative, grassroots approaches in a broad-based pay equity movement can further efforts to contest the gendered labor markets at the core of economic restructuring.

Notes

1. This U.S. Supreme Court decision upheld a lower court ruling that plaintiffs could sue for wage discrimination even if men and women were in similar, but not identical,

jobs. The case was based on a discrimination lawsuit filed by female guards in the county jail whose responsibilities varied slightly from those of male guards. The case was pursued under Title VII of the 1964 Civil Rights Act.

2. Job evaluation, a formal procedure for hierarchically ordering a set of jobs according to their worth within or value to an organization, is frequently used to ascertain whether jobs of comparable value are paid equitably. Both traditional and comparable worth job evaluation involve external wage comparisons with the labor market and internal wage comparisons within the organization.

3. For example, Albelda and Tilly (1994) point out that SSA's capital–labor accord periodizes the historical development of labor markets based on the experience of white male workers. Gordon, Edwards, and Reich (1982) view the postwar period as the most recent of three overlapping social structures of accumulation in U.S. economic history. Focusing on labor market structures, they identify a period of initial proletarianization (1820s–1890s); a period when conditions for wage workers became increasingly homogeneous as mechanization lowered the skill component of jobs (1870s through World War II); and a period of labor market segmentation from the 1920s to the present. Thus, SSA views the postwar period as marked by a shift from homogenization of labor to labor market segmentation, yet Albelda and Tilly note that labor markets were segmented by gender and race in the nineteenth century (see also Cherry 1991; Wagman 1995).

4. Some of the sources utilized for this section include Aglietta (1979); Gordon, Edwards, and Reich (1982); Bernstein and Adler (1994); Kotz, McDonough, and Reich (1994); Loader and Burrows (1994). Despite the broad similarities between the two frameworks, the causes of prosperity and stagnation, the nature of the relationship between economic and other social institutions, as well the exact dating of the recent decline vary among authors and countries under study. For comparison of key themes in the two schools, see Kotz (1994a) and O'Hara (1994). In this summary, we are focusing on critical approaches to the post-Fordist era; therefore we do not consider more optimistic work on flexible specialization such as Piore and Sabel (1984).

5. Underconsumptionist theories argue that economic crises develop when workers' real wages decline and they are unable to purchase goods and services, thus capitalists are not able to realize a profit from their investments. Profit squeeze theories attribute crises to economic expansion, which drives wages up, cutting into capitalists' profits.

6. For contrasting positions on globalization as cause or symptom, see Faux (1995b) and D. Gordon (1994b).

7. Analyses of global feminization are sometimes reproached for presupposing a uniform trajectory to contemporary economic restructuring. Critics argue that this formulation oversimplifies the diversity of women's experiences in specific national, regional, and cultural contexts (Cohen 1994). Yet Bakker (1996) argues that feminization indeed captures an important, though not inevitable, dimension of contemporary restructuring.

8. This is supported by Howell's (1992) case study of France during this period.

9. Smith, like Marx, believed that commodities had a "natural" price based upon the direct and indirect labor embedded in them during production; he believed market prices fluctuated around this price according to supply and demand.

10. In fact, raising the wages of such minority-concentrated jobs is entirely consistent with the pay equity mandate that jobs be remunerated according to their skill, *effort,* responsibility, and *working conditions.* According to the theory of compensating differentials, shining shoes and scrubbing floors should garner higher wages due, in part, to the unpleasant working conditions and physical effort required for each job.

8

Women and Labor Market Flexibility

The Cases of Japan and the Former West Germany in the Postwar Years

David Kucera

There are two primary reasons for the increased interest in labor market flexibility since the early 1970s: first, the interest in production flexibility, often associated with the just-in-time production techniques used by larger Japanese manufacturers; and, second, the worsening as well as diverging unemployment patterns in the advanced capitalist countries after the early 1970s. While unemployment increased in Japan and Europe as well as the United States after the early 1970s, the increase was considerably greater in Europe, for which the experience of the former West Germany was typical. (All data in this study refer to the former West Germany or, in most recent years, to the regions of the former West Germany.) Even though the rate of unemployment in 1990 was lower in West Germany than in the United States, it was the manifold increase in unemployment in the former that drew particular attention (Bureau of Labor Statistics 1994).

These differences are widely held to result from differences in labor market flexibility, and thus increasing flexibility is argued to be vital to improving the European unemployment problem. The supposed lack of labor market flexibility in Europe is often attributed to the effects of strong government social policies and is commonly referred to as Eurosclerosis. One of the most prominent recent studies on unemployment is the *OECD Jobs Study*. The emphasis that the *Study* gives to the issue of labor flexibility in accounting for the different unemployment experiences of Europe and

Japan is reflected in the following quotation, which considers the destabilizing effects in the 1970s and 1980s of the oil crises, the breakdown of Bretton Woods, financial market liberalization, the increased globalization of production, and the rapid pace of technical change: "[I]n the midst of this tumultuous period when so many forces were testing the flexibility of economies, policies to achieve social objectives were extended, with the unintended side-effect of making markets, including importantly labour markets, more rigid. This erosion of the ability to adapt to change was probably most pronounced in continental Europe and Oceania.... Only the Japanese economy handled the problems of this period of adjustment relatively well" (Organization for Economic Cooperation and Development) [hereafter OECD] 1994a, 30).

Reflecting an influential viewpoint, an editorial in the May 30, 1986, *Financial Times* stated that "Japan's low unemployment is primarily a reflection of very high internal mobility, America's a reflection of high external mobility. Europe suffers high unemployment because it lacks either sort of mobility," where internal refers to the mobility of workers within firms, the internal labor market, and external to the mobility of workers in the labor market at large (quoted in Metcalf 1987, 51–52).

A fundamental shortcoming with these points of view is that they neglect the very gendered nature of labor flexibility and labor market adjustment in Japan. Japan does in fact rely to a high degree on external labor flexibility, but this flexibility is disproportionately provided by women workers. These women serve very strongly as a buffer work force, moving in and out of employment and the labor force with much greater volatility than Japanese men. This study, by paying careful attention to the role of women in Japanese and West German labor markets, provides a substantially different view of both Japanese labor market flexibility and, just as important, Japanese macroeconomic performance since the early 1970s.

This study uses techniques drawn from *Women and Recession,* a 1988 volume edited by Jill Rubery, which provide a means of comparing men and women's labor force and employment volatility over business cycles. By using standardized data and tests for Japan and West Germany, this study reveals that women served more strongly as a buffer work force in Japan than in West Germany. More than that, this study reveals strongly diverging patterns of women's relative labor force and employment volatility over the post-1973 years of slower growth. There was a dramatic increase in these measures in Japan and no significant change in West Germany, indicating that Japanese women served more strongly as a buffer work force in the post-1973 years relative to Japanese men. Combined with data on the extremely high proportions of discouraged workers in Japan in recent years, 80 percent of whom are women, this study argues that the

Japanese unemployment picture is a good deal less favorable than indicated by standard measures and probably not so different from West Germany, once one more fully accounts for the role of Japanese women as a buffer work force. As a result, one should be cautious of policy proposals suggesting that the West German labor system become more like the Japanese, in terms of general labor flexibility as well as government social policy.

This study is noteworthy not only in that it is directly comparative but because Japan and West Germany particularly merit careful comparison. The postwar experience of these countries was broadly similar, from the rebuilding of devastated economies to rapid output and productivity growth and eventual world economic leadership. The similarities held not just for broad macroeconomic factors, but for patterns of female labor force participation. In the early 1950s, just over 40 percent of the labor force in Japan was female, compared with about 36 percent in West Germany. These measures converged by the mid-1970s at about 37 percent, after which they increased in nearly lockstep fashion to 40 percent in 1990.[1] In terms of overall parallel movement, the pattern is even more similar for all employees (all workers minus self-employed and family workers) and all nonagricultural employees, with female percentages in Japan consistently 2 to 3 percent below those in West Germany over the postwar years. Female percentages for all and nonagricultural employees showed overall increases throughout the postwar years, with more rapid increases since 1970 in West Germany and 1975 in Japan.

The next section of this chapter considers the data on unemployment and discouraged workers as well as different kinds of labor flexibility—internal, external, numerical, and functional—particularly as they apply to the Japanese labor system. The section after presents data and methods used, followed by a section presenting the results of the data analysis.

Unemployment and Labor Market Flexibility

Over the years 1983 to 1991, unemployment rates averaged 7.2 percent in West Germany and 2.5 percent in Japan. Counting discouraged workers as unemployed over these same years would increase the Japanese unemployment rate by 125 percent, to 5.6 percent (OECD 1993a, 35; 1993b, 32–33). As noted, fully 80 percent of these discouraged workers were women. Data on discouraged workers are not, unfortunately, collected in West Germany, making direct comparison impossible. However, it is worth noting that among the eighteen OECD countries for which data on discouraged workers are available, Japan and, to a lesser extent, Sweden, are truly anomalous. These are also the two OECD countries with the lowest official rates of unemployment in 1991, with unemployment rates of 2.1 percent in Japan and 2.7 percent in Sweden, compared with the OECD average of 7.1 percent (for twenty OECD countries). The proportion of discouraged to unemployed workers was 90.8 percent in Japan that year and 54.1 percent in Sweden, compared with the OECD average of 14.3 percent (including Japan and Sweden). In no other countries did the proportion of discouraged to unemployed workers exceed 25 percent (OECD 1993a, 10). Unless West Germany also had exceptionally high proportions of discouraged workers, then, counting discouraged workers as unemployed would bring substantial convergence between Japanese and West German rates of unemployment. In addition, a large majority of involuntary part-timers in Japan and West Germany were women (70 and 80 percent, respectively, in 1991), and there were nearly twice as many involuntary part-timers in relation to unemployed workers in Japan as in West Germany over the span of years from 1983 to 1991 (OECD 1993a, 10, 16–17).

Toshiaki Tachibanaki writes, "There is a common understanding outside of Japan that the Japanese labour market is more flexible than those of other industrialized nations, and that this flexibility has facilitated to lower the rate of unemployment and to provide a better performance of the macroeconomy in general" (1987, 647). The neoclassical theory of unemployment suggests that the primary cause of long-term, nonfrictional unemployment is wage rigidity and that this would account for the very low rates of unemployment in Japan compared with West Germany.

However, a study by Robert Gordon suggests the similarity between eleven Western European countries and Japan in terms of nominal wage flexibility in relation to output changes. Gordon writes that "the differences among the United States, Japan, and Europe are minimal. Responses of the nominal wage rate to the output ratio are of roughly the same order of magnitude in the three aggregate economies" (1987, 689). Ronald Schettkat is also skeptical of the role of labor market flexibility in accounting for the large increase in unemployment in West Germany. He writes: "Neither intersectoral wage rigidity nor intrasectoral wage rigidity increased over recent decades in West Germany and thus neither can explain the rise in unemployment.... International comparison shows that countries that developed their institutional framework in the direction suggested by the 'eurosclerosis' thesis came up with the worst unemployment results (e.g., Great Britain) whereas economies with a strong welfare state (e.g., Sweden) did very well" (1990, 207; cf. Abraham and Houseman 1994, and Blank 1994, for similar arguments regarding the relationship between government social policy and labor market flexibility and unemployment). Schettkat also notes that both the inflow and outflow ratios for employment (measured by gross flows divided by initial employment) increased in West Germany from 1970 to 1986 (in spite of the increase in long-term unemployment), at odds with the argument that the increase in West German unemployment rates were caused by labor market rigidity (1990, 210, 221).

Schettkat's mention of inflow and outflow ratios suggests the many aspects of labor flexibility. These ratios are related to external mobility or flexibility, noted above. Another widely used distinction is between functional and numerical flexibility, with functional flexibility referring to qualitative issues of labor flexibility within the firm and numerical flexibility referring to quantitative issues of labor flexibility both within and without the firm. Functional flexibility refers, more specifically, to issues of flexibility in job design and definition and the mobility of workers across tasks. In this sense, functional flexibility is closely associated with flexibility in production, such as the just-in-time system of production, for which functional flexibility is argued to be essential (Piore 1986, 162–63).

A recent OECD study describes what is seen as the increased emphasis of firms on functional rather than numerical flexibility, writing that functional flexibility "appears to have clearly outdistanced the Fordist overemphasis on numerical flexibility and the quantity of labor, controlling the number of hours worked and the organization of working time, regulation of hiring and dismissals, and the use of part-time and temporary workers" (quoted in Brodsky 1994, 59). The actual shift from numerical to functional flexibility is probably overstated, for the growing emphasis on functional flexibility is, at least in some circumstances, consistent with the growth of numerical flexibility. For example, some U.S. manufacturers have implemented alternative work schedules (breaking down the eight-hour day and five-day week) simultaneously with implementing so-called labor–management cooperation schemes such as quality circles, which generally emphasize aspects of production associated with functional flexibility. (Cf. Slaughter 1995, 3, regarding the Saturn Corporation's plant in Tennessee, and Lund 1994, 7, regarding the NUMMI plant, a GM–Toyota joint venture in California.)

The organization of production in larger Japanese manufacturing firms has provided a widely emulated model for functional flexibility. At the same time, Japanese firms make extensive use of numerical flexibility. This is one of the primary themes of this study: in terms of hiring and firing, numerical flexibility in Japan is provided disproportionately by women workers, as indicated by their greater employment volatility relative to men. And many of the Japanese women who provide such a buffer work force are among the growing number of part-time and temporary workers, which the OECD study associates with numerical flexibility.

This study follows up on the body of literature that argues that the Japanese lifetime employment system, which applies almost exclusively to men, imposes a rigidity in the labor adjustment process, a rigidity accommodated by the highly flexible nature of Japanese women's employment and labor force participation (Jones 1976–77, 592; Kawashima 1987, 611; Tachibanaki 1987, 669; Edwards 1988, 249; Carney and O'Kelly 1990, 127; Ono 1990, 87–88; Peterson and Sullivan 1990, 172–73; Hashimoto 1993, 141; Houseman and Abraham 1993, 45; Lam 1993, 198, 218). In a recent study, Susan Houseman and Katharine Abraham describe the relation of women to the lifetime employment system as follows: "The Japanese lifetime-employment system gives the average Japanese worker stronger job security than the average American worker. However, lifetime-employment guarantees apply only to the core, "regular" work force. Peripheral workers, including temporary, day, and part-time workers, are more vulnerable to contract termination. These workers are predominantly female and are widely believed to serve as a buffer for the regular workforce" (1993, 45). In a similar manner, Linda Edwards writes: "It should be pointed out that the present system of employing men in full-time jobs and women in more casual, part-time jobs serves the Japanese economy well. With this system, Japanese firms are willing to guarantee many of their male workers job security over the business cycle because the firms have access to a pool of transitory (female) workers who readily enter and exit the labor force and are able to take on part-time employment. . . . True employment equality between men and women would upset the way the Japanese labor market currently adjusts to cyclical variations in aggregate demand" (1988, 249).

Data and Methods

The primary data sources for this study are drawn directly from Japanese and West German government publications. For Japan, labor force and employment data are from the Japanese Ministry of Labor's *Yearbook of Labour Statistics* (based on household labor force surveys for aggregate data and on establishment surveys for manufacturing data, with results for the latter discussed in the section "Japanese Women as a Buffer Workforce in Recent Years"); for West Germany, labor force and employment data are from the Bundesministerium fuer Arbeit und Sozialordnung's *Arbeits- und Sozialstatistik: Hauptergebnisse* (based on a combination of household and establishment surveys; the surveys are combined in the data source itself[2]). All data are annual.

In order to derive measures of women's relative labor force and employment volatility, regressions are based on ordinary-least-squares estimates of the following equation:

$$\log F_t - \log F_{t-1} = \alpha + \beta(\log T_t - \log T_{t-1}) + \gamma \text{TIME} + \varepsilon, \quad (1)$$

where F is defined as the number of female employees or labor force participants; T, the number of male and female employees or labor force participants (with both F and T evaluated in terms of logarithmic growth rates); *TIME*, a linear time trend; and ε, an error term. The model is identical to that used in *Women and Recession*. The key issue in this model is whether estimates of β are significantly greater than 1, in which case it can be said that women function as a buffer work force.

A central element of this analysis is that the equation is also estimated with a dummy-modified T variable, providing a test of structural change for the post-1973 years of slower employment growth. In this case, the estimating equation is as follows:

$$\log F_t - \log F_{t-1} = \alpha + \beta(\log T_t - \log T_{t-1}) + \\ \theta(\log T_t - \log T_{t-1})(DUMMY) + \gamma \text{TIME} + \varepsilon, \quad (2)$$

where *DUMMY* is defined as 0 for years before and 1 for years after the slowdown. (The equation was also estimated by adding the dummy variable itself, allowing the intercept to vary, but coefficient estimates on the dummy variable did not prove significant.) In this model, estimates of β provide a measure of women's relative labor force or employment volatility for the pre-1973 period, estimates of θ provide a measure of the change in such volatility between the pre- and post-1973 periods, and, by inference, the sum of estimates of β and θ provide a measure of women's relative labor force or employment volatility for the post-1973 period. A key consideration in this second model is the sign and magnitude of estimates of θ. If, for example, an estimate of θ is positive, this indicates that women's relative labor force or employment volatility increased in the post-1973 years, with the extent of increase given by the magnitude of the estimate.

For estimates of α's, θ's, and γ's, the null hypothesis is that these equal zero and the non-null hypothesis that they do not; for estimates of β's, the null hypothesis is that these equal one and the non-null hypothesis that they are greater than one, with two-tailed tests for estimates of α's, θ's, and γ's, and one-tailed tests for estimates of β's, as well as for confidence intervals comparing women's relative labor force and employment volatility in Japan and West Germany. In the tables that follow, statistical significance is indicated by the number sign (#), one asterisk (*), and two asterisks (**) for 10,

5, and 1 percent significance, respectively (though a result deemed significant indicates at least 5 percent significance, unless indicated otherwise).

Last, standard deviations of the logarithmic growth rates of the time-series used in this model are derived, providing a different measure of women's labor force and employment volatility in Japan and West Germany.

Women in Japan and West Germany as Buffer Work Forces

Japan

Table 8.1 shows results at the aggregate level for Japan. Columns numbered 1 through 3 show results based on equation (1) above; columns numbered 4 through 7 show results based on equation (2). Estimates of β are shown in columns 1 and 4, headed by the span of years for which β's are estimated; estimates of γ are shown in columns 2 and 6, headed by "TIME"[3;] estimates of θ are shown in column 5, headed by "CHANGE." Below each of these coefficient estimates are their associated standard errors, in parentheses. To facilitate presentation, results for α estimates are not shown. In columns 3 and 7 are adjusted R-squares, below which are indicators of any autocorrelation (ARMA) corrections, in parentheses, as well as Durbin-Watson statistics.

Headings for levels of aggregation, to the leftmost, are followed by "(D)" when an additional level of differencing is required to attain stationarity. Below these headings are average female percentages for the entire period under estimation. (This format is also followed in Table 8.2 for West Germany.) Results are shown for the labor force, all workers, all employees (minus self-employed and family workers), and nonagricultural employees.

Estimates of Japanese women's relative labor force and employment volatility in column 1 of Table 8.1 indicate that Japanese women served as a buffer work force throughout the postwar years. Results are particularly striking for the entire labor force and all workers, with the estimates of women's relative volatility 86.7 and 71.9 percent greater, respectively, than if men's and women's volatility were identical (that is, if estimates of β were equal to one).

For each of the four aggregate levels, equation (2) with the test of structural change provides a better specification, as indicated by higher adjusted R-squares than for equation (1). Using 1973 as the turning point, tests of structural change are significant at the 5 percent level or better for the labor force, all workers, and nonagricultural employees, though at only the 10 percent level for all employees. Alternative and multiple turning points are

Table 8.1

Japan: Regression Results, 1952–1990

	Equation (1)			Equation (2)		
	(1) 1952–1990 (S.E.)	(2) TIME (S.E.)	(3) Adj. R-squared (ARMA) DW	(4) 1952–1973 (S.E.)	(5) CHANGE (S.E.)	(6) TIME (S.E.)	(7) Adj. R-squared (ARMA) DW
Labor force 40% Female	1.867** (0.126)	0.0004** (0.0001)	0.86 2.05	1.677** (0.097)	0.819** (0.139)		0.90 (MA1) 1.81
All workers 40% Female	1.719** (0.123)	0.0004** (0.0001)	0.84 2.01	1.539** (0.107)	0.677** (0.154)		0.86 (MA1) 1.92
All employees 33% Female	1.186* (0.101)		0.79 2.04	1.263** (0.107)	0.407# (0.224)		0.80 2.20
Nonagricultural employees 33% Female	1.219* (0.095)		0.81 1.92	1.304** (0.100)	0.439* (0.212)		0.83 2.09

Source: Japan Ministry of Labor, *Yearbook of Labour Statistics*.
Note: #, *, and ** indicate the significance at 10, 5, and 1 percent levels, respectively.

Figure 8.1 **Japan: Measures of Women's Relative Labor Force and Employment Volatility**

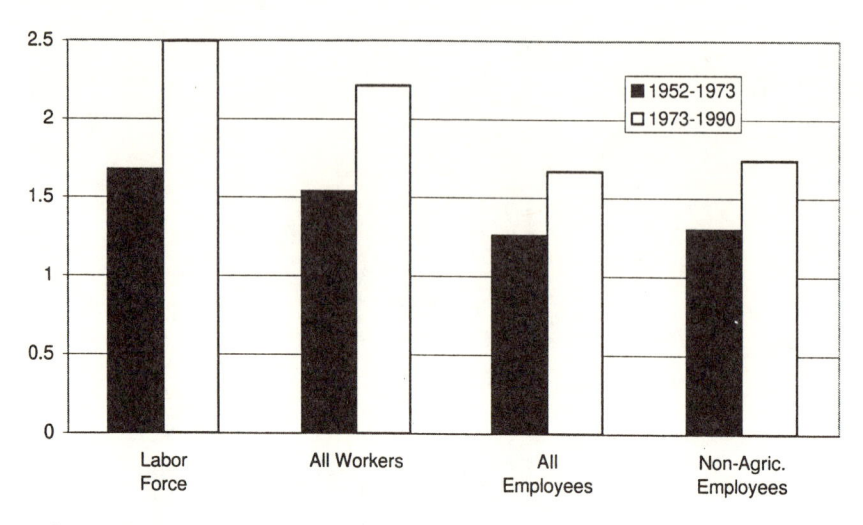

[Bar chart showing values for 1952-1973 (dark bars) and 1973-1990 (light bars):
- Labor Force: ~1.7 (1952-1973), ~2.5 (1973-1990)
- All Workers: ~1.55 (1952-1973), ~2.2 (1973-1990)
- All Employees: ~1.25 (1952-1973), ~1.65 (1973-1990)
- Non-Agric. Employees: ~1.3 (1952-1973), ~1.7 (1973-1990)]

Source: Japan Ministry of Labor, *Yearbook of Labor Statistics*.

also tested for years in the 1970s and early 1980s, based on recursive residuals tests as well as the more stable growth pattern following the second oil shock of the late 1970s. For the labor force and all workers, the 1973 turning point yields the largest coefficients of structural change. For all employees and nonagricultural employees, 1974 and 1975 turning points yield slightly larger coefficients of structural change, but not significantly so (at even the 10 percent level, based on confidence interval tests) and do not change the significance of regression results. The 1973 turning point was combined with turning points from the late 1970s and early 1980s, but only the 1973 turning point proved significant.

For ease of visual representation, coefficient estimates of women's relative labor force and employment volatility are shown in Figure 8.1. The dark bars represent coefficient estimates for the 1952 to 1973 years, and the light bars for the 1973 to 1990 years.

The result most worthy of notice is that for the labor force. As argued in the opening of this study, the success of labor adjustment processes is usefully evaluated in terms of differences by gender. Results for Japan indicate that women function more strongly as a buffer work force by a large and significant measure. Were Japanese women's labor force participation not so tenuous, Japan's unemployment rates would be a good deal higher. Just as important, Japanese women's relative labor force participation became a good deal more volatile after the 1973 slowdown in economic growth. For the 1952 to 1973 period, Japanese women's relative labor force volatility was 67.7 percent higher than if men's and women's volatility were identical; for the 1973 to 1990 period, the figure increased to 150 percent (based on the sum of estimates for the 1952–73 period and for the test of structural change, or β plus θ from equation [2]). That is, the volatility of Japanese women's labor force participation in the 1973 to 1990 period was an estimated two-and-one-half times greater than the volatility of total (men's and women's) labor force participation. This suggests that one should view Japan's seemingly favorable unemployment patterns with skepticism.[4]

West Germany

Results at the aggregate level for West Germany are shown in Table 8.2. For the labor force and all employees, there is significant evidence that women served as a buffer work force, though at only the 10 percent level for all employees over the entire 1952 to 1990 period. There is no significant evidence of structural change for the post-1973 period, and adjusted R-squares are identical across equations (1) and (2). For all workers, all employees, and nonagricultural employees, estimates of structural change are negative, such that estimates of women's relative employment volatility for the 1973 to 1990 period are all less than one.

Coefficient estimates of women's relative labor force and employment volatility are shown in Figure 8.2. As with the graph for Japan, the dark bars represent coefficient estimates for the 1952 to 1973 years, and the light bars for the 1973 to 1990 years. A comparison of Figures 8.1 and 8.2 makes apparent the strongly diverging patterns of women's relative labor force and employment volatility in Japan and West Germany, with substantial increases in these measures in the former and, generally, declines in the latter over the post-1973 years of slower employment growth.

Confidence Intervals Testing Differences Between Japan and West Germany

Coefficient estimates for women's relative labor force volatility are consistently and significantly larger in Japan than in West Germany. This is revealed most clearly in Table 8.3, which shows the results of confidence interval tests. For the entire span of years considered and for both the pre- and post-1973 subperiods, estimates for Japan are larger than for West Germany and larger at the 1 percent level of significance. The same pattern

Table 8.2

West Germany: Regression Results, 1952–1990

	Equation (1)			Equation (2)			
	(1) 1952–1990 (S.E.)	(2) TIME (S.E.)	(3) Adj. R-squared (ARMA) DW	(4) 1952–1973 (S.E.)	(5) CHANGE (S.E.)	(6) TIME (S.E.)	(7) Adj. R-squared (ARMA) DW
Labor force (D) 38% Female	1.130* (0.065)		0.89 2.08	1.117* (0.069)	0.142 (0.228)		0.89 2.09
All workers (D) 37% Female	1.018 (0.053)		0.91 2.11	1.030 (0.061)	−0.054 (0.135)		0.91 2.05
All employees (D) 36% Female	1.082# (0.049)		0.93 (MA1) 1.87	1.112* (0.057)	−0.140 (0.131)		0.93 (MA1) 1.86
Nonagricultural employees (D) 36% Female	1.026 (0.043)		0.94 2.00	1.037 (0.048)	−0.055 (0.116)		0.94 1.94

Source: Bundesministerium fuer Arbeit und Sozialordnung, *Arbeits- und Sozialstatistik.*
Note: #, *, and ** indicate significance at 10, 5, and 1 percent levels, respectively.

Figure 8.2 **West Germany: Measures of Women's Relative Labor Force and Employment Volatility**

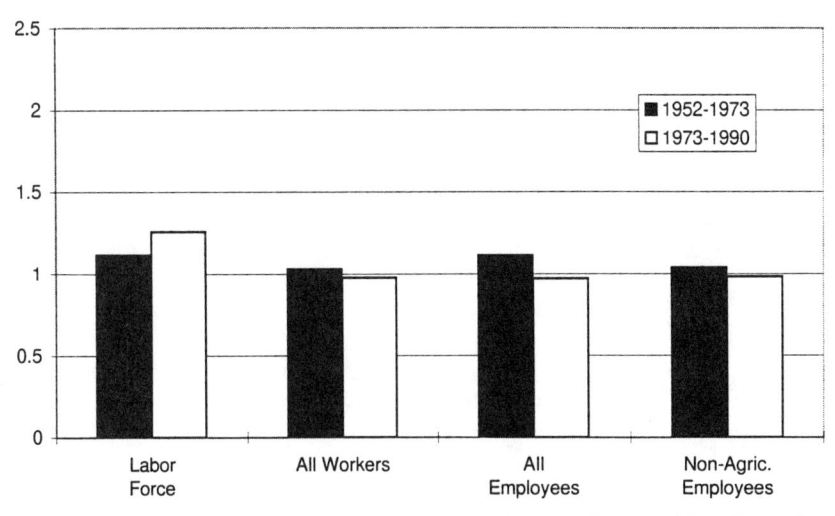

[Bar chart showing values for Labor Force, All Workers, All Employees, and Non-Agric. Employees, comparing periods 1952-1973 and 1973-1990]

Source: Bundesministerium fuer Arbeit und Sozialordnung, *Arbeits- und Sozialstatistik.*

is observed for all workers. For all employees, coefficient estimates of women's relative employment volatility are consistently larger, but significantly larger for only the post-1973 subperiod. For nonagricultural employees, coefficient estimates are significantly larger for both the pre- and post-1973 subperiods, though at only the 10 percent level for the entire 1952 to 1990 period. These confidence interval tests provide strong evidence that Japanese women served more as a buffer work force than did German women.

Japanese Women as a Buffer Work Force in Recent Years

In their 1993 article titled "Female Workers as a Buffer in the Japanese Economy," Houseman and Abraham test women's relative employment volatility in Japan and the United States for the manufacturing sector as a whole. Comparing the 1980s with the 1970s, their empirical work for Japan indicates that analogous measures of women's employment volatility *declined* relative to men's in the more recent period, though Japanese women continued to serve significantly more as a buffer work force than Japanese men even in the later period. Using monthly data, the authors construct a finite distributed lag model, regressing the logarithmic differences of, separately, women's and men's employment on the logarithmic differences of current and lagged manufacturing output.[5]

Table 8.3

Confidence Interval Results, 1952–1990

	(1)	(2) Subperiods	(3)
	1952–1990	1952–1973	1973–1990
Labor force	**	**	**
All workers	**	**	**
All employees	—	—	*
Nonagricultural employees	#	*	*

Sources: Japan Ministry of Labor, *Yearbook of Labour Statistics*, Bundesministerium fuer Arbeit und Sozialordnung, *Arbeits- und Sozialstatistik*.

Notes: #, *, and ** indicate significance at 10, 5, and 1 percent levels, respectively; "—" indicates no significant difference between coefficient estimates.

For the 1970 to 1979 period, the twelve-month elasticity (the sum of coefficient estimates on current output and output lagged through twelve months) is 0.456 and 0.160 for women's and men's employment, respectively; for the 1980 to 1989 period, the twelve-month elasticity is 0.316 and 0.195 for women's and men's employment, respectively. For both periods, women's employment elasticity is significantly greater than men's at the 5 percent level. Yet female-to-male ratios based on these elasticities declined substantially, from 2.85 in the 1970s to 1.62 in the 1980s (Houseman and Abraham 1993, 47).

In an effort to address this issue, equation (2) from above is estimated using data for the manufacturing sector with both 1973 and either 1979 or 1980 turning points. Consistent with Houseman and Abraham's findings, coefficient estimates for the 1979 and 1980 turning points are negative. They are not, however, significantly so, with t-statistics of 1.11 and 1.00 for the 1979 and 1980 turning points, respectively. Coefficient estimates for the 1973 turning point remain positive and significant at the 1 percent level, consistent with the view that the early 1970s marked a more decisive turning point over the span of the postwar years.[6]

That the 1980s represented only a temporarily altered situation for women workers in Japan is also suggested by comparing growth rates of male and female labor force participation and employment across the upswing of 1987 to 1991 and the downswing of 1991 to 1993. Table 8.4 shows average annual growth rates of labor force participation, total civilian

Table 8.4

Average Annual Growth Rates of Labor Force Participation and Employment in Japan: Comparing the 1987–1991 Upswing and the 1991–1993 Downswing

	Labor force		Total employment		Industrial employment	
	Male	Female	Male	Female	Male	Female
A: 1987–1991	1.33	2.21	1.55	2.37	2.20	2.69
B: 1991–1993	1.05	0.57	0.84	0.35	1.35	–1.47
C: Gap (B – A):	–0.29	–1.65	–0.70	–2.02	–0.85	–4.16
D: Ratio (female gap/male gap):	5.7		2.9		4.9	

Source: OECD, *Quarterly Labour Force Statistics*.

employment, and industrial employment for men and women over the 1987 to 1991 and 1991 to 1993 periods. The table shows both that women's labor force participation and employment grew more rapidly than men's in the 1987–91 upswing, and that women's labor force participation and employment grew less rapidly than men's in the 1991–93 downswing. This is also shown by the gap between employment growth in the up- and downswing years in row C, showing the difference between values in row B and row A. By all categories—labor force participation, total employment, and industrial employment—the gap is much larger for women, indicating the greater difference across periods. Last, ratios are constructed by dividing the female gap by the male gap, shown in row D of the table. These ratios reveal that the difference in average annual growth rates of labor force participation across the up- and downswing was 5.7 times greater for women than for men. For total employment, the ratio was 2.9 and for industrial employment 4.9. These measures reveal that women continue to serve strongly as a buffer work force in Japan into the present.

The continued role of women as a buffer work force in Japan is also suggested by examining the numbers of discouraged workers in relation to labor force participants over the 1987 to 1991 upswing and 1991 to 1993 downswing. As noted earlier, Japan had by far the highest ratios of discouraged to unemployed workers among the eighteen OECD countries for which data on discouraged workers are available, and from 1983 to 1991 the proportion of discouraged workers that were women averaged just over

80 percent (OECD 1993a, 10, 35; 1993b, 32–33).

Looking at discouraged workers as a percentage of the labor force, the proportions of discouraged workers declined by an average annual rate of 7.1 percent from 1987 to 1991. From 1991 to 1993, this pattern was reversed, with the proportions of discouraged workers increasing at an average annual rate of 4.5 percent (Sorrentino 1995, 34). These different patterns across the up- and downswing provide additional evidence indicating that women continue to play a vital role as a buffer work force in Japan, and that the difference in the employment situation of Japanese women in the 1980s was only temporary, resulting from the relatively favorable employment growth of the decade in the face of a labor shortage.

This continued role of Japanese women as a highly marginal buffer work force is also supported by more anecdotal evidence. In the December 1, 1992, *New York Times,* David Sanger wrote as follows:

> When Japan's economy boomed through the late 1980's, doors opened and women edged into choice jobs that freed them from serving tea and answering telephones, the traditional duties of the clerical workers known as "office ladies." But Japanese women today say that many of the changes were superficial, and that career opportunities are evaporating as the economy dries up. . . . . Many of those [women entering the workforce in the 1980s] were middle-aged women who re-entered the workforce after their children reached school age. And many were part of the huge corps of what Japan loosely terms its part-time workers, many of whom actually work more than 40 hours a week. When Japan's economy was humming, such workers were evident everywhere. . . . With the boom's abrupt end, though, part-time workers were the first to go.

Comparative Labor Force and Employment Volatility

Table 8.5 shows standard deviations of the logarithmic growth rates of labor force participation and employment for all workers, all employees, and nonagricultural employees, separating the 1952 to 1973 and 1973 to 1990 years as was done in the aggregate level regressions. These standard deviations are derived from the independent variables used in the time-series regressions. Examining these measures of volatility provides a somewhat different sense of women's relative labor force and employment volatility. More specifically, even though women's labor force and employment volatility relative to men's is significantly higher in Japan than in West Germany, this is often relative to substantially lower labor force or employment volatility. That is, even though women unambiguously function more as a buffer work force than men in Japan than in West Germany,

Table 8.5

Standard Deviations of Logarithmic Growth Rates of Total (Men plus Women) Labor Force Participation and Employment, 1952–1990

	1952–1973		1973–1990	
	Germany	Japan	Germany	Japan
Labor force	0.013	0.010	0.007	0.006
All workers	0.018	0.010	0.013	0.007
All employees	0.021	0.021	0.014	0.009
Nonagricultural employees	0.022	0.021	0.014	0.009

Sources: Japan Ministry of Labour, *Yearbook of Labour Statistics*; Bundesministerium fuer Arbeit und Sozialordnung, *Arbeits- und Sozialstatistik*.

Japanese women are less unambiguously worse off than German women in certain cases. This results when total (men plus women) labor force or employment volatility is substantially lower in Japan.

For the 1952 to 1973 period, the volatility of employment for all employees and nonagricultural employees was, by these measures, nearly identical in West Germany and Japan. For labor force participants and all workers, though, these measures are lower in Japan by 23.6 and 40.2 percent, respectively. In 1973 to 1990, years of slower employment growth, these measures of volatility are about the same for labor force participants but only half as high in Japan for all workers and 38.9 and 39.4 percent lower in Japan for all employees and nonagricultural employees, respectively. In those cases in which the measures of volatility are higher in West Germany, then, Japanese women's high labor force and employment volatility is moderated relative to German women though not, of course, relative to Japanese men.

This issue is examined by comparing standard deviations of the growth rates of women's labor force participation and women's employment, shown in Table 8.6. With the exception of all workers in both periods, standard deviations are consistently larger for Japan. This biggest gap is for the labor force in the 1973 to 1990 period, for which the standard deviation for Japan is 65.1 percent larger than in West Germany. For all workers, all employees, and nonagricultural employees, though, the standard deviations are not much larger in Japan, suggesting that women in Japan were not, in this sense, much more strongly affected by employment volatility than women in West Germany.

Table 8.6

Standard Deviations of Logarithmic Growth Rates of Women's Labor Force Participation and Employment, 1952–1990

	1952–1973		1973–1990	
	Germany	Japan	Germany	Japan
Labor force	0.017	0.018	0.008	0.013
All workers	0.020	0.018	0.015	0.014
All employees	0.025	0.031	0.015	0.016
Nonagricultural employees	0.026	0.032	0.015	0.016

Sources: Japan Ministry of Labour, *Yearbook of Labour Statistics*; Bundesministerium fuer Arbeit und Sozialordnung, *Arbeits- und Sozialstatistik*.

Conclusion

Takafusa Nakamura writes, "Is it perhaps true that without a cushion against business slowdowns in the form of some kind of labor force that can be readily sacrificed, Japan's employment system is untenable?" (1995, 162). This study provides evidence in the affirmative to Nakamura's question, suggesting that the impediments to numerical flexibility imposed by the predominately male lifetime employment system are accommodated by the role of Japanese women as a buffer work force. Japanese women served all the more strongly as a buffer work force after the early 1970s, during which the Japanese labor market was lauded for its low unemployment and its flexibility in adapting to dramatic change in the world economy.

This study does not argue against the importance of internal and functional flexibility to the Japanese labor system. Nor does it argue that the superiority of Japanese over West German macroeconomic performance was mere illusion. There is no question, for example, that the Japanese economy did much better at creating jobs in the post-1973 period of slower growth (OECD 1994b, 4). All the same, the gender-blind approach typical of comparative studies of labor market flexibility and unemployment neglects the importance of external numerical flexibility in the Japanese economy, provided by women entering and exiting employment and the labor force at much higher rates that Japanese men. Such flexibility, reflected in the exceptionally high rates of discouraged women workers in Japan in recent years, indicates than Japanese unemployment rates are greatly underestimated. Were discouraged workers counted as unemployed in Japan, the average annual rate of unemployment in Japan over the 1983 to 1991 period would be more than double the official rate, giving a significantly different view of the success of labor adjustment in Japan in the face of slower economic growth.[7]

Notes

1. The decline in Japanese women's labor force participation prior to the mid-1970s is accounted for by the declining importance of self-employed and family workers, particularly in agriculture.

2. In the 1991 volume of *Arbeits- und Sozialstatistik [Employment and social statistics]*, the data are described as follows: "aufgrund der Ergebnisse der Volks- und Arbeitsstaettenzaehlung" ["on the basis of population and employment census"](26); in the 1975 volume, the data are described similarly as follows: "auf Grund der Ergebnisse der Volks- u. Berufszaehlung " ["on the basis of population and occupational census"] (26).

3. The linear time trend was included only when significant at the 5 percent level, following the analyses in Rubery's *Women and Recession*.

4. The importance of the 1973 turning point is suggested by Fujita, who wrote that "in 1973's oil crisis, companies tried all kinds of measures not to lay workers off, including shuffling, shorter work hours, etc. However, this was not the case for women workers (particularly the part-time workers) who were the first to be laid off in a recession. The state did not intervene in this practice of firing the female labor force, nor did the company union protect women workers who were to them only temporary workers" (1987, 593–94).

5. Houseman and Abraham's model also includes a constant and a linear time trend.

6. Using 1973 and 1979 as turning points, the coefficient estimate for the 1973 turning point is 1.388, with an associated standard error of 0.260; the coefficient estimate for the 1979 turning point is −0.433, with an associated standard error of 0.389. Using 1973 and 1980 as turning points, the results are essentially the same.

7. See also Hamada and Kurosaka (1984, 72–76), Taira (1985), and Eatwell (1995) regarding other arguments that Japanese unemployment rates may be deceptively low.

9

Race, Class, and Occupational Mobility

Black and White Women in Service Work in the United States

Marilyn Power and Sam Rosenberg

The economic experience of women of different race-ethnicities is affected by the complex interaction of race, class, and gender. An analysis of these experiences must acknowledge the "interlocking, interactive nature of these systems" (Glenn 1992, 1), and a growing body of literature has begun the difficult process of understanding this dynamic in the United States as it is played out in many venues.[1] These studies demonstrate that class and racial-ethnic differences are reflected in different life experiences, different world views, and, important for the current study, different labor force experiences. Additionally, for all women, labor force experience cannot be understood without an understanding of unpaid labor in the household as well; but both the content and the impact of this unpaid labor may be affected by class and race-ethnicity (e.g., by the presence or absence of extended family; by the ability or inability to afford household help or commodity substitutes for family labor).

This study examines and compares the occupational mobility of black and white women who worked in service occupations in their late teens and twenties. Rather than focus on a narrow set of variables, the study replaces conventional hypothesis-testing with an exploratory, storytelling approach, which more effectively illuminates the complexity of the interaction of gender, race-ethnicity, and class in the lives of women. This descriptive methodology enables us to examine how being a service worker when

Table 9.1

Percentage of Black and White Women Employed in Service Occupations, 1960 and 1994

	White		Black	
	1960	1994	1960	1994
Private household workers	6.5	1.3	37.4	2.0
Other service workers	13.8	15.4	22.7	23.7
Total	20.3	16.6*	60.1	25.7

Source: Zalokar 1990, 45; *Employment and Earnings*, January 1995, 204.
*Discrepancy due to rounding.

young contributes to a different "life story" for women of different race and class.

Historically there has been considerable occupational segregation by race among women workers in the United States, with black women confined to the lowest level of manual occupations, especially domestic work, farm work, and unskilled factory jobs. However, black women achieved a dramatic improvement in their occupational distribution in the postwar period, largely through a movement out of service and into professional and clerical occupations (Albelda 1986; King 1992; Malveaux 1985b; Zalokar 1990). In this period, the proportion of black women employed in service occupations dropped dramatically, while white women experienced a much smaller decline (see Table 9.1).

Among black women who work full-time year-round, improved occupational distribution was reflected in a rapid increase in their median earnings relative to white women's, increasing from 74.6 percent of white women's earnings in 1967 to 96.3 percent in 1975. However, the ratio has declined somewhat since the mid-1970s, and has fluctuated in the past decade between 90 and 92 percent of white women's median earnings (U.S. Bureau of the Census 1992).

The convergence of median earnings between black and white women during the 1960s and 1970s has led some authors to conclude that occupational segregation by race is no longer an issue for women workers (cf. Fosu 1988). Yet, as the data indicate, black women remain considerably more likely to be service workers than white women. In addition, cross-sectional data on occupational distribution by race may understate differences in mobility patterns for black and white service workers. Because many service occupations are relatively easy to enter, they serve for some young women as a temporary means of earning money while preparing for other, more lucrative jobs. In other cases, women may be stuck in service employment over the long term. Longitudinal data allow us to investigate the extent to which black women are more likely than white women to get stuck in low-wage service employment.

The Current Study: Descriptive Characteristics

The focus of the current study is occupational mobility of black and white women working in service occupations. Service occupations have historically been a major source of employment for black women and continue to employ a significant, though declining, proportion of both black and white women. They are for the most part low-paid jobs with no clear promotional path (the exceptions by and large are the overwhelmingly male protective services). Their relatively easy entry and frequently flexible hours attract a diverse group of women.

Our sample consists of women surveyed by the National Longitudinal Survey (NLS) of Young Women who reported working in a service occupation in 1972, and who also reported an occupation in 1988. The women were 14 to 24 years of age in 1968. Our study picks them up in 1972 when they were 18 to 28, in order to examine a sample with greater labor market experience.[2] These women are a fascinating cohort to study because they were beginning their work lives just as the civil rights laws and affirmative action guidelines were beginning to be enforced (however inadequately). At the same time, labor force participation for women was becoming a long-term fact of life, and the civil rights and women's movements were challenging established racial and gender stereotypes. The sixteen years covered in this study take the cohort through the years when they would be likely to be completing education, forming families, and establishing labor force strategies.[3]

The women in our sample were employed at least one week in both 1972 and 1988, and worked in service occupations in 1972 (as defined by the 1960 BLS occupational codes). In total there were 261 white women and 135 black women in the sample. Mobility was measured in two ways.[4] First, we looked at the broad (one-digit) occupational category of 1988 occupations. Although there are differences in pay and prospects among service occupations, most female-dominated service jobs are very low paid with little room for advancement. Occupational mobility, in many cases, involves leaving the service category altogether. Second, we divided occupations into ranks based on 1970 census data on mean earnings in three-digit occupations in 1969 of the experienced female labor force who worked fifty to fifty-two weeks.[5] Mean earnings were used in developing our ranking system rather than the earnings of the members of the sample because mobility is better measured by potential earnings in an occupation than by the earnings of an individual at a moment in time (e.g., the earnings of a new law school graduate may not reflect the relative stature of her job). Occupations were divided by earnings into fifteen ranks as follows:

Rank	Earnings Range
1.	$0-$1,999
2.	$2,000-2,999
3.	$3,000-3,999
4.	$4,000-4,999
5.	$5,000-5,999
6.	$6,000-6,999
7.	$7,000-7,999
8.	$8,000-8,999
9.	$9,000-9,999
10.	$10,000-10,999
11.	$11,000-11,999
12.	$12,000-12,999
13.	$13,000-13,999
14.	$14,000-14,999
15.	$15,000-15,999

The direction of occupational mobility is defined as follows:
Upward mobility: Rank 1988 > Rank 1972
Downward mobility: Rank 1988 < Rank 1972
No change: Rank 1988 = Rank 1972

NLS Service Workers and Occupational Mobility

1. Mobility by Occupation

Of all the women in the NLS cohort who were interviewed in 1972, the black women were considerably more likely than the white to be service workers: 28 percent of the black women who reported occupations, and 17.4 percent of the white women, were in service work. For both groups of women the most common occupation was clerical work, which employed 42.4 percent of the white women and 31.5 percent of the black women.

White women were considerably more successful at leaving service work than were black women. By 1988, among our sample of 1972 service workers, 74 percent of the white women had left the service category, mostly for jobs in the professional/technical or clerical occupations. By contrast, only a minority, 48 percent, of black women had left service

Table 9.2

1988 Occupations of White and Black 1972 Service Workers (percentages)

Occupation	White (n = 261)	Black (n = 135)
Professional, technical, and kindred	23.0	11.1
Managers, officials, and proprietors	11.5	3.7
Clerical and kindred	24.5	15.6
Sales workers	3.8	1.5
Craftsmen, foremen, and kindred	1.1	0.7
Operatives and kindred	8.4	11.8
Private household workers	1.5	5.9
Other service workers	24.5	46.7
Laborers, including farm	1.5	2.9
Total	99.8*	99.9*

*Varies from 100 percent due to rounding.

occupations; and those who had were as likely to have moved into operative occupations as into clerical or professional/technical occupations. These observations suggest that service work may be more likely to serve as a temporary occupation for young white women who are preparing themselves for better jobs, while for black women service is more likely to become a long-term job category. Further, for those black women who did leave service work, a higher percentage than the white women moved into blue-collar occupations. It is important to note, however, that few women of either race entered highly paid predominately male occupations; among the white women who entered professional/technical occupations, half became noncollege teachers or nurses (as did nearly half of the much smaller number of black professional/technical workers). And for women of both races who left service work, the most represented occupational category was clerical work, itself relatively low paid and heavily female-dominated (see Table 9.2).[6]

2. Occupational Mobility by Rank

In addition to being more able to leave service occupations, white women started out in better paying service positions. Both the low pay and the low range of pay within service occupations are illustrated by our ranking system: traditionally female service occupations ranged in rank from 1 to 4 (representing mean earnings in 1969 of 0–$4,999). Only the male-dominated protective services rose above the rank of 4; three of the white

Table 9.3

Occupational Ranks in 1972 and 1988 of 1972 Service Workers
(percentages)

	White (n = 261)		Black (n = 135)	
Rank	1972	1988	1972	1988
1	16.9	1.5	28.1	5.9
2	24.9	5.4	18.5	3.7
3	25.7	16.5	42.2	36.3
4	31.4	23.5	11.1	23.7
5	1.1	19.5		14.8
6		17.2		8.9
7		11.5		6.7
8		3.1		
9				
10				
11				
12				
13		0.4		
14				
15		1.1		
	100	100	99.9*	100
Mean rank #	2.75	4.85	2.36	3.91
Standard deviation	1.11	1.98	1.01	1.47

Notes:
*Varies from 100 percent due to rounding.
#Difference in mean rank by race significant at the .01 level in both 1972 and 1988, two-tailed test.

women, and no black women, had entered these occupations, scoring ranks of 5. Nevertheless, even within this narrow range the white women were clustered in the higher-ranking occupations in 1972, with 31 percent at rank 4 (compared to 11 percent of the black women). The mean rank for white service workers was 2.75, significantly higher than the black women's mean of 2.36 (see Table 9.3).

Over the period in question both black and white female service workers moved up the occupational hierarchy. However, the extent of the upward mobility was considerably greater for the white women. By 1988, the gap in rank between the black and white women had increased and remained statistically significant. The mean rank for black women was now 3.91, while that for whites was 4.85. The highest rank attained by black women was 7, and 70 percent continued to work at occupations ranked 4 or below. And while 95 percent of the white women remained at or below rank 7, only

47.1 percent were working in jobs of rank 4 or less. In addition, eight white women achieved rank 8, one rank 13 (a lawyer), and three rank 15 (doctors) (see Table 9.3).

The more favorable labor market prospects facing white women can be seen further by controlling for initial occupational position. The likelihood of upward mobility is related to the job held at the beginning of the period. Individuals located near the bottom of an occupational hierarchy are, virtually by definition, more likely to move up since there is little room to fall further.

Thus, service workers are divided into two groups, those with 1972 ranks of 1 or 2 and those with a rank of 3 or above. For both black and white women, the likelihood of upward mobility is greater and the likelihood of downward mobility is smaller the lower the initial rank. For example, 89 percent of whites with a job in 1972 of either rank 1 or 2, but only 57.2 percent of those with a job in 1972 of rank 3 or above, were upwardly mobile.

However, regardless of the rank of initial job, white women fared better. For both high- and low-ranked groups, the white women began and ended at significantly higher ranks, with the gap widening over the period. For example, the racial gap in average rank rose from 0.2 in 1972 for service workers in ranks 1 and 2 to 1.29 in 1988 (see Table 9.4).

Furthermore, holding a low-paying service position in 1972 did not seem to negatively influence the jobs held by white women in 1988. There was no significant difference in 1988 rank between those in the higher- and lower-ranked jobs in 1972. The same was not true for black women. Rather, for black 1972 service workers, being in an occupation ranked 1 or 2 was a significant disadvantage. Women in the higher-ranked occupations achieved a 1988 rank of 4.21, compared to 3.57 for those in the lower-ranked groups.[7]

Thus, service jobs, even low-paid ones, may be more of a bridge to better positions for young white women and more of a trap for young black women. And as we will discuss below, most of the lower-ranked white women were babysitters and waitresses, and for many of them these occupations served as temporary jobs while they prepared themselves for better employment. Most of the lower-ranked black women were domestics not elsewhere counted and did not seem to have access to the same degree of upward mobility.

3. Methodology

Prior to investigating the role of specific occupations in influencing mobility, we analyze three factors—family size and family structure, education, and social class background—which may also affect women's job pros-

Table 9.4

Occupational Mobility by Rank, 1972–1988 (percentages; standard deviations for average ranks in parentheses)

Rank group	Average rank 1972		Rank increased		Rank same		Rank decreased		Average rank 1988	
	White	Black	White	Black	White	Black	White	Black	White	Black
1,2	1.6 (0.49)	1.4* (0.49)	89.0	87.3	9.2	11.1	1.8	1.6	4.86 (2.16)	3.57* (1.51)
3,4,5	3.58 (0.53)	3.21* (0.41)	57.2	54.2	32.9	34.7	9.9	11.1	4.84 (1.85)	4.21* (1.37)
Total	2.75 (1.11)	2.36* (1.01)	70.5	69.6	23.0	23.7	6.5	6.7	4.85 (1.98)	3.91* (1.47)

*Black–white differential is significant at the .01 level, two-tailed test.

pects. Our analysis is more exploratory than confirmatory.[8] We create a series of tables documenting racial differences in family size, educational attainment, and social class. We develop a "story" by interweaving these racial differences with the racial differences in occupational mobility. We complement this "story" with a discussion of two occupations—domestic work and waitressing—and the differential opportunities they provide black and white women for occupational advancement. We do not test specific hypotheses since we believe that existing theory is incomplete, not being sufficiently complex to account for race and class differences among women. Rather we feel that our exploratory analysis may help to develop hypotheses for confirmatory testing in the future.

Furthermore, we do not use the more conventional technique of regression analysis. First, we believe that family size and family structure, educational attainment, and social class background are intertwined, not amenable to being analyzed via a conventional linear regression. More complex modeling might be feasible, but given the existing state of theory, it too would be little more than an exploratory analysis. Second, the detailed analysis of domestic work and waitressing could not be integrated into the regression analysis. Third, in some categories, there are just a few individuals. These small cell sizes would make it very difficult to run meaningful regressions.

4. Work/Family Differences

Care of children is an important aspect of women's unpaid labor and can create work/family conflicts. Women's labor force strategies, and their ability to participate in wage work, are affected by their responsibilities for children. The presence of children may affect women differently by race and by class, partly for cultural reasons, but importantly because of the presence or lack of other economic resources. That is, it is possible that women with more access to resources may respond to child-care demands by reducing their labor force attachment, while women with fewer resources may increase their wage work, both in hours and in efforts to advance. On the other hand, their limited resources, combined with the pressures of work and family, are likely to seriously impede their upward mobility. Black women have a long history of combining work and family, unlike white women; and they also are likely to have more limited access to economic resources other than their own wage-earning ability.[9]

In our sample, the black women were more likely to face work and family conflicts than the white women, since they had more children and had them at a younger age (see Table 9.5).

Table 9.5

Number of Children per Family by Race, 1972 and 1988 (percentages)

Number of children	1972		1988	
	White	Black	White	Black
0	60.2	35.6	17.0	10.4
1	21.1	24.4	17.4	15.6
2	13.4	12.6	33.6	15.6
3	4.6	18.5	21.2	23.0
4	0.8	3.7	5.8	17.0
5	—	3.7	3.5	8.9
6	—	0.7	0.8	4.4
7	—	0.7	0.8	3.0
8				0.7
9				0.7
10				0.7
Mean	0.65	1.48*	1.99	2.96*
	(0.93)	(1.54)	(1.39)	(1.99)

*Difference significant at the .01 level, two-tailed test.

Although there was no significant difference in rank between women with and without children in 1972, the presence of children in 1972 was associated with lower mobility for both groups. By 1988, the white women who had children in 1972 had achieved a rank of 4.5, compared to 5.1 for those who had not had children in 1972. Black women who were parents in 1972 achieved a mean rank of 3.7 in 1988, compared to 4.2 for women who had not been parents.[10]

The black women in our sample were apparently much more likely to be single parents: only 56.3 percent of the black mothers, compared to 83.7 percent of the white mothers, reported being married in 1972. Single parenting can make it very difficult for young women to gain the training and experience that could help them advance in the labor force; indeed, the small group of white women who were single mothers in 1972 were at a significantly lower rank than other white women in both 1972 and 1988. However, the considerably larger group of black 1972 single mothers were not lower in rank than other black service workers in 1972, and only slightly, albeit significantly, lower in rank in 1988.[11] This difference may reflect greater cultural familiarity with combining work and single parenting among black women, and perhaps more acceptance and assistance from other family members; but it also reflects the poor mobility of the black

Table 9.6

Educational Attainment by Race, 1972 and 1988 (percentages)

	1972		1988	
	White	Black	White	Black
Mean educational attainment (years)	12.0 (1.69)	10.8* (1.86)	13.0 (1.83)	11.9* (1.59)
Percentage with less than 12 years	21.5 (.41)	53.6* (.50)	7.3 (.26)	24.4* (.43)
Percentage attending school in 1972	23.7 (.43)	15.6** (.36)		

*Difference significant at the .01 level, two-tailed tests.
**Difference significant at the .05 level, two-tailed tests.

women as a whole, whether or not they were single mothers. In addition, as we have seen, most of the black women were mothers, whether single or married, and the presence of children was associated with significantly lower mobility for both white and black women.

5. Education

Many service occupations have low educational requirements; few require more than a high school diploma, and for many even this is not necessary. We might expect, therefore, that both the white and black women in our sample would have relatively low levels of education. On the other hand, service work can be used as temporary employment by women preparing for more lucrative occupations (e.g., college students working as waitresses or babysitters during the year or in the summer); this group could be working in low-ranked service occupations despite relatively high levels of education. In addition, they may be more likely to be attending school at the same time that they are working as service workers. And they are likely to be more successful at leaving service work and achieving a higher occupational rank by 1988.

The educational variables show large and striking differences between the black and white women, with black women substantially lower in educational attainment at both the beginning and the end of the period. The black women were also significantly less likely to be attending school at the time of the 1972 interview (see Table 9.6).

Table 9.7

Rank in 1972 and 1988 by School Attendance (percentages)

	Attending school	Not attending school
White		
Rank in 1972	2.53	2.82***
	(1.11)	(1.10)
Rank in 1988	6.19	4.43*
	(2.45)	(1.60)
Black		
Rank in 1972	2.86	2.27**
	(.964)	(.998)
Rank in 1988	4.71	3.76**
	(1.98)	(1.31)

*Difference significant at the .01 level.
**Difference significant at the .05 level.
***Difference significant at the .10 level; all two-tailed tests.

White women were apparently more likely to be using the flexibility of service work to support further education, a strategy that seems to have paid off extremely well in terms of mobility. In fact, white women in school in 1972 held service jobs of significantly lower rank than white women not in school. The opposite was the case for black women. Black women also benefited from school attendance, but their upward mobility was considerably lower (see Table 9.7). This lower mobility may reflect in part the lower starting level of education for the black women: 38.1 percent of the black women attending school in 1972 were in grade 12 or lower, compared to only 3.2 percent of the white women.[12]

6. Class Differences

These observations about education may suggest underlying class differences between the black and white women (and, as we will discuss below, within each racial group). There are considerable disagreements among theorists about how to measure class position (and further disagreements about how to measure class position for *women*—cf. Power 1984). For the purposes of this project, our interest is in the differing access to economic resources. Because the women were still young in 1972, we will measure these resources by the resources of their families of origin, as measured by their fathers' occupations at the time of their first interviews in 1968. Mothers' occupations are obvi-

Table 9.8

Father's Occupation in 1968 for Women in Service Occupations in 1972 (percentages)

Occupation	White	Black
	5.0	17.0
Professional, technical, and kindred	12.3	2.21
Managers, officials, and proprietors	8.8	0
Clerical and kindred	6.9	1.5
Sales workers	3.4	0.7
Craftsmen, foremen, and kindred	20.7	6.7
Operatives and kindred	14.6	19.3
Private household workers	1.1	7.4
Other service workers	3.8	9.6
Farmers and farm managers	14.6	14.1
Farm laborers	1.5	5.2
Laborers	6.5	16.3
Armed forces	0.8	0
Total	100.0	100.0

ously also relevant,[13] and the discussion will refer to them as well, but almost half the white women and more than half of the black women did not report an occupation for their mothers.

There are striking occupational differences between the black and white fathers. Considerably more black than white respondents reported no occupation for their fathers, either because no father was present or because fathers were not working. Black fathers for whom occupations were reported were most likely to be factory operatives, service workers (including a substantial proportion in domestic work), laborers, and farmers and farm managers. Only three black fathers were reported to be in professional or technical occupations, and none were in managerial occupations. White fathers were likely to work in professional/technical or managerial occupations, in the crafts as operatives, or as farmers or farm managers (see Table 9.8).

Only 41.5 percent of the black women reported occupations for their mothers; but among mothers who were reported to be working, 82.1 percent were in service occupations, including 32.1 percent in domestic work. Among white women, 54 percent reported mothers' occupations; of these, 31.2 percent were in service occupations (including 7.8 percent in domestic service), 20.6 percent were clerical workers, and 15.6 percent were in professional/technical occupations.

This information about parents' occupations makes it clear that the black women came from families with fewer economic resources. Black parents were clustered in lower-paid occupational categories at a time in their daughters' lives (ages 14 to 24) when money to pay for college or further training would be particularly important. This, of course, is not a surprising finding, given a long history of discrimination in access to education and occupational segregation by race. But it does help explain why a substantial number of the white respondents were able to use service work as a temporary stopping place, while the majority of the black respondents became mired down.

Domestics and Waitresses

We have seen that for a substantial proportion of the white 1972 service workers, service work was a temporary occupation on the way to better-paid employment. This employment pattern was available to many fewer of the black women in our sample. The difference in ability to use service work as a stepping stone may begin with access to a different set of service occupations; the white and black women in our sample differed markedly in the service occupations they held. One-fourth of the white 1972 service workers were waitresses, with hospital attendants a distant second at 14.2 percent, followed by hairdressers and cosmetologists and private babysitters. One-fourth of the black women were hospital attendants (the only occupation with substantial representation from both races), closely followed by domestic workers not elsewhere classified; no other occupation employed as many as 10 percent of the black women (see Table 9.9).

Both babysitting and waitressing were low-ranked occupations: babysitting had a rank of 1, while waitressing had a rank of 2. But both occupations have the flexibility in hours that permits them to be combined with schooling or training to achieve upward mobility. This flexibility seemed to be a more important determinant of mobility for white women than the rank of the occupation: while black women with 1972 ranks of 1 or 2 were in significantly lower-ranked occupations in 1988 than black women who had started in higher-ranked service occupations, there was no difference in 1988 rank for white women from low- versus high-ranked service occupations.

1. Domestic Work

A number of authors have observed that domestic work may serve as a "bridging" occupation for white women, a transitional job on the way to better-paid work, while women of color are more likely to become ghettoized and unable to leave the occupation (cf. Glenn 1981; Rollins 1985;

Table 9.9

Top Four Service Occupations by Race, 1972

White		Black	
Occupation	Percent	Occupation	Percent
Waitresses	23.7	Hospital attendants	23.0
Hospital attendants	14.2	Private household, not elsewhere classified	21.5
Hairdressers and cosmetologists	12.6	Chambermaids	8.1
Private babysitters	11.9	Waitresses	8.1
Total	62.4	Total	60.7

Table 9.10

Education, Presence of Children, and Mobility by Occupational Rank for White and Black Women Working as Domestic Workers in 1972
(percentages)

	1972		1988	
	White	Black	White	Black
Attending school in 1972	29.5 (.462)	7.9* (.273)		
Educational attainment (years)	12.3 (1.41)	9.9* (1.97)	13.5 (2.39)	10.2* (2.10)
Percentage with children in 1972	27.3 (.451)	71.0* (.460)		
Mean rank in 1988			5.14 (2.56)	3.24* (1.48)

*Difference significant at the .01 level, two-tailed test.

Romero 1988; 1992). Our data seem to confirm these observations. While the majority of the black 1972 domestic workers in our sample were able to move out of housework, few escaped from low-ranked service occupations. The white 1972 domestic workers had a much more positive experience.

For both groups of women, recent arrivals in the labor force in 1972, private household work was a frequent occupation: 16.9 percent of the white women and 28.1 percent of the black women worked in private households. However, as we have seen, most of the white women worked as babysitters, while most of the black women were in the category "private household, not elsewhere classified," which includes all domestic workers except babysitters, housekeepers, and laundresses (two white women in our sample were housekeepers in 1972; there were no laundresses).

The white women in domestic work clearly fit a different pattern from the black women. In fact, they were among the most highly educated and upwardly mobile of the white women in our sample, while the black domestics had educational and mobility averages considerably below the mean for the black sample as a whole. The white women were also far less likely than the black women to be balancing work and family responsibilities (see Table 9.10).

Only 20.4 percent of the white domestics were still service workers in 1988 (and only one of those, or 2.3 percent of the sample, was still in domestic work), and 27.3 percent had become professional/technical workers. By contrast, only one of the black women (2.6 percent of the sample) had entered a professional/technical occupation, while 60.5 percent had remained in service work, including 15.8 percent still working as domestics.

2. Waitresses

Waitressing illustrates some of the differences in the experience of black and white women in service work, and also illuminates some of the differences within the sample of white service workers. The most striking observation is that this category, by far the most common occupation for white service workers in our sample, employing one-quarter of the white women, employed only eleven black women (8.1 percent of our sample). That black women were so much less likely to work as waitresses may be at least in part the result of a familiar form of racial discrimination, in which people of color are excluded from jobs involving direct contact with customers.[14] This exclusion is significant because waitressing may offer the flexibility of hours that enables it to be combined with education or training to achieve occupational mobility. It can also combine with child-rearing for the same reasons, a possibility that apparently attracted many of the white women in our sample. In our discussion, we will compare white and black waitresses on some variables, but it is important to note that the small number of black waitresses makes such comparisons problematic.

The white waitresses as a group did not vary significantly from the rest of the white 1972 service workers in the percentage in school in 1972, presence of children in 1972, educational degree, or rank attained in 1988; they had a slightly lower level of education in 1972, at 11.6 years compared to 12.2 for the rest of the white service workers.[15] These averages, however, conceal important distinctions among the white women. When we divide the sixty-two white waitresses in our sample by whether or not they had children in 1972, striking differences appear, suggesting the existence of class differences among white waitresses that may be both determined by and reflected in the presence of children. The thirty-three white waitresses without children began and ended our survey period with higher levels of education than the twenty-nine women with children, moving from a mean of 12.5 years in 1972 to an impressive 14.3 years in 1988, compared to 10.8 and 11.3 respectively for the women with children.[16] Half of those without children, and none of the women with children, were attending school in 1972; and by 1988 those without children in 1972 had achieved a considerably higher occupational rank, at 5.1 compared to 4.1 for the women with children.[17] These findings confirm casual observation: waitressing can be a temporary occupation for women who are continuing their education and training; and it can also be a dead end for less educated women with fewer economic resources. The apparent importance of children in this division is perhaps not surprising: the presence of children makes it difficult to further an education and work; in addition, women striving for upward mobility may postpone childbearing.

The small number of black waitresses were quite similar to the white waitresses; they diverged from the total black sample in their lower likelihood of having children (45.5 percent did), and higher level of education in 1988 (12.5 years). While their mean 1988 rank, at 4.12, was lower than white waitresses, it was higher than the black sample as a whole. The clear divergence from the white waitresses comes in the likelihood of combining the work with schooling: only one of the black waitresses was attending school at the time of the 1972 interview. There were none of the dramatic differences observed for the white waitresses between the five black women with and the six without children (perhaps not surprising given the tiny sample).

By 1988 only 24.2 percent of the white waitresses were still service workers, almost half of them still waitresses (a relatively high degree of occupational stability compared to other service occupations). The remainder were most likely to have moved into clerical work (25.8 percent) or professional/technical occupations (19.3 percent). Among the eleven black waitresses, five (45.4 percent) remained in service work, none of them as waitresses; four (36.4 percent) had become clerical workers, one (9.1 percent) had entered the professional/technical category, and one had become a laborer.

Conclusion

In summary, we found that the black women in our sample were considerably more likely to get stuck in service occupations than the white women, or to leave them for other low-ranked occupational categories. White women were often able to use service work, even the lowest-ranked occupations, as a temporary stopping place while preparing themselves for better-paying jobs (mostly in traditionally female clerical and professional occupations). For both white and black women, responsibility for children led to lower mobility; however, considerably fewer of the white women had children when the study began. Finally, the white women were more likely to come from families in which parents worked in higher-paid occupational categories, giving them potentially more access to the resources they needed for upward occupational mobility. For most of the black women, and some of the white women in our sample, service work was a dead end. For most of the white women, it was not.

The 396 women in our sample started out in the same occupational category. They were the same age and were living through the same political/economic era. Yet the outcomes they experienced in terms of economic mobility were clearly affected by race and by class background, complexly intertwined with parenthood and marital status. From a methodological point of view, these findings bring into question the meaningfulness of cross-sectional analysis of occupational distributions. From a theoretical point of view, they confirm the argument that the effects of race and gender oppression are not simply additive—the outcome is a vastly different life experience—and they emphasize the importance of considering class background as part of this analysis as well. The findings also suggest the importance of considering the presence of children, not unidirectionally as an impediment to economic mobility, but as part of the complex picture of women's differing economic prospects. Politically, the findings emphasize the continuing and substantial differences in access to economic mobility by race, differences that must be addressed through public policy.

Notes

This chapter is reprinted from Marilyn Power and Sam Rosenberg, "Race, Class and Occupational Mobility: Black and White Women in Service Work in the United States," *Feminist Economics* 1, no. 3 (fall 1995): 40–59, with permission from Routledge.

1. Cf. Zavella 1991; Zinn and Dill 1994; Andersen and Collins 1992. Specifically with regard to women working in service occupations, see Palmer 1989; Sacks 1988; Rollins 1985; Glenn 1981, 1992; Romero 1988; Cobble 1991.

2. The black women in our sample were one year older, on average, than the white women. Mean age in 1968 was 17.8 years for white women and 18.7 years for black women (difference significant at the 1 percent level, two-tailed test).

3. Black women were oversampled proportionally to the population, to allow for a significant sample size: of the 5,159 young women in the original sample, 1,459, or 28.3 percent, were black. Neither Hispanics nor any other racial-ethnic group than blacks were identified separately; 62 women in the total sample were identified as "other," and are not included in our study. The National Longitudinal Survey is a valuable, if flawed, tool to use to track the economic experience of black and white women. Some flaws (and frustrations) of this study come from holes in the data: the women were not interviewed every year, and retrospective questions were not consistently asked about the noninterview years. In addition, although the retention rate for the sample is very impressive, a quarter of our sample of service workers was missed for at least one interview year. As a result, while we can be sure what each of the women in our sample was doing in 1972 and 1988, our information about the intervening years is necessarily incomplete.

4. This study focuses on *occupational* mobility, which is defined as movement among occupations with differing earnings potentials. This is a more narrow focus than

that taken by studies of *social* mobility, which may include cultural and social characteristics (e.g., neighborhood of residence), as well as measures of the total array of resources (e.g., spouse's income) in a determination of mobility. Nor does this study address intergenerational mobility (cf. Tickamyer and Blee 1990), or the subjective experience of mobility, which may bring stress as well as rewards to women of color who find themselves separated from their communities of origin (cf. Higginbotham and Weber 1992).

5. Since the NLS uses the 1960 census occupational codes, it was first necessary to recode the occupations to the 1970 classification scheme. This was done using the system provided in John Priebe (1972).

6. Having escaped service work for clerical occupations, further, black women may again experience lower mobility than white women (cf. Power and Rosenberg 1993).

7. Difference significant at the 1 percent level, two-tailed test.

8. For a discussion of the differences between exploratory and confirmatory data analysis, see Erikson and Nosanchuk (1992) and Tukey (1977).

9. Cf. Geschwender and Carroll-Seguin (1990). Because respondents were not sampled every year, and because one-quarter of the sample missed at least one interview year, we cannot compare the amount of time the black and white women in our sample spent out of the labor force.

10. Differences for both black and white women significant at the 10 percent level, two-tailed test.

11. There were only seventeen white single parents in 1972; they held a rank of 2.3 in 1972 and 4.1 in 1988, compared to 2.8 in 1972 and 4.9 in 1988 for all other white women. Differences in both years were significant at the 10 percent level, two-tailed test. There were thirty-eight black single parents in 1972; their rank of 2.2 in 1972 was not significantly different from the rank of 2.4 achieved by all other black women. In 1988 black single parents held a rank of 3.6, compared to 4.0 for all other black women; this difference was significant at the 10 percent level, two-tailed test. This finding is consistent with Elaine McCrate's argument that young black women confined to the secondary labor market may have little incentive to postpone childbearing, since their chances for upward mobility are slight in any case (McCrate 1990).

12. A detailed analysis of relative returns to education is beyond the scope of this paper. However, we found that even the minority of black women who had achieved twelve or more years of education in 1972 experienced less upward mobility than their white counterparts, achieving a 1988 mean rank of 4.36, compared to 5.04 for white women with twelve or more years of education in 1972 (black/white difference significant at the .01 level).

13. Tickamyer and Blee (1990) find mother's occupation has a more significant effect than father's occupation in determining a daughter's occupational mobility.

14. According to data compiled by Dorothy Sue Cobble, waiting tables became a female-dominated occupation in the twentieth century, as white women displaced white and black men; black women were either relegated to the least desirable, lowest paid waitressing work or excluded entirely (Cobble 1991, 27–29). In 1993 the occupational category waiters and waitresses was 80 percent female, but only 4.6 percent black (*Employment and Earnings* January 1994, 207).

15. Difference significant at the 10 percent level, two-tailed test.

16. Differences significant at the 1 percent level, two-tailed test.

17. Difference in school attendance significant at the 1 percent level, difference in 1988 rank significant at the 5 percent level, two-tailed tests.

10

Embracing Discrimination?

The Interaction Between Low-Wage Labor Markets and Policies in Aid of the Poor

Heather Boushey

Poverty has been an enduring feature of the economic landscape in the United States. Welfare reform advocates and policymakers have continually debated the most effective and efficient way to eradicate, or at least ameliorate, American poverty. The current reform argument is that welfare policies have fostered dependence on the state, led to burgeoning out-of-wedlock births, and destroyed the sanctity of the two-parent family by supporting only single mothers. Critics of the welfare state see this as a drain on the nation's resources. Furthermore, the allocation of increasing amounts of taxpayers' money to welfare programs has not eliminated poverty. In this sense, many analysts appear to agree: policies to eradicate poverty have not been successful—the number of poor people in the United States has not dropped substantially over the past three decades.

This chapter will explore the failure of poverty policy by addressing the gaps in theories that underlie the current policy debate. A basic definition of poverty is to be without access to income—that is, to not have a well-paying job. One important aspect of the current debate is that it ignores the fact that access to good jobs is not gender or race neutral. Discrimination and inequality characterize the labor market. Social and economic policies are also not gender or race neutral and in fact often reinforce the discrimination that permeates labor markets. This analysis distinguishes itself by pointing out that discrimination in the labor market is linked to the construction of poor relief policy. Many analysts of the welfare state note that welfare support is meager and insufficient to provide for a decent standard of living (Albelda et al. 1996), and many also note that there are not necessarily adequate jobs to be found (Spalter-Roth et al. 1995). What is missing is an exploration of the interactive relationship between these two phenomena. It is no accident that women and minorities dominate both the welfare rolls and low-wage labor markets; in fact, it is because gender and race greatly influence labor market status that poor relief also acquired discriminatory tendencies.

The development of poor relief is a contingent, historical process grounded in the conditions of labor markets within a particular location. Policies in aid of the poor have not developed uniformly across nations, nor have they progressed consistently within nations. Rather, poor relief has taken on a distinctively national character and has expanded and contracted sporadically. The form of poor relief in general has been to provide subsistence or assistance where market relations fail or are deemed socially inappropriate, while the specific nature of poor relief varies with local conditions. Gender and race constructs are a historically contingent development that fundamentally impacts the form and purpose of poor relief in the United States. In particular, there is a clear interaction between low-wage labor markets, and their characterization as gendered and racialized, and the system of poor relief that has sprouted especially from the history of race relations in the southern states.

This chapter develops the theoretical underpinnings of the system of poor relief in the United States. The aim is to show how the development of poor relief follows from the construction of low-wage labor markets where accumulation is the driving force behind this process. The theoretical goal is to bring race and gender to the fore of the analysis of the labor supply process by explaining how differentiation by race and gender is an integral part of both the historical development of the welfare state and the continual recreation of low-wage labor markets. The first section outlines the theoretical approach. The second section describes the historical development of the system of poor relief in the United States. Both sections pay particular attention to how the constructs of gender and race impact the development of low-wage labor markets and poor relief, respectively. The final section discusses the implications and conclusions.

The Generation of Low-Wage Labor Markets and the Process of Gender and Race Discrimination

The process of accumulation in general entails the continual regeneration of a low-wage labor supply. Low-wage labor markets in the United States are disproportionately dominated by women and minorities. Work on labor market discrimination has found that the ascriptive characteristics of gender and race are determining factors in wages and employment (Albelda 1985; Boston 1988; Bergmann 1989; Fuchs 1988; Gittleman and Howell 1994; Kirschenman and Neckerman 1991; Reich 1981; Reskin and Hartmann 1986). Labor market discrimination against women and minorities is sustained and recreated through the creation of wage differentials (Williams 1991; Mason 1993). Thus, some workers are systematically excluded, on the basis of their gender or race, from higher paying segments of the labor market to sustain a constant supply of low-wage labor.

We begin this analysis with a general discussion of persistent wage inequality because the starting point of a complete theory of labor market discrimination must be to develop a lens through which we can see the simultaneous and interactive processes of oppression that occur within capitalism. Capitalism is, by its very nature, an oppressive process that breeds inequality. This is the core of Marx's critique of the capitalist economic system. Through explicating how capitalism differentiates among workers, we will be able to understand how discrimination is endemic to both labor markets and the poor relief system in the United States.

In the classical Marxian approach, it is through the process of competition that the laws of capitalism are realized. Competition, among labor and among capital, mitigates against the equalization of wage rates (Botwinick 1993). First, under capitalism, firms compete against one other for market shares and profits (Marx 1986b). Marx's distinctive analysis of capitalist competition allows us to see how persistent and substantial differentials in profit rates can be explained (Shaikh 1980). This is extended to an analysis of wage differentials in that "the overall range of wage differentiation in any particular labor market will largely depend on a particular firm and/or industry's conditions of access to its potential labor reserves" (Botwinick 1993, 114). Second, workers and capitalists compete against each other over the extraction of surplus value. In the initial stages of capitalist development, capitalists increased the rate of profit through absolutely increasing surplus value—increasing the length of the work day without equal increases in wages. In the modern era, surplus value is generally increased relatively[1] through increasing the productivity of labor (Marx 1986a). The struggle between labor and capital will determine how much of the surplus value capital is able to appropriate.

The dynamics of capitalist accumulation also regulate both the supply and the demand for labor such that an excess supply is always reproduced. Marx termed this process the continual regeneration of the reserve army of labor (Marx 1986a).[2] Once we recognize that underemployment—the reserve army of labor—is a permanent feature of the labor market, labor mobility will not operate as a sufficient condition to equalize wage rates. The constant pressure of desperate pools of unemployed workers will significantly weaken any potential upward pressure on wage rates at the low end of the labor market. Concurrently, this will tend to exert downward pressure on above-average wage rates at the upper spectrum of wages through the replacement of the high-wage workers by these cheaper and possibly more acquiescent workers in the reserve army of labor. Marx's analysis of aggregate labor markets suggests that movements in the wage level tend to be limited by both movements in the productivity of labor and movements in the reserve army of labor. Differential costs of production will essentially form "centers of gravity" around which actual wage rates will fluctuate. Labor organization is a crucial component of this process because it is only through struggle with capital that labor may be able to garner wage gains from increased productivity or limit the impact of the reserve army of labor on wages.[3]

Wage differentials are then the result of three dynamics: (1) capitalist competition and technical change, which creates differentials in the conditions of production, productivity, and profitability; (2) continual regeneration of the reserve army of labor of the unemployed; (3) uneven effects of organized labor.

Having established within the Marxian model that capitalism in general recreates wage and employment inequality, we can now explore the systematic method in which this occurs on the basis of ascriptive characteristics of workers. The generation of jobs with substandard working conditions and the assignment of women and minorities to these jobs are both consistent with capitalist competition. Thus, beginning with capitalism in general, we derive the conditions for discrimination to exist. Gender and race discrimination and income inequality are symptoms of the dynamics of wage differentials. In this view, the genesis of the reserve army of labor is not simply reducible to actions of the capitalist class. Workers compete with each other for good jobs and thus, they too, are implicated in the dynamics of the reserve army.

The classical Marxian analysis provides only a starting point for an analysis of gender and race discrimination in the labor market. Understanding why particular ascriptive characteristics of workers define labor market positions entails an understanding of the structures capitalism is embedded in. There is an extensive literature that covers discrimination by gender and race and addresses these aspects of our economy. The literature on discrimination is, for the most part, carefully sectioned into two tracks: work on gender discrimination and work on racial discrimination. What is needed is a theory that can explain how and why *both* gender and race discrimination coexist under competitive capitalism. In her critique of segmented labor market theory, Albelda (1985) argues that white women and black men and women have always been separated from white males in the labor force. Labor market segmentation is actually a process whereby white women and black men and women are being integrated directly into the capitalist work system. Both characteristics are important to understanding the structure of labor markets. Glenn (1985, 1992) notes that it is imperative that gender and race be not merely additive aspects of the model. Rather, "a necessary step is the development of models which view race and gender stratification as part of a larger system of inequality" (Glenn 1985, 47). There are well-developed models of patriarchy (Hartmann 1981) and of colonial subordination (Fanon 1967), but few theories that attempt to explain both processes simultaneously. Glenn argues that these two systems of oppression cannot be seen merely as parallel because there is a dialectic relationship between gender and race, if only because individuals belong to both groups. The fact that both groups experience similar oppression under capitalism should also lead us to question whether they can be analyzed as phenomena independent of each other or of capitalism in general. Glenn (1991) points out that even the analysis of social reproduction (Humphries and Rubery 1984) is limited by not acknowledging a racial component. Social reproduction is constructed around racial categories whereby white women have occupied white-collar and lower professional positions while women of color have been disproportionately employed as service workers carrying out public reproductive labor. The dynamics of gender and race are intertwined in the economic and social system whereby the relative privilege white women enjoy in the labor market is conditioned by the existence of women of color who provide social reproductive labor.

Another difficulty in the literature on discrimination is that much of it relies on a theoretical foundation that gender and race discrimination are temporary phenomena not endemic to capitalism (Phelps 1972). These models, then, cannot help us understand why discrimination persists in the face of educational or job tenure parity. One key to understanding the dynamics of gender and race discrimination as simultaneous and linked processes is to explain why they continue to exist under capitalism and why these populations are overrepresented in low-wage jobs. It is here that we return to the theory of differential wages. In this model, wage differentials are not dependent on particular forms of discrimination, but persistent inequalities are continually recreated under capitalism. There is space for a complete theory of discrimination, but the model cannot determine who will occupy the discriminated positions. Given the work on discrimination by race and gender, it makes sense to think how the strength of these workers vis-à-vis the capitalist system has crucial implications for whether or not they will be able to garner their share of income. One way is to think of gender and race as markers that identify groups of people who are more easily discriminated against, given the historical development of social structures. Looked at within this broader social construct, gender and race discrimination aimed at women and minorities in the labor market is linked to their disadvantaged position vis-à-vis capital relative to white men. Historically, these workers did not have the support of the more advantaged group in their struggles over wages.[4] Thus, the extensive work on gender and race dynamics can be integrated into the broader dynamics of capitalism in general and we can develop a model of gender and race discrimination embedded in the capitalist process of accumulation.

This strand of inquiry has been explored by political economists Rhonda Williams and Patrick Mason. Mason (1993) extends Botwinick's analysis of wage differentials to include the possibility of racial exclusion within competitive capitalism. Access to high-wage jobs is the concrete expression of discrimination based on the abstract understanding of discrimination as a labor allocation device for "determining service in the reserve army" (6). Williams draws on the way in which the competition among workers for access to good jobs is played out within the constructs of gender and race. She argues that "workers seeking to shelter themselves from bourgeoisie society's most fragile and despised existence—life among the low-waged and unemployed—have ample reason to create and wield weapons to shelter themselves from other members of the working class" (Williams 1991, 77). The competition among workers plays out along the lines of gender and race through, in addition to other ways, union exclusion. Williams and Smith (1990) analyzed the influence of gender and race in the determinants of salary grade and job assignment in the service and maintenance union at Yale University. Their empirical results "suggest that Local 35's wage setting process reproduces white supremacy within the union. All else equal, white men's jobs receive significant and large wage and grade premiums" (71). White workers employ their power as the dominant union members to maintain their privileges in the labor market.

The classical Marxian model finds inequality, both in terms of wages and employment, to be endemic to the general process of accumulation. The continual regeneration of a reserve army is a part of this process and maintains a steady labor supply. The model does not tell us which workers will occupy these positions in the labor market; in fact, it is entirely unclear whether these workers should be identified by any particular ascriptive characteristics. The work done on gender and race discrimination points to the hypothesis that women and minorities indeed occupy these positions in the labor market in the United States. These groups experience systematic and sustained discrimination in terms of both wages and employment. To understand why, we needed to understand the underlying dynamics of capital accumulation and how this process has interacted with the structure of social relations among people in the United States. When approached from this perspective, the logic of poor relief programs in the United States becomes clear. Poor relief policies reinforce the dynamics of gender and race exclusion that originate in the labor market. This analysis is a first step in heeding Mason's call to include state policy as a further level of concretization of policies of exclusion.

The Evolution of the United States' System of Poor Relief

Poor relief in general is designed to reinforce the poor's participation in paid labor while ensuring that mass upheaval does not erupt during economic downturns. Local control enables the consideration of local labor markets in the construction of poor relief policies. The U.S. labor market is characterized by wage and employment differentials based substantively on a worker's gender or race. These patterns in the labor market are mirrored in policies in aid of the poor. The concrete structure of poor relief is limited by the dynamics of capital accumulation forever in search of lower labor costs and conditioned by the historical development of divisions based on gender and race in the United States.

The emergence of policies to alleviate fluctuations of the market began soon after capitalism's first birth pangs (Polanyi 1944). At some point, every advanced capitalist economy developed programs to counteract the impact of the markets' downturns on workers. Since capitalism and poor relief developed in tandem, one could argue that welfare policies functionally follow capitalist development. This would not be the entire picture. In some nations, such as the United States and Great Britain, the form the welfare state took is less generous and less universal than in continental Europe.[5] The United States inherited its pattern of poor relief from the colonists' native England. There, although the system of poor relief established by the Poor Laws of 1601 was national in scope, individual parishes had ultimate responsibility for their local poor (Trattner 1984, 12). Poor relief in the United States continued the tradition of local responsibility and the notion that communities are only responsible for their own poor. The Social Security Act of 1935,[6] which nationalized poor relief in the United States, allowed the states to maintain control over many aspects of welfare programs—including benefit levels, work requirements, and the eligibility of childless individuals. Local control over these aspects both shifted responsibility from the federal government and allowed communities to regulate the poor relief with an eye to local labor market conditions and social structures characterized by gender and race divisions.

The variance in poor relief systems among nations is a function of many unique historical factors and the relationship between capital and the state in general. Esping-Andersen (1990) developed a typology for differentiating among welfare regimes in advanced capitalist nations where the differences among nations' welfare systems are based on the specific formation of alliances between social groups, including, but not limited to, economic classes. Varying responses to the commodification of human labor comprises the history of the maturation of the welfare state in advanced nations and explains the more specific traits of the different welfare systems. Thus, although the general nature of poor relief is similar across nations, the specific outcome of poor relief policies varies. This analysis can be extended to explore the differences between localities in the United States since one of the enduring aspects of poor relief is substantial local control over eligibility and benefit levels. Poor relief reinforces the traditional structures of power and does not interfere with the needs of accumulation in particular localities.

In the United States, the underlying dynamic of the development of poor relief followed a cyclical pattern, linked to the needs of capitalist accumulation and organized primarily to pacify and maintain a stable, low-wage labor supply (Piven and Cloward 1971). This is opposed to other analyses of the welfare state, which view it as part of a symbiotic, mutually beneficial relationship with capitalism or as the evolutionary outcome of the simultaneous development of capitalism and liberal democracies (see Bowles and Gintis 1986; Offe 1984).[7] The antagonistic interpretation of the history of the U.S. welfare state, well developed by Piven and Cloward, rejects the idea that symbiosis is the defining characteristic of the relationship between the state and the poor (see also Gough 1979). Poor relief is instead the result of the state's response to cyclical changes in the labor market. Under capitalism, work is the primary means of organizing social life so that the breakdown of the employment structure—high unemployment or underemployment—leads to social upheaval. In general, poor relief is provided in times of economic and social turmoil and cut back when stability is reinstated. In effect, the state steps in to adjust labor supply when labor demand has shifted. State policies in aid of the poor are implemented to maintain civil order and sustain attachment to the labor force in times of economic turbulence. More specifically, the role of relief arrangements is to promote work at any wage, thus, "relief arrangements . . . have a great deal to do with maintaining social and economic inequalities" (Piven and Cloward 1971, xvii).

Poor relief is concretely structured by the specific gendered and racialized nature of the United States' labor market. In the first analysis, social programs in the United States make a clear distinction between the deserving and the undeserving poor, which is traceable to the individual's relationship to the labor market (Katz 1989). Programs such as Social Security and unemployment compensation reward labor market participation and are allocated for the deserving poor. These programs are universal, carry relatively generous benefit levels, and enable recipients to live above the level of abject poverty. Benefits are available to all citizens, regardless of income (up to a limit), personal habits, or individual characteristics. The programs for the undeserving poor, such as Aid to Families with Dependent Children (AFDC) and the Food Stamp program, are only available to citizens who qualify, based on their level of income, and carry stipulations concerning personal behavior. The benefits provided by these programs are sparse at best and are not meant to induce people to continue economic dependence on the state. This is clear when benefit levels of different types of programs are compared: in 1982, a foster parent would, on average, receive four times the amount of money an AFDC recipient would receive to raise one child (Pearce 1990). Although both programs are aimed explicitly at supporting children, the income support for a child in an AFDC recipient's home is only a quarter of what a child can expect when living in a foster home where the parents' employment status is not considered relevant to the child's level of support.

Discrimination by gender and race both structure individuals' relationships to the labor market and are interwoven into the construction of poor relief policies. Poor relief policies not only discipline low-wage labor in general, but more specifically, these policies reinforce the gendered and racialized character of low-wage labor markets in the United States. The development of this dynamic is a complicated historical process. Tracing this history will show how the dominant-class interest in "reproducing the members of society as gendered and racially conscious beings" plays out in the construction of policies in aid of the poor (Janiewski 1991, 71). Class interests in reproducing gender and race systems go beyond individual capitalists' need for low-wage workers. The two systems, the labor market and poor relief, reinforce the continual regeneration of low-wage workers based on the ascriptive characteristics of individuals. Simultaneously, both systems reinforce the privileged nature of white male employment through both keeping minority and female wages down and, where necessary, keeping these individuals out of the capitalist labor market entirely. In reinforcing women's domesticity, for example, the system of poor relief has helped reserve well-paid jobs for (white) men, further perpetuating women's secondary position in the labor market. As noted above, competition among workers has often taken the form of exclusion where policies enacted by workers and their unions strive to reserve jobs for white men at the expense of working women and minorities. The implication of poor relief policies in the maintenance of low-wage labor markets is not, however, reducible to their interaction with the capitalist labor market. Poor relief policies that neglect workers outside the capitalist labor market help to maintain these workers' dependency on their employers. Janiewski (1991) notes that this stabilizes the gender and race system by maintaining white male privilege (see also Glenn 1992). Poor relief in the United States has reinforced participation in low-wage labor markets in both the capitalist and noncapitalist sectors of the economy.

The undeserving poor includes women and minorities both because this serves a need for capital and because it is possible to discriminate against these individuals within the construct of American civil society. The literature on the undeserving poor, however, generally splits into three levels. The focus is to examine the potential recipient in terms of relationship to the labor market, gender, or race.[8] These are not—as they are often portrayed—mutually exclusive categories. The differentiation of recipients by their gender or race follows both from the structure of labor markets and from the broader social constructions of gender and race. The characterization of undeserving poor as a gendered and racialized concept was institutionalized into national poor relief policy during the New Deal and continues in the discourse and practice of poor relief up to the current day.

The Social Security Act was implemented almost thirty years before the Civil Rights Act, and while it extended social rights to many Americans it also incorporated the nation's racial divide. Southern congressional leaders were able to use their considerable committee power to shape the Social Security Act so that it did not interfere with labor supply patterns in the South (Quadagno 1994).[9] Race became a significant factor in the allocation of poor relief under the act because it contained two important concessions to the southern leaders. The first was continued local discretion over benefit levels and terms of recipiency, and the second was the exclusion of black-dominated occupations from the Old Age Assistance program. Both concessions substantially reinforced the power of the southern elite over the black masses by making the latter entirely dependent on the wages and jobs the white elite offered. While working-class white males garnered a substantial safety net through the act's programs, black Americans were unable to tap into these benefits.

Although the Social Security Act nationalized poor relief in the United States, individual states retained substantial control over the income maintenance programs for the able-bodied poor including, most importantly, AFDC. The states have discretion over benefit levels, the terms of recipiency, and whether or not they enact programs to provide income support for single men. Historically, the race component of the structure of poor relief played out most vividly in the southern United States. There, the definition of undeserving explicitly included all blacks—both men and women—who could work in the fields during harvest time for poverty wages (Lemann 1992, 5). Many states either denied benefits altogether to blacks or only allowed them to receive aid in the winter when there was no work in the fields. The United States Commission of Civil Rights found that this pattern prevailed as far north as southern Illinois. In the words on one poor relief recipient who testified in 1966:

> I am a resident of Cairo. Soon as the month of May, the public aid would start sending letters to the recipients. Due to seasonal work, your grant is cut and you are supposed to make it up by doing this seasonal work....
>
> The public aid recipient is a source of cheap labor for the farmer. We have asked my superintendent of public aid about forcing the people to the fields, why didn't he wait and let us stay back until labor rise [i.e., until labor shortages forces wage levels up], and he said the poor farmers couldn't pay any more, we'd have to go along with this going rate, and this going rate has been the same thing ever since I been in Cairo. (Quoted in Piven and Cloward 1971, 125)

Southern states also used exclusion clauses to deny welfare assistance to mothers who were deemed to be employable if "suitable" employment were available. Such employment, for a southern black woman, could be almost anything. In Georgia, a 1952 rule directed county welfare boards to deny all welfare benefits to mothers during the peak cotton-picking season (Piven and Cloward 1971, 135). Local leaders were able to sustain a strong labor supply because federal government poor relief policies did not interfere with local labor markets.

The second concession to southern congressional leaders was that blacks became ineligible for the programs designed for the "deserving poor." Quadagno (1994, 1988) has documented how the Social Security Act also excluded the vast majority of blacks from the Old Age Assistance programs. In 1935, more than three-quarters of the nation's blacks lived in the South, and 76 percent of black women were employed as either farmworkers or domestics in 1940 (Albelda 1985, 77). The bargain the southern congressional delegation struck denied old-age assistance to domestic and agricultural workers, and, as a result, only about 10 percent of the black labor force initially was covered by Old Age Insurance (Quadagno 1988). Where white

Americans could wait out a spell of unemployment with the new unemployment insurance, most blacks were ineligible and thus more likely to work for white planters and industrialists at less than living wages.

Blacks still continue to receive less from Social Security than whites while proportionally paying more taxes for the program.[10] Because Social Security coverage and benefits are lower for blacks, they are more likely than white parents to be a financial burden on their children in their old age (Oliver and Shapiro 1995). Black children, in turn, are less able to amass wealth (to buy homes or pay for a good college education) and move solidly into the middle class. This reinforces blacks' status in the labor market as low-wage workers and makes their move into the middle class more difficult because they do not have the income supports that in general are given to whites. The construction of these policies never directly forced blacks into low-wage labor markets through legislative edict, but they did make it more difficult for blacks to escape poverty and low-wage work.

The consideration of gender adds another dimension to the concept of the undeserving poor and further complicates the relationship between capital and poor relief. There is a tension between the structure of the gender system, whereby women are supposed to remain in the home to care for children, and policies in aid of poor women. On the one hand, single mothers are provided with welfare benefits, but on the other hand, these benefits have never been substantial enough to enable poor women to live far above abject poverty. Many policymakers and reformers have stressed that welfare should not promote marital dissolution, nor should it be a substitute for male income. This has promoted analysts to suggest that poor relief policies punish women who are single mothers (L. Gordon 1994). However, another way to approach this tension is to see that women face labor market discrimination, which is reinforced by poor relief policies. The construction of poor relief discriminates against women by not providing a substantive safety net for unemployed women similar to the way it discriminates against black Americans. The outcome is the same: women are disadvantaged relative to (white) men in both the labor market and in the poor relief programs that support them in times of unemployment. These structures are mutually reinforcing.

Women form the bulk of welfare recipients, and, in the United States, the majority of poor relief programs are geared toward the maintenance of women with children to rear.[11] Sapiro (1990) points out that not only are women the majority of poor relief recipients, but "it is not possible to understand the underlying principles, structures, and effects of our social welfare system and policies without understanding their relationship to gender roles and gender ideology" (Sapiro 1990, 37). She asserts that the welfare state fosters economic dependency on the part of women: "Our social policies assume that women are the primary caregivers, which means there is little assistance to be offered to women who are, in addition, breadwinners. Our social welfare system depends on women either being dependent or taking on what has become to be known as the 'double burden' " (Sapiro 1990, 47).

Gender played a substantial role in the construction of poor relief from the dawn of the early Mother's Pension programs instituted during the Progressive Era. In these programs, women were only deserving of relief if they were widowed or abandoned by their husbands, and even then they were subject to stringent housekeeping and chastity rules (L. Gordon 1994). Programs implemented to reduce female poverty at the turn of the century did not question the legitimacy of women's economic dependence on men within the family. The Children's Bureau was established in 1912 as the result of the efforts of white women in the Progressive movement who wanted society to recognize the value of mothering and to acknowledge that the public had a responsibility to assist mothers who were in financial need due to the absence of a spouse (Skocpol 1993; L. Gordon 1994). The Children's Bureau opposed collective child-care policies; they believed they were a disservice to women for they would allow more women to work and be detrimental to the development of the nation's children (L. Gordon 1994, 52).[12] The early programs for mothers and widows strove to reconcile the implicit tension between supporting mothers' right to aid and encouraging shiftlessness in men. Programs were developed with the idea that women and their children who were deprived of income through the dissolution of marriage by death or separation should be cared for by the state. This care, however, came with stipulations on the behavior of the woman in question; a woman's dependence on the state was not to enable her to be truly economically independent and should under no circumstances promote men to shirk their familial responsibilities.[13] Mother's aid was always meager and was never intended to allow single mothers to live far above absolute poverty (L. Gordon 1994; Sapiro 1990). "Man-in-the-house" rules further enforced the conception that men, not the state, should provide economic support for women and children. If a welfare recipient consorted with men she would lose her benefits and be told that her boyfriend should support her and her children (Abramovitz 1988). States implemented these rules to ensure men were not shirking their familial responsibilities and were participating in productive, paid employment. In 1968, however, the Supreme Court struck these rules down: "Destitute children who are legally fatherless cannot be flatly denied federally funded assistance on the transparent fiction that they have a substitute father" (quoted in Piven and Cloward 1971, 308).

The Social Security Act not only institutionalized the racial divide into American poor relief policy but also enshrined the notion of women's domesticity by maintaining the presupposition that women's economic role was secondary to that of men's. This reinforced women's secondary role in the labor market by not providing women with the same safety net as (white) men. The act did not cover women's primary occupations—teachers, nurses, hospital employees, librarians, and social workers—and therefore systematically denied working women Social Security benefits that were generally available to working men (Quadagno 1994, 157). The act limited a homemaker's ability to claim her husband's Social Security benefits: until 1977, a woman had to be married for twenty years to qualify for spousal benefits, and still she must be married for ten years (Quadagno 1994, 229). AFDC's program structure also assumes that women are not the primary breadwinners, that they are responsible for childrearing, and that children should be raised in a two-parent home. Each of these stipulations reduces the power of women in the labor market relative to white men through extending the concept of undeserving poor to include women without men to support them.

Poor relief reforms in the 1960s and 1970s continued to ensconce the racialized and gendered nature of the definition of undeserving poor. The War on Poverty programs still presumed that women should be financially dependent on male income. For example, Daniel Moynihan's report entitled *The Negro Family* (U.S. Department of Labor 1965) argued that the breakdown of the black family was responsible for disproportionate numbers of black women on welfare. To solve the problem, black *men* needed to be given jobs so that they could support their families (Quadagno 1988, 17). Implicitly, the logic was that if black men had jobs, the family would remain intact. Women cannot support the family or are not breadwinners. In the late 1960s, the Work Incentive Program established that welfare mothers should work rather than remain in the home, but the program's job training was still aimed at poor men (Sapiro 1990).

This logic is still at work: job training programs continually target poor men more often than poor women even though women are more likely to be poor and to have responsibility for children (Rose 1995). Further, to this day it is the poor woman who is punished if her man refuses to support her. At times, this has taken the form of criminalizing women's sexuality. For example, in Boise, Idaho, in May of 1996: "A 17-year-old Emmett girl, nearly nine months pregnant, has been given a 30-day suspended sentence and three years' probation for having sex. She was handed the sentence on Wednesday by Gem County magistrate Gordon Petrie after being found guilty of fornication, a state law that makes sex between unmarried people a crime.... The girl said prosecutors explained the charge was not about sex; it was about welfare and the high costs it puts on tax-payers" (*The Nation* 1996, 7). Most recently, President Clinton has "ended welfare as we knew it." The congressional Republicans' "Contract with America" had asked: "Isn't it time for the government to encourage work rather than rewarding dependency? The Great Society has had the unintended consequence of snaring millions of Americans into the welfare trap. Government programs designed to give a helping hand to the neediest of Americans have instead bred illegitimacy, crime, illiteracy, and more poverty" (*Contract with America,* 65)

Welfare policy critics voiced two overriding concerns: rising illegitimate birthrates and the disincentive welfare provides to work. It is the latter that permeates the introduction to the Personal Responsibility and Work Opportunity Reconciliation Act of 1996, while the former provides the substance of the act: "Therefore, in light of this demonstration of the crisis in our Nation, it is the sense of the Congress that prevention of out-of-wedlock pregnancy and reduction in out-of-wedlock birth are very important. Government interests and the policy contained ... is intended to address the crisis" (HR 3734, Title I, Sec. 101.10). The substantive change from previous legislation is that all states must require a "parent or caretaker receiving assistance under the program to engage in work ..." (HR 3734, Title I, Sec. 402.A.1.A.ii). The aim is self-evident: make the poor work and maintain the sanctity of the two-parent family. What the act does not note is that this policy will impact women and minorities more than white men, given that these groups are excluded from other types of social insurance.[14]

Conclusion

Proponents of poor relief argue that it guarantees citizen welfare and provides a safety net in times of economic need. Welfare programs are seen for their positive impact in providing subsistence beyond the market. It is for these very qualities that conservatives decry welfare state policies.[15] A fundamental issue, however, is the purpose of welfare: is it state benevolence designed to uphold the dignities of citizenship, or is there some other underlying determinant of poor relief implementation and practice? The argument here is that poor relief policies are not (nor have they ever been) designed to impede labor market participation. Further, these policies articulate existing patterns of gender and race oppression. Janiewski has stated that "Employers never recruited or managed workers as though they were colorless and sexless. They drew upon tradition to allocate work, power, honor, and resources while modifying the preexisting pattern to their purposes" (1991, 90). In this way, the structure of employment and the need of employers to have access to a continual supply of low-wage labor has played into the construction of poor relief. The privileged members of the labor market—predominantly white men—are eligible for the generous poor relief programs aimed at the deserving poor. The disadvantaged members of the labor market—predominantly women and minorities—have not historically been eligible for the substantive programs and, rather, have been recipients in programs that have explicitly aimed at pushing these workers back into the labor market at the lowest wages. The gender and race components of poor relief policies stem from discrimination embedded in the labor market. Poor relief policies reinforce a preceding parallel structure in the labor market. Linking these parallel developments shows the relationship between poor relief, labor market conditions, and gender and race exclusion.

Policymakers must acknowledge the link between the labor markets and poor relief in order to eradicate the gender and race bias in the composition of the poor. This endeavor is increasingly politically relevant as Congress has recently enacted a welfare reform program explicitly aimed at pushing welfare recipients toward employment in low-wage labor markets—even if this means welfare recipients must perform (unpaid) work for the state. This interactive dynamic between poor relief and labor market structures must be explored especially as welfare reform presupposes that all Americans have access to jobs at living wages. Policies such as pay equity, living wages, and affirmative action are a step in this direction because they strive to reduce labor market discrimination. This lessens the impact gender and race can play in the granting of poor relief since, without discrimination, these characteristics may not allocate women and minorities to the bottom of the labor market.

Notes

1. Recent strikes, such as the Staley workers in Illinois who battled over the length of the working day, were over absolute surplus value.
2. Humphries and Rubery (1988) point out that there are many ways in which women as a group may function as a labor reserve. If women's labor is a buffer in the labor market, where relative female employment varies with cyclical and secular economic trends, then there should be procyclical variation in participation rates and wages. If women are entirely segmented, then women's labor may fluctuate differently than men's because they are not competing in the same labor markets. If women are substitutes, then their employment may increase cyclically as they are substituted for more expensive male labor. My chapter is beginning with the *general* hypothesis of the reserve army and is leaving these finer distinctions to a later work.
3. Note that skilled labor will receive higher wage rates than unskilled because of the extra costs of training skilled labor (Marx 1986a, 172). This does not suggest, however, that all workers with similar skills will receive a uniform wage.
4. There is an extensive literature on the history of discrimination by unions and the

fight for the family wage. Brenner and Ramas (1984) argue that women were less able than men to defend their skills and were more constrained by domestic tasks, especially since adult women workers often had children to support or were widowed and were therefore very desperate. Without the spare time to organize, and with their lack of mobility due to the responsibilities of child care, it was difficult to search for work if the local employer paid low wages. Young women were more likely to organize but since they were usually only working temporarily, it was difficult to sustain union activity. The gendered division of labor, however, existed long before unions began their discriminatory policies. At the time of the drive for a family wage, in the 1840s, the unions were concerned about the competition they were experiencing from women, due to their lower salaries. They argue that the movement was more an effect of women's lower wages rather than a cause. See also Sen (1980).

5. This is not to argue that the state is functional for capital as there have been programs, such as Affirmative Action, which attempt to address labor market inequalities. On another level, the programs examined here do enable people to exist without wage labor. Thus, even if poor relief does not eradicate inequality, it does decrease the percentage of the population of women and minorities that are absolutely destitute. These caveats aside, this chapter explores the darker side of poor relief.

6. The Social Security Act created most of the social programs we associate with the American "welfare state," such as Unemployment Insurance, Social Security, and Aid to Dependent Children (ADC). ADC later became Aid to Families with Dependent Children (AFDC) in recognition of the fact that the state transfers income to a family, not directly to a child (Sapiro 1990). In this chapter, the program is always referred to by its current name, AFDC.

7. The symbiotic approach has been extended to analyses of the development of social policy in the less developed economies with the argument that these nations will create social welfare policies as their economies grow. See MacPherson and Midgley (1987).

8. This is to say that analyses tend to focus on one issue, rather than all three simultaneously.

9. In the 1930s, southern political power was ensconced in the Democratic party. Poll taxes and literacy tests for voter registration meant that blacks and many poor whites were disenfranchised. This reduced opposition to the Democratic party majority; with no political opposition for congressional seats, southern Democrats were able to attain seniority and thus control key committees in the House and Senate (Quadagno 1994, 21).

10. Quadagno (1994) points out that because (1) there is a cap on the level of income that is taxable for Social Security, and (2) blacks earn on average less than whites, "black men were taxed on 100 percent of their income, on average, while white men earned a considerable amount of untaxed income" (161).

11. For further discussion of the composition of welfare recipients, see Albelda et al. (1996).

12. Collective child care was also deemed inappropriate for women because it would engender greater exploitation of female wage labor: "Some [settlement workers] feared that child care would makes things harder for women, allowing greater exploitation of their labor.... A quarter of a century later Grace Abbott, head of the Children's Bureau, was arguing that such provision might lead mothers to collapse under the double burden of earning and domestic labor" (L. Gordon 1994, 52).

13. Linda Gordon (1994) has yet another insightful quote: when Hull House women discussed Chicago in 1895, they wrote "The theory that 'every man supports his own family' is as idle in a district like this as the fiction that 'every one can get work if he wants' " (53).

14. Yoon and Spalter-Roth (1995) found that 74 percent of all unemployed male workers and 80 percent of all unemployed female workers do not receive Unemployment Insurance benefits. A higher proportion of women than men are likely to be screened out by basic criteria such as required weeks of work in previous job, base earnings, or necessary high quarter earnings.

15. This includes black conservatives such as Thomas Sowell and Glenn Loury, both economists, who argue that self-help, rather than government programs, constitutes the proper path for black economic progress in the United States. They believe that a "culture of poverty" was spawned by welfare state policies that hamper black progress through enabling dependence on the state, rather than the market, and propelling the "crisis" of the black family. For a critique of their views see Gooding-Williams (1987).

11

Reversing the Great U-Turn

Pay Equity, Poverty, and Inequality

Deborah M. Figart and June Lapidus

Empirical research by labor economists as well as sociologists interested in wage discrimination has demonstrated that a significant portion of the gender-based wage gap can be attributed to occupational gender segregation. A wage penalty exists for male and female incumbents in traditionally female occupations, even after accounting for human capital and institutional variables (England 1992; Sorensen 1989a, 1989b, 1994; Treiman and Hartmann 1981). Feminist researchers have studied the processes that perpetuate and exacerbate this wage penalty, including biased job evaluation systems (Steinberg 1992; Wajcman 1991), socially designated conceptions of skill (Steinberg 1990), organizational characteristics (Acker 1990; Baron 1991; Buswell and Jenkins 1994; Anderson and Tomaskovic-Devey 1995), as well as the influence of market forces (Bridges and Nelson 1989). The relationship between wage inequality by gender and occupational segregation has been used to document the need for comparable worth policies designed to reduce the portion of the gender-based wage gap due to the undervaluation of female-dominated occupations (England 1992; Sorensen 1994; Treiman and Hartmann 1981). Pay equity or comparable worth has thus been viewed primarily as a strategy to address gender-based wage differentials.[1]

Evidence on recent trends in earnings inequality suggests that policies targeting female-dominated occupations for wage increases could also have an impact on overall wage dispersion. Since 1979, there has been an observed increase in overall earnings inequality, what Harrison and Bluestone (1988) have termed "The Great U-Turn."[2] Two studies indicate that approximately one-fifth of the increase in earnings inequality appears to be explained by the shift from manufacturing to more female-intensive service sector employment (Harrison and Bluestone 1988, 120; Karoly 1992, 114).[3] Between 1979 and 1989, the U.S. economy lost 1.2 million manufacturing and mining jobs and gained 19.3 million jobs in the service sector for a net creation of 18.1 million (Mishel and Bernstein 1994, 153). This trend both continued and accelerated into the 1990s. While the service sector has produced more professional and managerial jobs than existed in manufacturing, it has also expanded employment in low-wage occupations, especially for workers without college degrees. Concerns have been expressed that middle-class jobs are disappearing. Further, the expansion of traditionally female industries has been accompanied by the "feminization" of occupations within industries due to the restructuring of work to reduce labor costs (Kuhn and Bluestone 1987; Jenson, Hagen, and Reddy 1988; Reskin and Roos 1990). Thus, policies that raise the wages of female-dominated sectors could mediate rising inequality.

Within-group inequality has also increased for both women and men. For example, Wagman and Folbre (1988) point out that while some women have moved into higher-paid professional and managerial occupations, the simultaneous expansion of low-wage women's jobs has yielded an increase in the percentage of women at both the upper and lower tails of the earnings distribution (see also Katz and Murphy 1992). Among men, the middle of the earnings distribution also declined, while the upper and lower tails grew (Burtless 1990; Harrison and Bluestone 1988; Levy and Murnane 1992). The increase in inequality among men can be largely explained by the loss of jobs paying a so-called family wage. In fact, the gender-based wage gap declined with a fall in men's real wages, as well as the relative increase in women's education and experience (Grubb and Wilson 1989; Karoly 1992; Levy and Murnane 1992; Mishel and Bernstein 1994).

Despite the influence of the social construction of gender on these earnings trends, the relationship between the gender pay gap and overall earnings inequality has been relatively unexplored. Studies linking gender to inequality generally emphasize changing family structure, such as the rise of female-headed families, rather than gendered labor markets (see, for example, Karoly 1996). In their comparative work, Blau and Kahn (1992, 1994) found that women benefit from a lower wage gap in countries with less overall earnings inequality. This chapter examines whether the converse is also true. That is, would a comparable worth policy designed to decrease the gender-based wage differential reduce other measures of earnings inequality?

While intuition would lead to the presumption of a positive finding, the issue is complex. Pay equity is sometimes perceived as a middle-class women's issue, primarily benefiting jobs requiring relatively higher levels of education. Although supporting the policy, Malveaux (1985a) questions whether it would assist the lowest-paid workers. Brenner (1987) argues that "comparable worth is a relatively conservative approach to women's low pay" because it accepts the existence of occupational wage hierarchies (457). Pay equity is frequently omitted from progressive policy agendas intended to address rising inequality, as in the Economic Policy Institute's *Reclaiming Prosperity,* for example (see Schafer and Faux 1996). Therefore, the question posed above must be refined to ask which forms of earnings inequality might be alleviated by comparable worth. Would the policy largely decrease inequality between women and men, or would it also narrow intragroup inequality? Are the improvements greater for the middle ranges of the earnings distribution or the lowest-paid workers?

In this research, we estimate the potential effect of a national comparable worth or pay equity policy on earnings inequality, both among and between women and men.[4] Thus, we ask what would happen if the negative correlation between wages and the "percent female" in occupations were eliminated economywide. Although eliminating this wage penalty represents a narrow interpretation of a national comparable worth policy, this estimate provides insight into its potential impact. We have previously undertaken similar empirical analyses to estimate the impact of a nationwide comparable worth policy on poverty among workers. In that work, we found that comparable worth would significantly reduce the percentage of women among the working poor by as much as 40 percent and significantly reduce the percentage of men among the working poor by about 10 percent (Lapidus and Figart 1994). A follow-up study compared two policy proposals aimed at low-wage labor markets: national pay equity coverage and an increase in the minimum wage to $5.15 per hour. These policies address two reasons for poverty-level wages among working poor women: women are overrepresented in low-wage jobs, and work done primarily by women is undervalued throughout the economy. We concluded that comparable worth does a better job at reducing the gender-based component of working poverty, although both policies benefit women workers (Figart and Lapidus 1995).

To extend this research beyond poverty measures, we assess whether pay equity can be one policy to reverse "The Great U-Turn" in earnings distribution. We found a decrease in overall earnings inequality, inequality between women and men, and inequality among women. These outcomes held across choice of inequality index. Although the finding that comparable worth would reduce between-gender-group inequality was expected, the estimated reduction in overall and within-group inequality demonstrates the potential of comparable worth to reverse the so-called "declining middle" by revaluing historically devalued women's occupations. The implication of these findings is that gender inequality is an important dimension of overall inequality. Applications within political economy that marginalize gender analysis may neglect vital policy options.

Data and Research Design

Wages and Comparable Worth

Occupational segregation by gender has had a measurable effect on wages. To estimate the effect of percent female in an occupation on wages, we replicated the multiple regression methodology used in previous studies. However, we also employed a technique to hypothetically eliminate the negative effect of percent female on earnings to estimate wages under a comparable worth scenario, ex ante. Studies that estimate the potential impact of comparable worth implemented at the establishment level across the United States are ex ante studies. Ex post studies measure wages and the wage gap after realization of comparable worth wage adjustments. Some ex ante studies estimate the potential impact of comparable worth on other aspects of the labor market including labor supply and employment (see Aldrich and Buchele 1986; Ehrenberg and Smith 1987; Killingsworth 1985, 1987; Smith 1988). None of these studies examines the potential impact of comparable worth on earnings inequality.

Most prior empirical research estimates that the negative impact of percent female on wages is in the 10 to 17 percent range, depending upon model specification (Aldrich and Buchele 1986; Johnson and Solon 1986; England 1992; Gerhart and El Cheikh 1991). Two longitudinal investigations employing regression models with fixed effects report coefficients in the 3 to 10 percent range, although the negative effect of working in a female-dominated job is higher for African American women (Kilbourne, England, and Beron 1994; Kilbourne, Farkas, Beron, Weir, and England 1994). On the higher end of cross-sectional studies, Blau and Beller (1988) and Sorensen (1989a, 1989b, 1990, 1994) estimated the impact at 15 to 20 percent for women and 20 to 27 percent for men, ceteris paribus. Studies on the low end of the spectrum emphasize that most of the difference in men's and women's occupational earnings is accounted for by industry or compensating differentials associated with job traits or characteristics. The addition of numerous measures of jobs traits (strength, working conditions, and so forth) from the *Dictionary of Occupational Titles* (DOT) reduces the explanatory power of the percent female variable (see England 1992; Filer 1985, 1989).

However, there is considerable disagreement about including job traits in the analysis. The more jobs traits (strength, working conditions, and so forth) included in the regression equation, the more likely they are to capture how the market remunerates such characteristics. In other words, characteristics of work are themselves historically associated with the gender composition of the job and will reduce the direct effect of gender composition on wages. Therefore, the inclusion of job characteristics maintains some of the bias comparable worth advocates seek to avoid. Since job characteristics also correlate with human capital variables, overuse can result in multicollinearity, according to Sorensen (1990, 1994). Furthermore, research by Jacobs and Steinberg (1990, 1994) found that little of the gender gap in earnings was accounted for by compensating differentials, especially undesirable working conditions.

Using the March 1992 *Current Population Survey* (CPS), we estimated wage regressions based upon Sorensen's methodology (1989a, 1990). Our sample included individuals ages sixteen to sixty-four with earnings in the survey week. Earnings are expressed hourly (HRSPAY). Because returns to independent variables have historically differed for men and women, it is customary to run separate earnings equations for men and women. The semilogarithmic earnings equations for women and men, respectively, are

$$ln\ W_F = \alpha_F + \beta_F X_F + \gamma_F Z_F + \varepsilon_F \tag{1}$$

$$ln\ W_M = \alpha_M + \beta_M X_M + \gamma_M Z_M + \varepsilon_M \tag{2}$$

where X is a vector of human capital, demographic, regional, industrial/firm, and occupational characteristics that influence earnings, and γ is the coefficient for percent female, Z, in three-digit occupation.[5] This coefficient is interpreted as the percent change in earnings with a one-point increase in percent female in each occupation.

A significantly negative γ is indicative of wage discrimination. The potential impact of comparable worth is then estimated by setting the percent female coefficient equal to zero. Specifically, new wages (NEWPAY) are calculated using the estimated coefficients from the women's and men's equations respectively (β_{Fs} and β_{Ms}) to generate a new wage equation in which $\gamma = 0$. Thus, women and men would be compensated as if percent female in the occupation were not depressing the wage. This process assumes that wage penalties in occupations that are 99 percent female are greater than in occupations that are 70 percent female and that this relationship is linear. A potential drawback of the approach is allowing the rates of returns to characteristics, the β's in equations (1) and (2), to differ between women and men; this underestimates the interaction between occupational segregation and returns to human capital and demographic variables.

The wage adjustment process we define, setting γ equal to zero, is not procedurally equivalent to a comparable worth compensation policy of raising wages in female-dominated occupations up to a male, nonfemale (male plus neutral), or neutral pay line. There are several ways in which this methodology of assessing and correcting for wage discrimination differs from conventional comparable worth implementation. First, individuals and not jobs are the unit of analysis. Separate equations for individual women and men are substituted for female-dominated and male-dominated jobs. (In studies of gender- and race-based wage discrimination, four equations for race–gender groups have been used. See Cotton 1988; Gyimah-Brempong and Fichtenbaum 1993.) This methodology was chosen in order to allow for pre– and post–comparable worth comparisons of wage inequality. Earnings inequality indexes are calculated with individuals as the unit of analysis. Further, this approach permits use of a national sample, rather than firm-level data.

To replicate Sorensen and again contrast estimated coefficients with previous research, we have added those job traits from the *Dictionary of Occupational Titles* that are summarized as scale variables in addition to conventional explanatory variables capturing human capital, demographic, industrial, and regional differences. The added job characteristics are cognitive skills, specific vocational training, strength, environment, and working conditions.[6] In addition, the inclusion of both full-time and part-time workers in the sample and allowing for the effect of both voluntary and involuntary part-time work on earnings, as we do, yields a lower coefficient for percent female. In a related article, we discussed the effects of modeling full-time workers only and the potential impact of eliminating the depreciation of wages for part-time workers (Figart and Lapidus 1996, 306). The net effect of these methodological qualifications is that from a comparable worth perspective, the regression model will understate the effect of percent female for women and likely overestimate it for men. The model intentionally biases γ against a hypothesis of a significantly negative impact of female occupational composition on earnings. Such restrictions incorporated into the methodology may produce a lower-bound estimate of the effect of comparable worth on earnings and inequality.

With those conditions stipulated, we estimated comparable worth wage adjustments under a scenario that mirrors pay equity implementation and the parameters of similar social policies in the United States as much as possible. For example, the benefits of comparable worth wage increases are restricted to women and men in female-dominated occupations, defined as

70 percent or more female. This threshold is the most commonly used, although some jurisdictions, such as New York State, have used more inclusive definitions. However, occupations that are less than 70 percent female nationally may qualify for comparable worth wage adjustments at the firm level due to intraoccupational segregation. Examples include social workers, bill or account collectors, office supervisors, food counter clerks, electrical assemblers, educational or vocational counselors, and psychologists. Because public policies such as Title VII of the U.S. Civil Rights Act of 1964 and the Family and Medical Leave Act of 1993 have excluded small firms, NEWPAY results assume that firms with fewer than twenty-five employees (at all locations) are excluded from a comparable worth mandate.[7] Finally, no one individual's wage is allowed to drop, mirroring historical precedent in compliance with the Equal Pay Act. Based upon previous research, we assume that comparable worth wage adjustments would not have major disemployment effects (see, for example, Ehrenberg and Smith 1987; Hartmann and Aaronson 1994; Kahn 1992; O'Neill, Brien, and Cunningham 1989).

Inequality Measures

Most studies of inequality have used the popular Gini coefficient. To assess the robustness of our results, we employed a variety of indexes. We calculated the following measures of earnings inequality: the coefficient of variation (CV); the variance of the natural log of earnings (VLN); the Gini coefficient (Gini); the Theil-Entropy Index (Theil); and Atkinson's measure when $\varepsilon = 1.5$ and 2.0 (ATK). For Atkinson, ε measures the relative sensitivity of an underlying social welfare function to transfers at different income levels. As ε increases, more weight is attached to transfers at the lower end of the distribution and less to transfers among top earnings recipients (Atkinson 1970; Jenkins 1991). We chose $\varepsilon = 1.5$ and 2.0 to emphasize those reductions in inequality that would result from increased earnings at the lower end of the distribution. Although there is heterogeneity among measures, studies that use a variety of scalar indexes for longitudinal analysis show consistent trends across measures (Karoly 1992; Levy and Murnane 1992).[8]

The CV is most sensitive to changes in the upper tail and is therefore least preferred if, a priori, we expect comparable worth to help women in the lower to middle ranges of the distribution. Deciles and the Gini coefficient are used to better examine distribution at the middle ranges, although no measure is ideal for distinguishing what happens in the middle from other kinds of inequality. The VLN and Theil measures, and Atkinson when $\varepsilon = 1.5$ and 2.0, are well suited to analyzing changes in the lower tail of the earnings distribution. In studying family income inequality, Treas (1983) selected the Theil index due to this property. VLN, Theil, and Atkinson are also exemplary because they can be decomposed into inequality within group and inequality between groups. We apply the decomposition methodology to ask, ex ante: How would comparable worth alter inequality *among* women and men as well as *between* women and men?[9]

Results

This section first describes the results of the regression models used to calculate new, predicted wages. The effect of the comparable worth wage adjustments on pay and earnings inequality is then presented. A summary of the estimated effect on overall earnings inequality is followed by a comparison of the decomposition of intergroup and intragroup inequality. The impact of comparable worth on measures of wage dispersion for women and men separately is discussed last.

Wages and Percent Female

The estimated coefficients for the semilogarithmic equations for women and men are consistent with previous researchers' estimates, with the exception that marital status did not have a significant impact on women's earnings.[10] For example, human capital acquisition had a highly positive and significant effect on earnings, and more for high school– and college-educated men than women. The wage penalty for voluntary part-time work was higher for men than for women, and significant for both. The effect of marital status on men's earnings was positive and higher for men who were currently married. The negative impact on earnings of being African American, Latino/a, or a member of another minority group was higher for men than women (see also Albelda 1986; Sorensen 1989b, 1990). Finally, the relative wage advantage of union membership is also slightly higher for men than women, although the effect seems to be converging across gender groups compared to earlier studies. Our estimates for the relative wage effect of unionization, 16 percent, were closer to Johnson and Solon (1986) than to Sorensen (1990). However, the magnitude of the estimates reflected those in the literature (see Lewis 1986).

To predict what women and men would earn with comparable worth, the impact of an occupation's percent female composition on wages was used. The estimated coefficients for percent female were $-.118$ for women and $-.193$ for men, and are significant at the 1 percent level. This means that as the percent female in an occupation rises by 1 percent, wages for women

Figure 11.1 **Hourly Wages Before and After Comparable Worth**

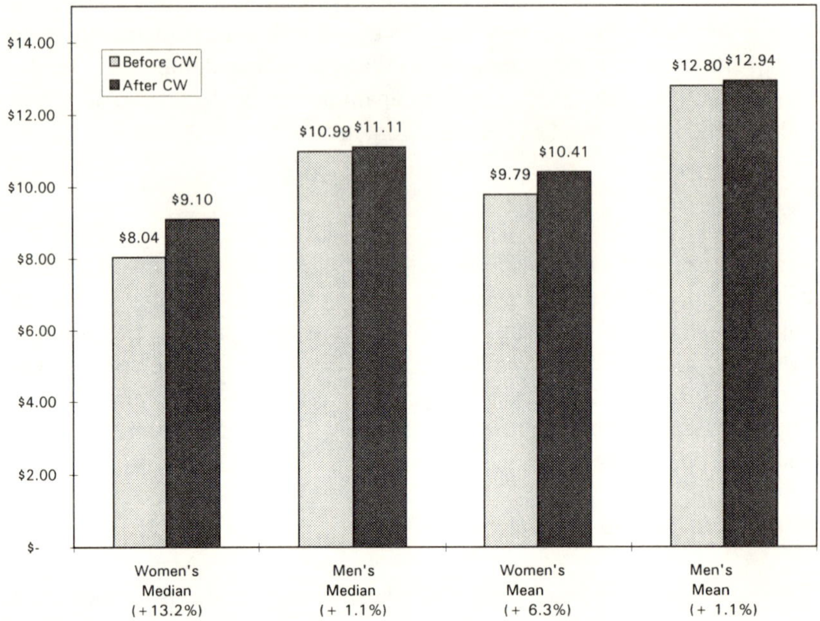

	Before CW	After CW
Women's Median (+13.2%)	$8.04	$9.10
Men's Median (+1.1%)	$10.99	$11.11
Women's Mean (+6.3%)	$9.79	$10.41
Men's Mean (+1.1%)	$12.80	$12.94

and men fall by .118 percent and .193 percent respectively, all other things equal. Another way of stating this is that a 10 percent increase in the percentage of women in a job category yields a decline in earnings of 1.18 percent for women and 1.93 percent for men. Looking at the coefficients in the extreme, a female incumbent in a job that is 100 percent female would earn almost 12 percent less than she would in an occupation with virtually all men. Therefore, the higher the percent female in the occupation in which the person is employed, the greater the wage depreciation and hence the higher the comparable worth wage increase in percentage terms. Using the customary practice of separate wage equations for women and men, the penalty of being employed in a female-dominated occupation is greater for men.

When post–comparable worth wages were estimated by setting $\gamma = 0$, we found that comparable worth could have a significant impact on women's hourly earnings and on the gender-based wage differential. The effects are shown in Figures 11.1 and 11.2. Women's median hourly earnings increased from $8.04 to $9.10, or 13.2 percent. As Figure 11.2 portrays, this translates into a relative increase in the female-to-male wage ratio of nearly 14 percent, from 72 cents on the dollar to 82 cents. At the mean, women's hourly earnings increased from $9.79 to $10.41, or 6.3 percent. These estimates conform to earlier research by Sorensen (1987) on the effect of comparable worth policies on earnings in five states. Although the wage

Figure 11.2 **Female-to-Male Median Wages**

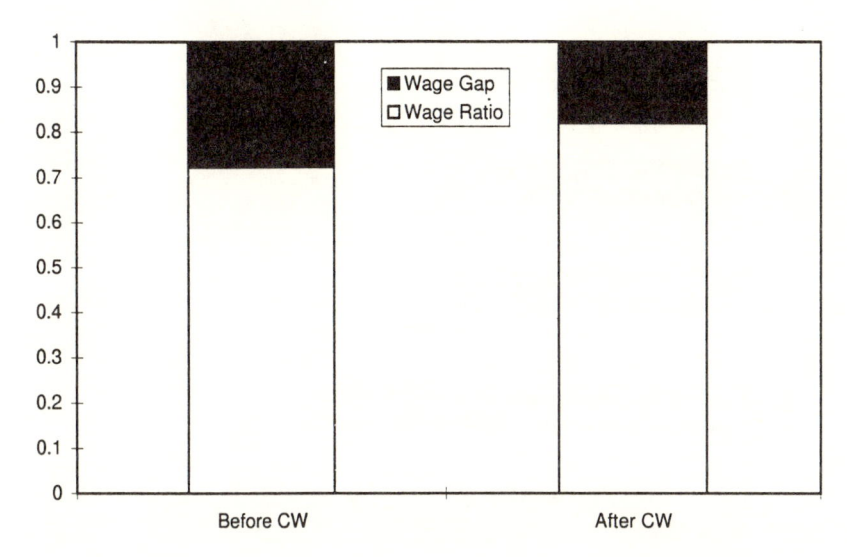

[Bar chart showing Wage Gap and Wage Ratio Before CW and After CW]

depreciation for men working in female-dominated occupations was relatively larger, the percentage increase in average and median pay for men was less, 1.1 percent, reflecting the smaller number of men in female-dominated occupations (see Figure 11.1).

The approximate increase in hourly wage costs as modeled by these comparable worth wage adjustments was 3.67 percent. This estimate of comparable worth expenditure corresponds with the average and median cost of implementation across twenty state governments found by Hartmann and Aaronson. This is lower than the cost as a percentage of payroll incurred by implementation of pay equity for civil service employees in Washington, Oregon, Iowa, Connecticut, Vermont, New Mexico, Massachusetts, and Michigan (Hartmann and Aaronson 1994; Figart and Kahn 1997).

Comparable Worth's Effect on Measures of Earnings Inequality

All five measures of earnings inequality registered a decline with comparable worth. Figure 11.3 summarizes the decrease in the inequality indexes with the change from HRSPAY to NEWPAY.[11] The largest relative declines were in Theil and VLN, two of the indexes capturing transfers at the lower tail. In order to test the significance of the declines, jackknife standard errors were calculated for CV, VLN, Theil, and Atkinson, using formulas derived by Karoly (1989).[12] The declines in CV, VLN, and Theil are significant at the 5 percent level. While standard errors are not available for

Figure 11.3 **Relative Decrease in Wage Dispersion and Inequality**

CV*	4.7%
Gini	4.4%
Atkinson	5.2%
VLN*	7.4%
Theil*	10.3%

*Indicates change in index is significant at the .05 level (one-tailed t test).

the Gini coefficient (Karoly 1992 indicates that computational costs are too high), the unambiguous improvement in the Lorenz curve discussed below also suggests that this decline is due to something other than sampling variability.

Comparison with results of longitudinal changes in the distribution of earnings in Karoly (1992) suggests that declines in the indexes in Figure 11.3 are dramatic. For example, Karoly reports that the 1.7 percent increase in the Theil-Entropy Index from .353 in 1976 to .359 in 1986 cannot be attributed to sampling variability (1992, 109–11). As a comparison, the decrease in Theil we report in Figure 11.3 is 10.3 percent. Similarly, the 5.2 percent decline in Atkinson for $\varepsilon = 1.5$ is greater than a 4.8 percent change from 1976 to 1986 measured and reported significant by Karoly (1992, 109).

Whereas comparable worth appears to reduce overall inequality, it is a policy that targets gender-based occupational segregation. Therefore, we decomposed VLN, Theil, and Atkinson (for $\varepsilon = 1.5$ and 2.0) by gender group to assess the potential effect of comparable worth on earnings inequality between as well as among women and men. Results of our decomposition analysis for intergroup (IR) and intragroup (IA) inequality are reported in Table 11.1.

Previous researchers who decomposed changes in inequality have found that inequality within gender (and race, age, or industry, and so on) group is greater than between groups. For example, Grubb and Wilson (1989) dem-

Table 11.1

Decomposition of Inequality Indexes

Measure	Overall*	Intergroup	Intragroup
VLN:			
HRSPAY	.352	.0214	.3369
NEWPAY	.326	.0081	.3177
% Δ	−7.4%	−62.1%	−5.7%
Theil:			
HRSPAY	.175	.0129	.1622
NEWPAY	.157	.0059	.1509
% Δ	−10.3%	−54.3%	−7.0%
Atkinson:			
if ε = 1.5			
HRSPAY	.231	.0100	.2230
NEWPAY	.219	.0050	.2148
% Δ	−5.2%	−50.0%	−3.7%
if ε = 2.0			
HRSPAY	.340	.0103	.3335
NEWPAY	.330	.0016	.3263
% Δ	−2.9%	−84.5%	−2.2%

*Sum may vary due to rounding; for Atkinson, ATK = IA + IR − IA*IR.

onstrated that inequality within gender group, measured by decomposing the Theil index, is higher than between groups. Using Atkinson's measure, Conrad (1993) also found inequality within racial groups is far greater than inequality between groups. Consider height as an analogy. The difference between the tallest woman and the shortest woman is greater than the difference between the average woman and the average man.

We also found that within-group inequality was greater than between-group inequality. Intragroup inequality accounts for over 90 percent of total inequality. In their survey of the literature on U.S. earnings levels and inequality, Levy and Murnane (1992) encourage researchers to explore this aspect of inequality.[13] As shown in Table 11.1, intragroup inequality would decline with comparable worth, but by much less than intergroup inequality in percentage terms. Consistent with a decline in the male–female wage gap under a comparable worth policy, inequality between women and men naturally declines for each of the measures used. Yet the magnitude of the relative change is striking. Intergroup inequality declined by 62.1 percent for VLN, by 54.3 percent for Theil, and by 50.0 percent and 84.5 percent for Atkinson (when ε = 1.5 and 2.0, respectively).

However, it is not possible to discern the differential effects of comparable worth on women and men from the decomposition analysis. Intragroup declines capture the combined effect of reductions in inequality among men and among women. We therefore calculated each index for men and women separately and report the results in Table 11.2. For women, each index declined markedly in absolute and relative terms. The percentage decreases in inequality ranged from 5.9 percent for the CV to 16.7 percent for the Atkinson (when $\varepsilon = 1.5$). With the exception of the Gini, indexes for men declined, but by a more modest amount. The average decrease was 2 percent, as measured by CV, Theil, Atkinson, and VLN. Changes in the CV and VLN are significant at the 10 percent level for women; none of the index declines for men are statistically significant.[14] It is unlikely that the increase in the third decimal place of the Gini for men is significant (see Karoly 1992).

The indexes that exhibit the largest percentage decreases for women and men are those that best capture changes in the lower tail of the earnings distribution. In fact, the share of hourly earnings received by each of the first four deciles increases under comparable worth. This indicates that comparable worth potentially reduces earnings inequality by increasing the income of the lowest-wage workers. This is consistent with our earlier findings that comparable worth wage adjustments could reduce the percentage of women and men earning poverty-level wages (see Lapidus and Figart 1994). The estimated decline in the value of the Gini coefficient among women indicates that comparable worth could also affect the proportion of women in the middle earnings quintiles. Wagman and Folbre (1988) note that, for women, the relative share of middle-wage jobs declined between 1970 and 1986. Since the Gini is most sensitive to changes in the middle of the earnings distribution, the nonintersecting Lorenz curves in Figure 11.4 suggest that a comparable worth policy has the potential to reverse this decline.

Let us put the changes in these indexes into some context. Although the magnitude of the changes varies according to the different measures, they are not moderate. In longitudinal studies, large and pivotal shifts in U.S. income distribution in the past three decades, including an increase in earnings inequality called "The Great U-Turn," have been noted when the inequality indexes change 5 percent to 10 percent, or movement occurs in the second decimal place. The overall changes in wage dispersion we estimated are within this range. The reduction in inequality among women noted in Table 11.2 exceeds this range for the Theil and Atkinson indexes. Further, in longitudinal and economic development research, an immense shift in income distribution is needed to alter the Lorenz curve. It appears that comparable worth would have this profound effect.

Table 11.2

Disaggregated Measures of Inequality

	CV	VLN	Gini	Theil	Atkinson (ε = 1.5)	Atkinson (ε = 2.0)
Women (n = 7,280)						
HRSPAY =	.607 (.012)	.309 (.009)	.300	.154 (.012)	.210 (.044)	.311 (.030)
NEWPAY =	.571[a] (.011)	.280[a] (.009)	.280	.134 (.024)	.175 (.010)	.283 (.034)
Δ =	−.036	−.029	−.020	−.020	−.035	−.028
% Δ =	−5.9%	−9.4%	−6.7%	−13.0%	−16.7%	−9.0%
Men (n = 7,538)						
HRSPAY =	.625 (.012)	.364 (.010)	.323	.168 (.010)	.239 (.006)	.354 (.029)
NEWPAY =	.615 (.012)	.354 (.010)	.326	.164 (.010)	.233 (.009)	.349 (.029)
Δ =	−.010	−.010	+.003	−.004	−.006	−.005
% Δ =	−1.6%	−2.7%	+0.9%	−2.4%	−2.6%	−1.4%

Note: Jackknife standard errors in parentheses.
[a]Indicates the change from HRSPAY to NEWPAY is significant at the .10 level (one-tailed t-tests).

Figure 11.4 **Lorenz Curves for Women**

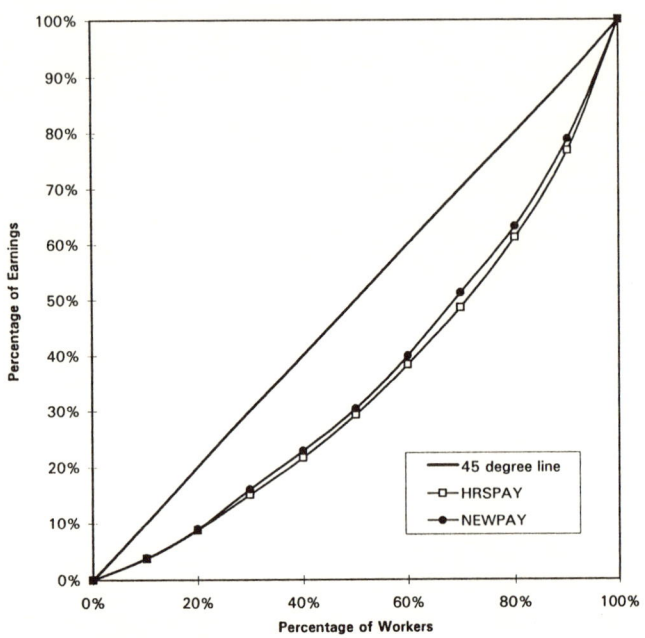

[Chart showing Lorenz curves with Percentage of Earnings on y-axis (0%–100%) and Percentage of Workers on x-axis (0%–100%). Three curves: 45 degree line, HRSPAY, and NEWPAY.]

Conclusions and Extensions

Under the comparable worth scenario presented here, eliminating the wage penalty associated with employment in occupations that are at least 70 percent female increases women's mean and median earnings and the gender-based wage ratio. Beyond this, an economywide comparable worth policy would decrease overall earnings inequality, inequality between women and men, and inequality among women. For three of four indexes for which jackknife standard errors are calculable, the overall decline in inequality is statistically significant. In the case of the Gini coefficient, examination of the Lorenz curves indicates a clear improvement under comparable worth. In comparison with previously reported research, the declines in all of the inequality indexes are notable.

Comparable worth is sensitive to class as well as gender inequality, addressing intragroup as well as intergroup inequality. By focusing on inequality within gender groups, this analysis disputes the contention that comparable worth primarily benefits middle-class women. In fact, a comparison of indexes indicates that reductions in inequality are concentrated in the lowest tails of the earnings distribution, raising wages of workers at the bottom of the ladder. Our findings therefore indicate that a commitment to pay equity could serve to offset longitudinal trends of rising inequality brought about by industrial and occupational restructuring in the U.S. economy. Female-dominated occupations targeted by pay equity—in administrative support, sales, and service—are typical of the expanding, low-wage sectors frequently imputed to skew the earnings distribution downward. Comparable worth can be conceptualized as a means for minimizing the disappearing middle in a feminizing labor force. It is a "low pay campaign" in addition to an equity policy for the labor market.

One major problem remains, however. As originally conceived, pay equity sought to eliminate both race- and gender-based wage discrimination. In an overwhelming majority of actual cases of comparable worth implementation across the United States, Canada, and Great Britain, the analysis of the racial composition of jobs has been omitted. Out of more than thirty U.S. states that have implemented comparable worth by a variety of means, only three (New York, New Jersey, Wisconsin) have included an examination of the racial composition of pay. The comparable worth pilot study for the federal government's workforce also examined possible wage discrimination by race. Of 100 U.S. counties, including the counties mandated by Minnesota legislation to enact comparable worth, the few that have included an analysis of race-based wage discrimination are Contra Costa County (CA), Montgomery County (MD), Suffolk County (NY), and King County (WA). Further, there are proportionately more employees who work in minority-concentrated jobs in U.S. cities, yet only Philadelphia and Washington, D.C., have investigated possible race bias. Finally, in several Canadian provinces (Ontario and Manitoba, for example), all private and public employers over a certain size must implement pay equity by gender, but not by race (see National Committee for Pay Equity [hereafter NCPE] 1989; McDermott 1991).

This exclusion of race inquiry needs to be remedied in order to expand the base of the pay equity movement. We are currently undertaking an analysis of hypothetical pay equity implementation by race as well as gender and would like to propose some guidelines for investigating earnings inequality due to occupational segmentation by race. First, researchers and activists must be sensitive to the fact that earnings experiences of racial and ethnic groups differ. For example, African Americans or Americans of Latin descent have lower earnings, on average, than Asian Americans. Therefore, the variable "nonwhite" (in contrast to "white") should not be used for an empirical examination of earnings of racial groups. Second, the widely used definition of 70 percent or higher for female-dominated jobs is inappropriate because African Americans are a substantially smaller percentage of the labor force. Since the threshold for female-dominated jobs is 1.4 times (or 40 percent higher than) the groups' participation in the general labor force, it seems appropriate to define African American–concentrated jobs as 14 percent or more black, or 1.4 times the group's participation in the labor force, a figure suggested by the National Committee for Pay Equity (see NCPE 1993 for a discussion). Imagine the possibilities for raising incomes of the working poor if a pay equity policy were implemented by race and gender. Stated more strongly, we cannot possibly hope to reverse "The Great U-Turn" by ignoring the role of race as well as gender in contemporary labor markets.

Notes

This chapter is adapted from Deborah M. Figart and June Lapidus, "The Impact of Comparable Worth on Earnings Equality," *Work and Occupations* 23, no. 3 (1996): 297–318, with permission from Sage Publications.

1. In this chapter, the terms *comparable worth* and *pay equity* are used interchangeably, although elsewhere one of the authors has argued that there is an analytical distinction between the two. As implemented, comparable worth has traditionally meant removing bias in job evaluation or classification systems and revaluing the wages in female-dominated jobs accordingly. Pay equity is a broader policy encompassing several alternative ways to reduce the gender-based wage gap, only one method of which is comparable worth (see Figart and Kahn 1997).

2. See Levy and Murnane (1992) for a review of the literature on increasing earnings inequality. The focus is on wages, rather than changes in the distribution of capital and labor's share of income.

3. However, growth of military spending and the expansion of male-dominated defense industries during the post–Vietnam War period, especially from 1980 to 1986, have also been found to increase income inequality, especially between gender and race groups (Abell 1994).

4. Our research is similar to Grubb and Wilson (1989), who calculate hypothetical changes in Theil measures of inequality under assumptions of change in, for example, the composition of the labor force, mean income ratios, or within-group inequality, ceteris paribus.

5. Tenure was omitted from the model because it is not included in the March CPS. Age and its square are proxies for experience. Marital status, presence of a younger child, and number of children are included in multiple regression analysis as proxies for supply-side variables that are not measured, such as time spent out of the labor force and other productivity-enhancing variables.

6. GED includes reasoning, mathematical, and language development, and measures the formal/informal education required to perform the job; scores range from 1 to 6. SVP is specific vocational training required to perform the job and ranges from 1 to 9. SVP includes training in school, at work, and in the military, institutional training, and training in the vocational environment. STRENGTH ranges from 1 to 5 for work ranging from sedentary to very heavy, and includes standing, walking, sitting, lifting, carrying, pushing, and pulling. ENVIRONMENT is a measure of working conditions indicating the absence or presence of environmental factors; it includes extreme heat and cold, wet or humid conditions, noise, hazards, and atmospheric conditions, and ranges from 1 to 6. PHYSICAL DEMANDS is a scale of 4 indicators gauging the absence or presence of physically demanding tasks; it includes climbing, stooping, reaching, and seeing.

7. With the *Current Population Survey,* the possible choices for number of employees of the firm (at all locations) was under 10, 10–24, and 25–99. The Ontario, Canada, legislation is less restrictive; it covers private sector employers with ten or more employees.

8. For discussion of the criteria or properties these indexes satisfy, such as independence of unit of measurement and the principle of transfers, see Slottje (1989), Jenkins (1991), Karoly (1992), and Levy and Murnane (1992).

9. Equations used to compute these inequality measures and their decomposition are available from the authors, or, alternatively: for the Gini, see Lerman and Yitzhaki (1984, 1989); for decomposing the VLN, see Karoly (1989); for decomposing the Theil, see Slottje (1989); for the Atkinson and its decomposition, see Conrad (1993).

10. A complete table of coefficients was originally reported in Figart and Lapidus (1996).

11. Because a large part of the variation in annual wage and salary income is due to variation in hours worked, our index measures based on hourly earnings are consistently lower than estimates presented in studies focusing on wage and salary income (see, for example, Blackburn 1990; Conrad 1993; Grubb and Wilson 1989; Karoly 1992). By focusing on hourly wages, our estimates are net of differences in hours worked. The effect of being employed part-time is reflected indirectly in the value of γ.

12. The jackknife standard error procedure is based on sequentially omitting each observation in a data set, and then calculating the desired statistic. In the case of inequality measures used, this would involve creating n–1 new estimates of each index and using those new estimates to in turn calculate the standard error (by summing the squared difference between the omitted value and the mean of the distribution without the omitted value and using a degrees of freedom correction). This can be quite costly and time consuming in the case of very large data sets. Karoly (1989) has shown that jackknife estimates can be calculated with only a few passes through the data.

13. In Levy and Murnane's (1992) review of recent literature, inequality between gender groups was stable in the 1970s and grew in the 1980s, while inequality within groups has grown steadily since 1970. In fact, the increase in inequality within groups defined by gender was greater and dominated the decline in inequality between men and women (see Grubb and Wilson 1989; Karoly 1992).

14. Though the magnitude of our estimated changes is quite large, it is difficult to show statistical significance. Overall, the decision to use hourly earnings as the dependent variable limited our sample to the outgoing rotation (one-quarter of the CPS). Second, when indexes are calculated separately for women and men, the sample size is further reduced, increasing our jackknife estimates of standard errors.

Bibliography

Abell, John D. 1994. "Military Spending and Income Inequality." *Journal of Peace Research* 31, 1: 35–43.
Abraham, Katherine, and Susan Houseman. 1994. "Does Employment Protection Inhibit Labor Market Flexibility? Lessons from Germany, France, and Belgium." In *Social Protection Versus Economic Flexibility,* ed. Rebecca Blank, 58–93. Chicago: University of Chicago Press.
Abramovitz, Mimi. 1988. *Regulating the Lives of Women: Social Welfare Policy from Colonial Times to the Present.* Boston: South End Press.
Acker, Joan. 1990. "Hierarchies, Jobs, Bodies: A Theory of Gendered Organizations." *Gender & Society* 4, 2: 139–58.
Adams, Donald R., Jr. 1982. "Industrialization: Evidence from the Brandywine Region." *Journal of Economic History* 42, 4: 903–15.
Aglietta, Michel. 1979. *A Theory of Capitalist Regulation: The U.S. Experience.* London: Verso.
Albelda, Randy. 1985. " 'Nice Work If You Can Get It': Segmentation of White and Black Women Workers in the Post-War Period," *Review of Radical Political Economics* 17, 3: 72–85.
———. 1986. "Occupational Segregation by Race and Gender: 1958–1981." *Industrial and Labor Relations Review* 39, 3: 404–11.
Albelda, Randy, Nancy Folbre, and the Center for Popular Economics. 1996. *The War on the Poor.* New York: The New Press.
Albelda, Randy, and Chris Tilly. 1994. "Towards a Broader Vision: Race, Gender, and Labor Market Segmentation in the Social Structure of Accumulation Framework." In *Social Structures of Accumulation: The Political Economy of Growth and Crisis,* ed. David M. Kotz, Terrence McDonough, and Michael Reich, 212–30. Cambridge: Cambridge University Press.
Aldrich, Mark, and Robert Buchele. 1986. *The Economics of Comparable Worth.* Boston: Ballinger.
Amariglio, Jack, Stephen Resnick, and Richard Wolff. 1990. "Division and Difference in the 'Discipline' of Economics." *Critical Inquiry* 17, 1 (autumn): 108–37.
Amott, Teresa, and Julie Matthaei. 1991. *Race, Gender and Work: A Multicultural Economic History of Women in the United States.* Boston: South End Press.
Andersen, Margaret. 1988. *Thinking About Women.* New York: Macmillan.
Andersen, Margaret L., and Patricia Hill Collins. 1992. *Race, Class, and Gender: An Anthology.* Belmont, CA: Wadsworth.

Anderson, Cynthia D., and Donald Tomaskovic-Devey. 1995. "Patriarchal Pressures: An Exploration of Organizational Processes that Exacerbate and Erode Gender Earnings Inequality." *Work and Occupations* 22, 3: 328–56.

Anderson, Robert M. 1993. "EP Seeks EP: A Review of *Sex and Reason* by Richard A. Posner." *Journal of Economic Literature* 31 (March): 191–98.

Appelbaum, Eileen. 1995. "New Work Systems in the New World Order." In *Beware the U.S. Model: Jobs and Wages in a Deregulated Economy*, ed. Lawrence Mishel and John Schmitt, 37–66. Washington, DC: Economic Policy Institute.

Aries, Philippe. 1962. *Centuries of Childhood*. London: Cape.

Armstrong, Nancy. 1987. *Desire and Domestic Fiction*. Oxford: Oxford University Press.

Armstrong, Pat. 1996. "The Feminization of the Labour Force: Harmonizing Down in a Global Economy." In *Rethinking Restructuring: Gender and Change in Canada*, ed. Isabella Bakker, 29–54. Toronto: University of Toronto Press.

Atack, Jeremy, and Peter Passell. 1994. *A New Economic View of American History*. 2nd ed. New York, London: W. W. Norton.

Atkinson, Anthony B. 1970. "On the Measurement of Inequality." *Journal of Economic Theory* 2, 3: 244–63.

Austen, Jane. 1814. *Mansfield Park*. In *The Complete Novels of Jane Austen*. Vol. 1. New York: Vintage Books, 1976.

Badgett, M.V. Lee. 1994a. "Civil Rights and Civilized Research." Presented at the 1994 Association for Public Policy Analysis and Management Research Conference.

———. 1994b. "Equal Pay for Equal Families." *Academe* 80, 3 (May/June): 26–30.

———. 1994c. "Lesbian and Gay Campus Organizing for Domestic Partner Benefits." Proceedings of the 22nd Annual Conference of the National Center for the Study of Collective Bargaining in Higher Education and the Professions. Baruch College, City University of New York.

———. 1995. "The Wage Effects of Sexual Orientation Discrimination." *Industrial and Labor Relations Review* 48, 4 (July): 726–39.

Badgett, M.V. Lee, and Rhonda M. Williams. 1992. "The Economics of Sexual Orientation: Establishing a Research Agenda." *Feminist Studies* 18, 3 (fall): 649–57.

———. 1994. "The Changing Contours of Discrimination: Race, Gender, and Structural Economic Change." In *Understanding American Economic Decline*, ed. Michael A. Bernstein and David E. Adler, 313–29. Cambridge: Cambridge University Press.

Bakker, Isabella. 1991. "Pay Equity and Economic Restructuring: The Polarization of Policy?" In *Just Wages: A Feminist Assessment of Pay Equity*, ed. Judy Fudge and Patricia McDermott, 254–80. Toronto: University of Toronto Press.

———. 1996. "Introduction: The Gendered Foundations of Restructuring in Canada." In *Rethinking Restructuring: Gender and Change in Canada*, ed. Isabella Bakker, 3–25. Toronto: University of Toronto Press.

———, ed. 1994. *The Strategic Silence: Gender and Economic Policy*. London: Zed Books.

Balibar, E., and I. Wallerstein. 1991. *Race, Nation, Class*. London: Verso.

Baran, P., and P. Sweezy. 1966. *Monopoly Capital: An Essay on the American Economic and Social Order*. New York: Monthly Review Press.

Barker, Diana Leonard. 1978. "The Regulation of Marriage: Repressive Benevolence." In *Power and the State*, ed. Gary Littlejohn et al., 239–66. London: Croom Helm for the British Sociological Association.

Baron, James N. 1991. "Organizational Evidence of Ascription in Labor Markets." In *New Approaches to Economic and Social Analyses of Discrimination*, ed. Richard A. Cornwall and Phanindra V. Wunnava, 113–43. New York: Praeger.

Barrett, Michèle. 1988. *Women's Oppression Today: The Marxist/Feminist Encounter.* London: Verso.
———. 1991. *The Politics of Truth.* Stanford, CA: Stanford University Press.
Barrett, Michèle, and Anne Phillips, eds. 1992. *Destabilizing Theory.* Stanford, CA: Stanford University Press.
Baty, S. Paige. 1995. *American Monroe.* Berkeley: University of California Press.
Becker, Gary S. 1991. *A Treatise on the Family.* Cambridge, MA: Harvard University Press.
Beechey, Veronica. 1988. "Rethinking the Definition of Work: Gender and Work." In *Feminization of the Labor Force: Paradoxes and Promises,* ed. Jane Jenson, Elisabeth Hagen, and Ceallaigh Reddy, 45–62. New York: Oxford University Press.
Bendroth, Margaret Lamberts. 1993. *Fundamentalism and Gender, 1875 to the Present.* New Haven, CT: Yale University Press.
Benenson, Harold. 1984. "Victorian Sexual Ideology and Marx's Theory of the Working Class." *International Labor and Working Class History* 25 (spring): 1–23.
Benería, Lourdes, and Martha Roldán. 1987. *The Crossroads of Class and Gender.* Chicago: University of Chicago Press.
Benería, Lourdes, and Catharine R. Stimpson, eds. 1987. *Women, Households, and the Economy.* New Brunswick, NJ: Rutgers University Press.
Benston, Margaret. 1969. "The Political Economy of Women's Liberation." *Monthly Review* 21, 4: 13–27.
Berger, Brigitte. 1984. "Comparable Worth at Odds with American Realities." In *Comparable Worth: Issue for the 80's,* ed. U.S. Commission on Civil Rights, 65–71. Washington, DC.
Bergmann, Barbara R. 1986. *The Economic Emergence of Women.* New York: Basic Books.
———. 1989a. "What the Common Economic Arguments Against Comparable Worth Are Worth." *Journal of Social Issues* 45 (fall): 67–80.
———. 1989b. "Does the Market for Women's Labor Need Fixing?" *Journal of Economic Perspectives,* 1: 43–60.
Bernstein, Michael A. 1994. "Understanding American Economic Decline: The Contours of the Late-Twentieth-Century Experience." In *Understanding American Economic Decline,* ed. Michael A. Bernstein and David E. Adler, 1–33. Cambridge: Cambridge University Press.
Bernstein, Michael A., and David E. Adler, eds. 1994. *Understanding American Economic Decline.* Cambridge: Cambridge University Press.
Blackburn, McKinley L. 1990. "What Can Explain the Increase in Earnings Inequality Among Males?" *Industrial Relations* 29, 3: 441–56.
Blank, Rebecca. 1994. "Does a Larger Social Safety Net Mean Less Economic Flexibility?" In *Working Under Different Rules,* ed. Richard Freeman. New York: Russell Sage Foundation.
Blau, Francine D., and Andrea H. Beller. 1988. "Trends in Earnings Differentials by Gender, 1971–1981." *Industrial and Labor Relations Review* 41, 4: 513–29.
Blau, Francine D., and Lawrence M. Kahn. 1992. "The Gender Earnings Gap: Learning from International Comparisons." *American Economic Review* 82, 2: 533–38.
———. 1994. "Rising Inequality and the U.S. Gender Gap," *American Economic Review* 84, 2: 23–33.
Blewett, Mary H. 1988. *Men, Women, and Work: Class, Gender, and Protest in the New England Shoe Industry, 1780–1890.* Urbana and Chicago: University of Illinois Press.
Block, Fred. 1990. *Postindustrial Possibilities: A Critique of Economic Discourse.* Berkeley: University of California Press.

Blumstein, Philip, and Pepper Schwartz. 1983. *American Couples: Money, Work, Sex.* New York: William Morrow.

Bordo, Susan. 1987. *The Flight to Objectivity.* Albany: State University of New York Press.

———. 1993. *Unbearable Weight: Feminism, Western Culture, and the Body.* Berkeley: University of California Press.

Boris, Eileen. 1994. *Home to Work: Motherhood and the Politics of Industrial Homework in the United States.* Cambridge: Cambridge University Press.

Bose, Christine. 1987. "Devaluing Women's Work: The Undercount of Women's Employment in 1900 and 1980." In *Hidden Aspects of Women's Work,* ed. Christine Bose, Roslyn Feldberg, and Natalie J. Sokoloff, 95–115. New York: Praeger.

Boston City Council. 1834–1839. Boston, Massachusetts: City Council, Records of the City of Boston. Boston Public Library, Microfilm JS13.B6, Reels 1, 2, 3.

Boston, Thomas. 1988. *Race, Class, and Conservatism.* Boston: Unwin Hyman.

Botwinick, Howard. 1993. *Persistent Inequalities: Wage Disparity Under Capitalist Competition.* Princeton, NJ: Princeton University Press.

Bowles, Samuel, and Herbert Gintis. 1986. *Democracy and Capitalism.* New York: Basic Books.

Bowles, Samuel, David M. Gordon, and Thomas E. Weisskopf. 1989. "Business Ascendancy and Economic Impasse: A Structural Retrospective on Conservative Economics." *Journal of Economic Perspectives* 3 (winter): 107–34.

Brantlinger, Patrick. 1977. *The Spirit of Reform.* Cambridge, MA: Harvard University Press.

Braverman, Harry. 1974. *Labor and Monopoly Capital.* New York: Monthly Review.

Brennan, T. 1977. "Women and Work." *Journal of Australian Political Economy* 11, 1: 8–30.

———. 1996. "Economy for the Earth." *Journal of Ecological Economics,* p. 442.

Brenner, Johanna. 1987. "Feminist Political Discourses: Radical Versus Liberal Approaches to the Feminization of Poverty and Comparable Worth." *Gender & Society* 1, 4: 447–65.

Brenner, Johanna, and Maria Ramas. 1984. "Rethinking Women's Oppression," *New Left Review,* no. 144 (March/April): 33–40, 68–71.

Bridges, William P., and Robert L. Nelson. 1989. "Markets in Hierarchies: Organizational and Market Influences on Gender Inequality in a State Pay System." *American Journal of Sociology* 95, 3: 616–58.

Briggs, Rex. 1994. Data from *Yankelovich Monitor,* telephone interview.

Brodie, Janine. 1996. "Restructuring and the New Citizenship." In *Rethinking Restructuring: Gender and Change in Canada,* ed. Isabella Bakker, 126–40. Toronto: University of Toronto Press.

Brodsky, Melvin. 1994. "Labor Market Flexibility: A Changing International Perspective." *Monthly Labor Review,* 117 (November): 53–60.

Brody, Michael. 1984. "New Era in Pay Scales? The Push for 'Comparable Worth' Could Destroy the Job Market." In *Equal Pay for UNequal Work,* ed. Phyllis Schlafly, 257–61. Washington, DC: Eagle Forum Education & Legal Defense Fund.

Brown, Dee. 1970. *Bury My Heart at Wounded Knee.* New York: Holt, Rinehart & Winston.

Brown, Doug. 1991. "An Institutionalist Look at Postmodernism." *Journal of Economic Issues* 25 (December): 1089–104.

Bruegel, Irene. 1979. "Women as a Reserve Army of Labour: A Note on the Recent British Experience." *Feminist Review* 3: 12–23.

Bruegel, Irene, and Diane Perrons. 1995. "Where Do the Costs of Unequal Treatment for Women Fall? An Analysis of the Incidence of the Costs of Unequal Pay and Sex Discrimination in the UK." *Gender, Work and Organization* 2 (July): 110–21.

Bryson, Valerie. 1992. *Feminist Political Theory: An Introduction.* New York: Paragon House.

Bundesministerium fuer Arbeit und Sozialordnung. 1962, 1965, 1975, 1980, 1991. *Arbeits- und Sozialstatistik: Hauptergebnisse.* Bonn.

Burawoy, Michael. 1979. *Manufacturing Consent.* Chicago: University of Chicago Press.

Bureau of Labor Statistics. 1994. *Comparative Labor Force Statistics, 10 Countries, 1959–93.* Washington, DC: Bureau of Labor Statistics.

Burk, Martha, and Heidi Hartmann. 1996. "Beyond the Gender Gap." *The Nation* 262 (June 10): 18–21.

Burke, Phyllis. 1993. *Family Values: Two Moms and Their Son.* New York: Random House.

Burris, Val. 1982. "The Dialectic of Women's Oppression: Notes on the Relation Between Capitalism and Patriarchy." *Berkeley Journal of Sociology* 27: 51–73.

Burtless, Gary. 1990. "Earnings Inequality over the Business and Demographic Cycles." In *A Future of Lousy Jobs,* ed. Gary Burtless, 77–122. Washington, DC: The Brookings Institution.

Buswell, Carol, and Sarah Jenkins. 1994. "Equal Opportunities Policies, Employment, and Patriarchy." *Gender, Work and Organization* 1, 2: 83–93.

Çağatay, Nilüfer, and Sule Özler. 1995. "Feminization of the Labor Force: The Effects of Long-Term Development and Structural Adjustment." *World Development* 23 (November): 1883–94.

Cameron, Barbara. 1996. "From Equal Opportunity to Symbolic Equity: Three Decades of Federal Training Policy for Women." In *Rethinking Restructuring: Gender and Change in Canada,* ed. Isabella Bakker, 55–81. Toronto: University of Toronto Press.

Carey, H.C. (Henry). 1835. *Essay on the Rate of Wages: With an Examination of the Causes of the Differences in the Condition of the Labouring Population Throughout the World.* Philadelphia: Carey, Lea & Blanchard; London: Longman, Rees, Orme, Green & Longman. Kress Collection. Baker Library at Harvard.

Carey, Henry C. [1847] 1967. *The Past, the Present, and the Future.* New York: Augustus M. Kelley.

Carey, Mathew. [1819–1828] 1970. *The American Journalist Autobiographical Sketches: Mathew Carey.* New York: Gregg Press.

———. 1830. *Essays on the Public Charities of Philadelphia, Intended to Vindicate the Benevolent Societies of this City from the Charge of Encouraging Idleness.* Philadelphia: Carey and Hart. Kress Collection. Baker Library at Harvard.

———. 1833. "Appeal to the Wealthy of the Land, Ladies as Well as Gentlemen, on the Character, Conduct, Situation, and Prospects of Those Whose Sole Dependence for Subsistence Is on the Labour of Their Hands." 2d ed. Philadelphia: L. Johnson, No. 6 George Street. Kress Collection. Baker Library at Harvard.

Carney, Larry, and Charlotte O'Kelly. 1990. "Women's Work and Women's Place in the Japanese Economic Miracle." In *Women Workers and Global Restructuring,* ed. Kathryn Ward. Ithaca, NY: ILR Press.

Cherry, Robert. 1991. "Race and Gender Aspects of Marxian Macromodels: The Case of the Social Structure of Accumulation School, 1948–68." *Science and Society* 55 (spring): 60–78.

Clark, Anna. 1995. *The Struggle for the Breeches: Gender and the Making of the British Working Class.* Berkeley: University of California Press.

Clarke, A. [1919] 1982. *Working Life of Women in the Seventeenth Century.* London: Routledge and Kegan Paul.
Cobble, Dorothy Sue. 1991. *Dishing It Out: Waitresses and Their Unions in the Twentieth Century.* Urbana and Chicago: University of Illinois Press.
Cockburn, Cynthia. 1991. *In the Way of Women: Men's Resistance to Sex Equality in Organizations.* Ithaca, NY: ILR Press.
Cohen, Marjorie Griffin. 1994. "The Implications of Economic Restructuring for Women: The Canadian Situation." In *The Strategic Silence: Gender and Economic Policy,* ed. Isabella Bakker, 103–16. London: Zed Books.
Cole, Arthur Harrison, and William Buckingham Smith. 1935. *Fluctuations in American Business 1790–1860.* New York: Russell & Russell.
Colley, Linda. 1992. *Britons: Forging the Nation 1707–1837.* New Haven, CT: Yale University Press.
Collier, Jane, Michelle Z. Rosaldo, and Sylvia Yanagisako. 1992. "Is There a Family? New Anthropological Views." In *Rethinking the Family: Some Feminist Questions,* revised ed., ed. Barrie Thorne with Marilyn Yalom. Boston: Northeastern University Press.
Colquhoun, Patrick. 1796. *A Treatise on the Police of the Metropolis.* London: H. Fry for C. Dilly.
Conrad, Cecilia A. 1993. "A Different Approach to the Measurement of Income Inequality." *Review of Black Political Economy* 22, 1: 19–31.
Corrigan, Philip. 1980. *Capitalism, State Formation and Marxist Theory.* London: Quartet Books.
Cott, Nancy, ed. 1972. *Roots of Bitterness.* New York: E.P. Dutton.
———. 1977. *Bonds of Womanhood: "Woman's Sphere" in New England, 1780–1835.* New Haven, CT: Yale University Press.
Cotton, Jeremiah. 1988. "Discrimination and Favoritism in the U.S. Labor Market: The Cost to a Wage Earner of Being Female and Black and the Benefit of Being Male and White." *American Journal of Economics and Sociology* 47, 1: 15–28.
Cowan, Ruth Schwartz. 1983. *More Work for Mother.* New York: Basic Books.
Cox, R. 1987. *Power, Production and World Order.* New York: St. Martin's Press.
Coxe, Tench. [1812] 1990. *Census of 1810.* Vol. 4. New York: Norman Ross.
Crow, Duncan. 1971. *The Victorian Woman.* London: George Allen & Unwin.
Curtin, Michael. 1987. *Propriety and Position: A Study of Victorian Manners.* New York: Garland Press.
Cushman, John H., Jr., 1995. "Dole Rivals Say Welfare Plan Is Weak on Curbs." *New York Times,* August 7, A1, B6.
Dalla Costa, M. 1973. *The Power of Women and the Subversion of the Community.* Bristol: Falling Wall.
Davidoff, Leonore. 1995. *Worlds Between: Historical Perspectives on Gender and Class.* New York: Routledge.
Davidoff, Leonore, and Catherine Hall. 1987. *Family Fortunes: Men and Women of the English Middle Class, 1780–1850.* Chicago: University of Chicago Press.
Davis, Ann. 1995. "Household Transformations: Value Categories, Historical Change, and Critique," Paper presented at the Allied Social Science Associations, Washington, DC, January.
Delphy, C. 1977. *The Main Enemy.* London: Women's Research and Resources Center.
de Marchi, Neil, ed. 1988. *The Popperian Legacy in Economics.* Cambridge: Cambridge University Press.
Dentith, Simon. 1983. "Political Economy, Fiction and the Language of Practical Ideology in Nineteenth-Century England." *Social History* 8 (May): 183–99.

DeParle, Jason. 1996. "What Does the Religious Right Really Want? And What is Bob Dole Going to Do About It?" *New York Times Magazine,* July 14, 18–25, 32, 38, 42, 44.
Derrida, J. 1980. *La Carte Postale: Socrates a Freud et au dela.* Paris: Flammarion.
———. 1994. *Specters of Marx.* Tr. Peggy Kamuf. New York and London: Routledge.
Dill, Bonnie Thornton. 1983. "Race, Class and Gender: Prospects for an All-Inclusive Sisterhood." *Feminist Studies* 9 (spring): 131–50.
Di Stefano, Christine. 1991. "Masculine Marx." In *Feminist Interpretations and Political Theory,* ed. Mary Shanely and Carole Pateman, 146–63. University Park: Pennsylvania State University Press.
Douglas, Ann. 1977. *The Feminization of American Culture.* New York: Alfred A. Knopf.
Douglas, Susan J. 1994. *Where the Girls Are.* New York: Random House.
Dublin, Thomas. 1991. "Women, Work, and Protest in Early Lowell Mills: The Oppressing Hand of Avarice Would Enslave Us." In *Women and Power in American History: A Reader, Volume I to 1880,* ed. Kathryn Kish-Sklar and Thomas Dublin, 144–57. Englewood Cliffs, NJ: Prentice-Hall.
———. 1994. *Transforming Women's Work.* Ithaca, NY and London: Cornell University Press.
DuBois, Ellen. 1978. *Feminism and Suffrage.* Ithaca, NY: Cornell University Press.
Earle, Peter. 1989. *The Making of the English Middle Class.* London: Methuen.
Eatwell, John. 1995. "Disguised Unemployment: The G7 Experience." *UNCTAD Discussion Papers,* no. 106.
Edgeworth, Maria. 1800. *Castle Rackrent.* London: J. Johnson.
———. 1802. "The Cherry Orchard." In *Early Lessons* (1857). London: G. Routledge.
———. 1811. "Prudence and Economy." In *On Practical Education,* 3rd ed., ed. Maria Edgeworth and Richard Edgeworth, 380–409, London: J. Johnson.
Edwards, Linda. 1988. "Equal Employment Opportunity in Japan: A View from the West." *Industrial and Labor Relations Review,* 41 (January): 240–50.
Edwards, Richard. 1979. *Contested Terrain: The Transformation of the Workplace in the Twentieth Century.* New York: Basic Books.
Ehrenberg, Ronald, and Robert Smith. 1987. "Comparable Worth Wage Adjustments and Female Employment in the State and Local Sector." *Journal of Labor Economics* 5, 1: 43–62.
Ehrenreich, Barbara. 1983. *The Hearts of Men.* Garden City: NY: Anchor Press.
Eisenstein, Zillah. 1979. "Developing a Theory of Capitalist Patriarchy and Socialist Feminism." In *Capitalist Patriarchy and the Case for Socialist Feminism,* ed. Zillah R. Eisenstein, 5–40. New York: Monthly Review Press.
Elliot, B.J. 1991. "Demographic Trends in Domestic Life 1945–87." In David Clark, ed., *Domestic Life and Social Change,* 85–100. London: Routledge.
Engels, Frederick. 1942. *Origin of the Family, Private Property, and the State.* New York: International.
England, Paula. 1992. *Comparable Worth: Theories and Evidence.* New York: Aldine de Gruyter.
———. 1993. "The Separative Self: Androcentric Bias in Neoclassical Assumptions." In *Beyond Economic Man,* ed. Marianne A. Ferber and Julie A. Nelson, 37–53. Chicago: University of Chicago Press,.
Erickson, B.H., and T.A. Nosanchuk. 1992. *Understanding Data Analysis,* 2d ed. Toronto and Buffalo: University of Toronto Press.
Esping-Andersen, Gøsta. 1990. *The Three Worlds of Welfare Capitalism.* Princeton, NJ: Princeton University Press.

Ettelbrick, Paula. 1989. "Since When Is Marriage a Path to Liberation?" *OUTLOOK National Gay and Lesbian Quarterly* 6, 9 (fall): 14–17. (Reprinted in Rubenstein 1993 and Sherman 1992.)

Ewen, Stuart. 1976. *Captains of Consciousness.* New York: McGraw-Hill.

Faludi, Susan. 1991. *Backlash: The Undeclared War Against American Women.* New York: Crown.

Fanon, Frantz. 1967. *Black Skin, White Masks.* New York: Grove Press.

Farley, Harriet. 1850. "Operatives' Reply to Hon. Jere. Clemens, Being a Sketch of Factory Life and Factory Enterprise, and a Brief History of Manufacturing by Machinery." Lowell: S.J. Varney. Kress Collection. Baker Library at Harvard.

Faux, Jeff. 1995a. "Preface." In *Beware the U.S. Model: Jobs and Wages in a Deregulated Economy,* ed. Lawrence Mishel and John Schmitt, ix–xii. Washington, DC: Economic Policy Institute.

———. 1995b. "Social Democracy and the Global Marketplace." In *Beware the U.S. Model: Jobs and Wages in a Deregulated Economy,* ed. Lawrence Mishel and John Schmitt, 3–14. Washington, DC: Economic Policy Institute.

Ferber, Marianne A., and Julie A. Nelson, eds. 1993. "Introduction: The Social Construction of Economics and the Social Construction of Gender." In *Beyond Economic Man: Feminist Theory and Economics,* ed. Marianne A. Ferber and Julie A. Nelson, 1–22. Chicago: University of Chicago Press.

Ferdinand, Theodore. 1992. *Boston's Lower Criminal Courts, 1814–1850.* Newark: University of Delaware Press. London and Toronto: Associated University Presses.

Ferguson-Clement, Priscilla. 1992. "Nineteenth-Century Welfare Policy, Programs, and Poor Women: Philadelphia as a Case Study." *Feminist Studies* 18, 1: 35–58.

Figart, Deborah M., and Peggy Kahn. 1997. *Contesting the Market: Pay Equity and the Politics of Economic Restructuring.* Detroit: Wayne State University Press.

Figart, Deborah M., and June Lapidus. 1995. "A Gender Analysis of U.S. Labor Market Policies for the Working Poor." *Feminist Economics* 1, 3: 60–81.

———. 1996. "The Impact of Comparable Worth on Earnings Inequality." *Work and Occupations* 23, 3: 297–318.

Filer, Randall K. 1985. "Male-Female Wage Differences: The Importance of Compensating Differentials." *Industrial and Labor Relations Review* 38, 3: 426–37.

———. 1989. "Occupational Segregation, Compensating Differentials, and Comparable Worth." In *Pay Equity: Empirical Inquiries,* ed. Robert T. Michael, Heidi I. Hartmann, and Brigid O'Farrell, 153–70. Washington, DC: National Academy Press.

Fine, Ben. 1992. *Women's Employment and the Capitalist Family.* London: Routledge.

Fine, Ben, and E. Leopold. 1993. *The World of Consumption.* London: Routledge.

Flax, Jane. 1990. *Thinking Fragments: Psychoanalysis, Feminism, and Postmodernism in the Contemporary West.* Berkeley: University of California Press.

Folbre, Nancy. 1982. "Exploitation Comes Home: A Critique of the Marxian Theory of Family Labor." *Cambridge Journal of Economics* 6 (4): 317–29.

———. 1993, "Socialism, Feminist and Scientific." In *Beyond Economic Man,* ed. Marianne A. Ferber and Julie A. Nelson, 94–110. Chicago: University of Chicago Press, 1993.

———. *Who Pays for the Kids? Gender and the Structures of Constraint.* New York: Routledge.

Fontana, Biancamaria. 1985. *Rethinking the Politics of Commercial Society: the Edinburgh Review 1802–1832.* Cambridge: Cambridge University Press.

Fosu, Augustin Kwasi. 1988. "Trends in Relative Earnings Gains by Black Women: Implications for the Future." *Review of Black Political Economy* 17, 1: 31–45.
Foucault, Michel. 1990. *The History of Sexuality. Volume 1: An Introduction.* New York: Vintage Books.
Fox-Genovese, Elizabeth, and Eugene Genovese. 1983. *The Fruits of Merchant Capital,* New York: Oxford University Press.
Fraad, Harriet, Stephen Resnick, and Richard Wolff. 1994. *Bringing It All Back Home.* London: Pluto.
Fraser, Nancy, and Linda Gordon. 1994. "A Genealogy of *Dependency:* Tracing a Keyword of the U.S. Welfare State." *Signs: Journal of Women in Culture and Society* 19 (winter): 309–36.
Friedan, Betty. 1963. *Feminine Mystique.* New York: W.W. Norton.
Friedman-Goldstein, Leslie. 1989. *The Constitutional Rights of Women: Cases in Law and Social Change.* Madison: University of Wisconsin Press.
Fuchs, Victor. 1988. *Women's Quest for Economic Equality.* Cambridge, MA: Harvard University Press.
Fujita, Kuniko. 1987. "Gender, State, and Industrial Policy in Japan." *Women's Studies International Forum,* 10, 6: 589–97.
Galenson, David W. 1984. "The Rise and Fall of Indentured Servitude in the Americas: An Economic Analysis." *Journal of Economic History* 44, 1: 3–26.
Gardiner, Jean. 1975. "Women's Domestic Labor." *New Left Review* 89: 47–58.
Garrett, G., and P. Lange. 1991. "Political Responses to Interdependence: What's 'Left' for the Left?" *International Organization* 46, 4 (autumn): 539–64.
Garza, Melita Marie. 1996. "Wage Warriors." *Chicago Tribune,* May 9.
Geoghegan, Thomas. 1996. "The State of the Worker." *New York Times,* January 25.
Gerhart, Barry, and Nabil El Cheikh. 1991. "Earnings and Percentage Female: A Longitudinal Study." *Industrial Relations* 30, 1: 62–77.
Geschwender, James A., and Rita Carroll-Seguin. 1990. "Exploding the Myth of African-American Progress," *Signs* 15, 2: 285–99.
Gilbert, Nigel, Roger Burrows, and Anna Pollert. 1992. *Fordism and Flexibility: Divisions and Change.* New York: St. Martin's Press.
Gilfoyle, Timothy J. 1992. *City of Eros: New York City, Prostitution, and the Commercialization of Sex, 1790–1920.* New York: W.W. Norton.
Gillespie, Ed, and Bob Schellhas, eds. 1994. *Contract with America: The Bold Plan by Representative Newt Gingrich, Representative Dick Armey and the House Republicans to Change the Nation.* New York: Times Books.
Gilman, Charlotte Perkins. 1966. *Women and Economics.* New York: Harper & Row.
Gittleman, Maury B., and David R. Howell. 1995. "Changes in the Structure and Quality of Jobs in the United States: Effects by Race and Gender, 1973–1990." *Industrial and Labor Relations Review* 48, 3: 420–40.
Glenn, Evelyn Nakano. 1981. "Occupational Ghettoization: Japanese-American Women and Domestic Service, 1905–1970," *Ethnicity* 8: 352–86.
———. 1985. "Racial Ethnic Women's Labor: The Intersection of Race, Gender, and Class Oppression," *Review of Radical Political Economics,* 17, 3: 86–108.
———. 1987. "Gender and the Family." In *Analyzing Gender: A Handbook of Social Science Research,* ed. Beth B. Hess and Myra Marx Ferree, 348–80. Newbury Park, CA: Sage Publications.
———. 1992. "From Servitude to Service Work: Historical Continuities in the Racial Division of Paid Reproductive Labor." *Signs* 18, 1: 1–43.

Goffman, Irving. 1976. *Gender Advertisements.* Cambridge, MA: Harvard University Press.

Goldin, Claudia. 1986. "The Economic Status of Women in the Early Republic: Quantitative Evidence." *Journal of Interdisciplinary History* 16 (winter): 375–404.

———. 1990. *Understanding the Gender Gap: An Economic History of American Women.* New York: Oxford University Press.

Goldman, M., and J. O'Connor. 1988. "Ideologies of Environmental Crisis: Technology and Its Discontents." *Capitalism, Nature, Socialism* No. 1: 91–106.

Goldthorpe, J.H. 1964. "Social Stratification in Industrial Society: The Development of Industrial Society." *Sociological Review.* Monograph, No. 8, 97–122.

Gooding-Williams, Robert. 1987. "Black Neoconservatism: A Critical Introduction," *Praxis International* 7, 2: 133–42.

Gordon, David M. 1994a. "Chickens Come Home to Roost: From Prosperity to Stagnation in the Postwar U.S. Economy." In *Understanding American Economic Decline,* ed. Michael A. Bernstein and David E. Adler, 34–76. Cambridge: Cambridge University Press.

———. 1994b. "The Global Economy: New Edifice or Crumbling Foundations?" In *Social Structures of Accumulation: The Political Economy of Growth and Crisis,* ed. David M. Kotz, Terrence McDonough, and Michael Reich, 292–305. Cambridge: Cambridge University Press.

Gordon, David M., Richard Edwards, and Michael Reich. 1982. *Segmented Work, Divided Workers: The Historical Transformation of Labor in the United States.* Cambridge: Cambridge University Press.

Gordon, Linda. 1994. *Pitied But Not Entitled.* New York: The Free Press.

———. 1996, "What Comes After Patriarchy? Comparative Reflections on Gender and Power in a 'Post-Patriarchal Age'," Session 129, Tenth Berkshire Conference on Women's History, Chapel Hill, North Carolina, June.

Gordon, Robert. 1987. "Productivity, Wages, and Prices Inside and Outside of Manufacturing in the U.S., Japan, and Europe." *European Economic Review* 31 (April): 685–739.

Gossett, Charles. 1994. "Domestic Partnership Benefits: Public Sector Patterns," *Review of Public Personnel Administration* 14, 1: 64–84.

Gough, Ian. 1979. *The Political Economy of the Welfare State.* London: Macmillan Education.

Gourevitch, P.A. 1986. *Politics in Hard Times: Comparative Responses to International Economic Crises.* Ithaca, NY: Cornell University Press.

Gove, Philip. 1941. *The Imaginary Voyage in Prose Fiction.* New York: Columbia University Press.

Gramm, Wendy Lee. 1994. "The Economy, A Women's Issue." *Wall Street Journal,* March 22, A14.

Granovetter, M. 1985. "Economic Action, Social Structure, and Embeddedness." *American Journal of Sociology* 91, 3: 481–510.

Grappard, Ulla. 1995. "Robinson Crusoe: The Quintessential Economic Man?" *Feminist Economics* 1, 1: 33–52.

Greenwood, Daphne. 1984. "The Institutional Inadequacy of the Free Market in Determining Comparable Worth." *Journal of Economic Issues* 18 (June): 457–64.

Grub, Farley. 1985. "The Incidence of Servitude in Trans-Atlantic Migration, 1771–1804." *Explorations in Economic History* 22: 316–39.

Grubb, W. Norton, and Robert H. Wilson. 1989. "Sources of Increasing Inequality in Wages and Salaries, 1960–1980." *Monthly Labor Review* 112, 4: 3–13.

Gutman, Herbert G. 1989. *Who Built America? Volume One: From Conquest and Colo-*

nization Through Reconstruction and the Great Uprising of 1877. New York: Pantheon Books.

Gyimah-Brempong, Kwabena, and Rudy Fichtenbaum. 1993. "Black–White Wage Differential: The Relative Importance of Human Capital and Labor Market Structure." *Review of Black Political Economy* 21, 4: 19–52.

Hall, Catherine. 1979. "The Early Formation of Victorian Domestic Ideology." In *Fit Work for Women*, ed. Sandra Burman, 15–32. New York: St. Martin's Press.

———. 1992. *White, Male, and Middle Class*. Cambridge: Polity Press.

Hall, S., D. Held, and T. McGrew, eds. 1992. *Modernity and Its Futures*. Cambridge: Polity Press.

Hamada, Koichi, and Yoshio Kurosaka. 1984. "The Relationship Between Production and Unemployment in Japan: Okun's Law in Comparative Perspective." *European Economic Review* 25, 1: 71–94.

Harrison, Bennett, and Barry Bluestone. 1988. *The Great U-Turn: Corporate Restructuring and the Polarizing of America*. New York: Basic Books.

Harrison, J. 1973. "Political Economy of Housework." *Bulletin of the Conference of Socialist Economists* 3, 1.

Harrison, Rachel, and Frank Mort. 1980. "Patriarchal Aspects of Nineteenth-Century State Formation: Property Relations, Marriage and Divorce, and Sexuality." In *Capitalism, State Formation and Marxist Theory: Historical Investigations*, ed. Philip Richard Corrigan, 79–109 London: Quartet Books.

Harth, Erica. 1988. "The Virtue of Love: Lord Hardwicke's Marriage Act," *Cultural Critique* (spring): 123–54.

Hartmann, Heidi. 1976. "Capitalism, Patriarchy, and Job Segregation by Sex." *Signs: Journal of Women in Culture and Society* 1, 3.

———. 1979. "The Unhappy Marriage of Marxism and Feminism: Towards a More Progressive Union." *Capital and Class* 8: 1–33.

———. 1981. "The Unhappy Marriage of Marxism and Feminism: Towards a More Progressive Union." In *Women and Revolution*, ed. Lydia Sargent, 1–41. Boston: South End Press.

———. 1987. "Changes in Women's Economic and Family Roles in Post–World War II United States." In *Women, Households, and the Economy*, ed. Lourdes Benería and Catharine R. Stimpson, 33–64. New Brunswick, NJ: Rutgers University Press.

Hartmann, Heidi, and Stephanie Aaronson. 1994. "Pay Equity and Women's Wage Increases: Successes in the States, A Model for the Nation." *Duke Journal of Gender Law and Policy* 1: 69–87.

Hartmann, Heidi I., and Ann R. Markusen. 1980. "Contemporary Marxist Theory and Practice: A Feminist Critique." *Review of Radical Political Economics* 12, 2: 87–94.

Hartsock, Nancy. 1983. *Money, Sex, and Power: Toward a Feminist Historical Materialism*. New York: Longman.

Harvard Law Review Editors. 1991. *Sexual Orientation and the Law*. Cambridge, MA: Harvard University Press.

Harvey, David. 1989. *The Condition of Postmodernity: An Enquiry into the Origins of Cultural Change*. Oxford: Basil Blackwell.

———. 1991. "Flexibility: Threat or Opportunity." *Socialist Review* 21 (January/March): 65–77.

Hashimoto, Masanori. 1993. "Aspects of Labor Market Adjustments in Japan." *Journal of Labor Economics* 11 (January): 136–61.

Hayden, Dolores. 1981. *The Grand Domestic Revolution*. Cambridge, MA: MIT Press.

———. 1984. *Redesigning the American Dream*. New York: W.W. Norton.

Headley, Joel Tyler. 1970 [1873]. *The Great Riots of New York: 1712–1873.* New York: Bobbs-Merrill.

Herbert, Christopher. 1991. *Culture and Anomie: Ethnographic Imagination in the Nineteenth Century.* Chicago: University of Chicago Press.

Higginbotham, Elizabeth, and Lynn Weber. 1992. "Moving Up with Kin and Community: Upward Social Mobility for Black and White Women," *Gender and Society* 6, 3: 416–40.

Hildebrand, George. 1980. "The Market System." In *Comparable Worth: Issues and Alternatives,* ed. E. Robert Livernash, 81–106. Washington, DC: Equal Employment Advisory Council.

Hill, Marilyn Wood. 1989. *Prostitution in New York City, 1830–1870.* Ann Arbor, MI: University Microfilms International Press.

Hilton, Boyd. 1988. *The Age of Atonement.* New York: Oxford University Press.

Himmelweit, Susan, and Simon Mohun. 1977. "Domestic Labour and Capital." *Cambridge Journal of Economics* 1, 1: 15–31.

Hobsbawm, E.J. 1964. *Labouring Men: Studies in the History of Labour.* New York: Basic Books.

Holmes, Steven A. 1996. "Income Disparity Between Poorest and Richest Rises." *New York Times,* June 20, A1.

Homer, Steven. 1994. "Against Marriage." *Harvard Civil Rights–Civil Liberties Law Review* 29, 2: 505–30.

hooks, bell. 1981. *Ain't I a Woman: Black Women and Feminism.* Boston: South End Press.

Horrell, Sara, and Jane Humphries. 1995. "Women's Labour Force Participation and the Transition to the Male-Breadwinner Family, 1790–1865." *The Economic History Review* 48, 1 (February): 89–117.

Houseman, Susan, and Katharine Abraham. 1993. "Female Workers as a Buffer in the Japanese Economy." *AEA Papers and Proceedings* 83 (May): 45–51.

Howell, Chris. 1992. "The Dilemmas of Post-Fordism: Socialists, Flexibility, and Labor Market Deregulation in France." *Politics & Society* 20 (March): 71–99.

Humphries, Jane. 1977a. "Class Struggle and the Persistence of the Working Class Family." *Cambridge Journal of Economics* 1, 3: 241–58.

———. 1977b. "The Working Class Family, Women's Liberation, and Class Struggle: The Case of Nineteenth-Century British History," *Review of Radical Political Economics* 9, 3: 25–41.

———. 1983. "The Emancipation of Women in the 1970s and 1980s: From the Latent to the Floating." *Capital and Class* 20 (summer): 6–28.

Humphries, Jane, and Jill Rubery. 1984. "The Reconstitution of the Supply Side of the Labour Market: The Relative Autonomy of Social Reproduction." *Cambridge Journal of Economics* 8: 331–46.

———. 1988. "Recession and Exploitation: British Women in a Changing Workplace, 1979–1985." In *Feminization of the Labor Force: Paradoxes and Promises,* ed. Jane Jenson, Elisabeth Hagen, and Ceallaigh Reddy, 85–105. New York: Oxford University Press.

Hunt, Margaret. 1993. "The Commercial Gaze." *Journal of British Studies* 32, 4: 333–57.

Hymowitz, Carol, and Michaele Weissman. 1978. *A History of Women in America.* New York: Bantam Books.

Jackson, Kenneth T. 1985. *Crabgrass Frontier.* New York: Oxford University Press.

Jacobs, Jerry A., and Ronnie J. Steinberg. 1990. "Compensating Differentials and the

Male–Female Wage Gap: Evidence from the New York State Pay Equity Study. *Social Forces* 69, 2: 439–68.
———. 1994. "Further Evidence on Compensating Differentials." Unpublished manuscript.
Jacobson, Paul H. 1964. "Cohort Survival for Generations Since 1840." *The Milbank Memorial Fund Quarterly* 42, 3, Part 1: 36–53.
Janiewski, Dolores. 1991. "Southern Honor, Southern Dishonor: Managerial Ideology and the Construction of Gender, Race, and Class Relations in Southern Industry." In *Work Engendered: Toward a New History of American Labor,* ed. Ava Baron. Ithaca, NY: Cornell University Press.
Japan Ministry of Labor. 1952–1990. *Yearbook of Labour Statistics.* Tokyo.
Jenkins, Stephen. 1991. "The Measurement of Income Inequality." In *Economic Inequality and Poverty: International Perspectives,* ed. Lars Osberg, 3–38. Armonk, NY: M.E. Sharpe.
Jenson, Jane. 1996. "Part-Time Employment and Women: A Range of Strategies." In *Rethinking Restructuring: Gender and Change in Canada,* ed. Isabella Bakker, 92–108. Toronto: University of Toronto Press, 1996.
Jenson, Jane, Elisabeth Hagen, and Ceallaigh Reddy. 1988. *Feminization of the Labor Force: Paradoxes and Promises.* New York: Oxford University Press.
Jervis, Robert. 1991. "The Future of World Politics." *International Security* 16, 3: 39–73.
Jessop, Bob. 1994. "The Transition to Post-Fordism and the Schumpeterian Workfare State." In *Towards a Post-Fordist Welfare State?* ed. Roger Burrows and Brian Loader, 13–37. London: Routledge.
Johnson, George, and Gary Solon. 1986. "Estimates of the Direct Effects of Comparable Worth Legislation." *American Economic Review* 76, 4: 1117–25.
Jones, H.J. 1976–77. "Japanese Women and the Dual-Track Employment System." *Pacific Affairs,* 49 (winter): 589–606.
Joseph, Gloria. 1981. "The Incompatible Menage à Trois: Marxism, Feminism, and Racism." In *Women and Revolution: A Discussion of the Unhappy Marriage of Marxism and Feminism,* ed. Lydia Sargent, 91–107. Boston: South End Press.
Kahn, Shulamit. 1992. "Economic Implications of Public-Sector Comparable Worth: The Case of San Jose, California." *Industrial Relations* 31, 2: 270–91.
Karoly, Lynn. 1989. "Computing Standard Errors for Measures of Inequality Using the Jackknife." Department of Economics, RAND Corporation. Photocopy.
———. 1992. "Changes in the Distribution of Individual Earnings in the United States, 1967–1986." *Review of Economics and Statistics* 74, 1: 107–15.
———. 1996. "Anatomy of the U.S. Income Distribution: Two Decades of Change." *Oxford Review of Economic Policy* 12, 1: 76–95.
Katz, Lawrence, and Kevin Murphy. 1992. "Changes in Relative Wages, 1963–1987: Supply and Demand Factors." *Quarterly Journal of Economics* 107, 1: 34–78.
Katz, Michael B. 1986. *In the Shadow of the Poorhouse: A Social History of Welfare in America.* New York: Basic Books.
———. 1989. *The Undeserving Poor.* New York: Pantheon Books.
———. 1995. *Improving Poor People.* Princeton, NJ: Princeton University Press.
Kawashima, Yoko. 1987. "The Place and Role of Female Workers in the Japanese Labor Market." *Women's Studies International Forum* 10, 6: 599–611.
Kelso, Robert W. 1922, 1969. *The History of Public Poor Relief in Massachusetts, 1620–1920.* Montclair, NJ: Paterson Smith.

Kerber, Linda. 1980. *Women of the Republic.* Chapel Hill: University of North Carolina Press.
Kessler-Harris, Alice. 1981. *Women Have Always Worked.* New York: The Feminist Press.
———. 1982. *Out to Work: A History of Wage-Earning Women in the United States.* Oxford: Oxford University Press.
———. 1990. *A Woman's Wage: Historical Meanings and Social Consequences.* Lexington: University Press of Kentucky.
Kessler-Harris, Alice, and Karen Brodkin Sacks. 1987. "The Demise of Domesticity in America." In *Women, Households and the Economy,* ed. Lourdes Benería and Catharine R. Stimpson, 65–84. New Brunswick, NJ: Rutgers University Press.
Kilbourne, Barbara, Paula England, and Kurt Beron. 1994. "Effects of Individual, Occupational, and Industrial Characteristics on Earnings: Intersections of Race and Gender." *Social Forces* 72, 4: 1149–76.
Kilbourne, Barbara, George Farkas, Kurt Beron, Dorothea Weir, and Paula England. 1994. "Returns to Skill, Compensating Differentials, and Gender Bias: Effects of Occupational Characteristics on the Wages of White Women and Men." *American Journal of Sociology* 100, 3: 689–719.
Killingsworth, Mark R. 1985. "The Economics of Comparable Worth: Analytical, Empirical, and Policy Questions." In *Comparable Worth: New Directions for Research,* ed. Heidi I. Hartmann, 86–115. Washington, DC: National Academy Press.
———. 1987. "Heterogeneous Preferences, Compensating Wage Differentials, and Comparable Worth." *Quarterly Journal of Economics* 102, 3: 727–41.
King, Mary C. 1992. "Occupational Segregation by Race and Sex, 1940–88," *Monthly Labor Review.* 115, 4: 30–37.
Kirschenman, Joleen, and Kathryn M. Neckerman. 1991. "'We'd Love to Hire Them, But . . .': The Meaning of Race for Employers." In *The Urban Underclass,* ed. Christopher Jencks and Paul Peterson. Washington, DC: The Brookings Institute.
Kitching, Gavin. 1995. *Marxism and Science: Analysis of an Obsession,* University Park, PA: Pennsylvania State University Press.
Klamer, Arjo. 1988. "Economics as Discourse." In *The Popperian Legacy in Economics,* ed. Neil de Marchi. Cambridge: Cambridge University Press.
Kotz, David M. 1994a. "The Regulation Theory and the Social Structure of Accumulation Approach." In *Social Structures of Accumulation.* ed. Kotz, McDonough, and Reich, 85–97. Cambridge: Cambridge University Press.
———. 1994b. "Interpreting the Social Structure of Accumulation Theory." In *Social Structures of Accumulation,* ed. Kotz, McDonough, and Reich, 50–71. Cambridge: Cambridge University Press.
Kotz, David M., Terrence McDonough, and Michael Reich, eds. 1994. *Social Structures of Accumulation: The Political Economy of Growth and Crisis.* Cambridge: Cambridge University Press.
Koven, Seth, and Sonya Michel, eds. 1993. *Mothers of a New World.* London: Routledge.
Kowaleski-Wallace, Elizabeth. 1991. *Their Fathers' Daughters: Hannah More, Maria Edgeworth, and Patriarchal Complicity.* New York: Oxford University Press.
Krugman, Paul. 1990. *The Age of Diminished Expectations.* Cambridge, MA: MIT Press.
Kuhn, Sarah, and Barry Bluestone. 1987. "Economic Restructuring and the Female Labor Market: The Impact of Industrial Change on Women." In *Women, Households, and the Economy,* ed. Lourdes Benería and Catharine R. Stimpson, 3–32. New Brunswick, NJ: Rutgers University Press.

Kuiper, Edith, and Jolande Sap, eds. 1995. *Out of the Margin: Feminist Perspectives on Economics.* London: Routledge.
Kurdek, Lawrence A. 1993. "The Allocation of Household Labor in Gay, Lesbian, and Heterosexual Married Couples." *Journal of Social Issues* 49, 3: 127–39.
Kuttner, Robert. 1995. "A Decent Minimum Wage." *Washington Post,* January 29.
Kuznets, Simon. 1965. *Economic Growth and Structure.* New York: W.W. Norton.
Laibman, David. 1992. *Value, Technical Change, and Crisis.* Armonk, NY: M.E. Sharpe.
Lam, Alice. 1993. "Equal Employment Opportunities for Japanese Women: Changing Company Practice." In *Japanese Women Working,* ed. Janet Hunter. London: Routledge.
Lamphere, Louise. 1987. *From Working Daughters to Working Mothers: Immigrant Women in a New England Industrial Community.* Ithaca, NY: Cornell University Press.
Langland, Elizabeth. 1992. "Nobody's Angels: Domestic Ideology and Middle-Class Women in the Victorian Novel." *PMLA* 107 (March): 290–304.
———. *Domestic Angels.* Ithaca, NY: Cornell University Press.
Lapidus, June, and Deborah M. Figart. 1994. "Comparable Worth as an Anti-Poverty Strategy: Evidence from the March 1992 CPS." *Review of Radical Political Economics* 26, 3: 1–10.
Larson, Kathryn. 1992. "The Economics of Lesbian Households." In Third Women's Policy Research Conference Proceedings. Institute for Women's Policy Research, Washington, DC.
Lasch, Christopher. 1977. *Haven in a Heartless World.* New York: Basic Books.
Layer, Robert G. 1955. *Earnings of Cotton Mill Operatives, 1825–1914.* Cambridge, MA: Harvard University Press.
Lazonick, William. 1990. *Competitive Advantage on the Shop Floor.* Cambridge, MA: Harvard University Press.
Lebergott, Stanley. 1964. *Manpower in Economic Growth: The American Record Since 1800.* New York: McGraw-Hill.
Lee, Everett S., and Michael Lalli. 1967. "Population." In *The Growth of Seaport Cities 1790–1825,* ed. David T. Gilchrist, 25–31. Charlottesville: University Press of Virginia.
Lemann, Nicholas. 1992. *The Promised Land: The Great Black Migration and How It Changed America.* New York: Vintage Books.
———. 1996. "Reed in the Wind." *The New Republic,* July 8, 32–36.
Lemons, J. Stanley. 1973. *The Woman Citizen: Social Feminism in the 1920's.* Chicago: University of Illinois Press.
Lerman, Robert I., and Shlomo Yitzhaki. 1984. "A Note on the Calculation and Interpretation of the Gini Index." *Economics Letters* 15, 3–4: 363–68.
———. 1989. "Improving the Accuracy of Estimates of Gini Coefficients." *Journal of Econometrics* 42, 1: 43–47.
Lerner, Gerda. 1986. *The Creation of Patriarchy.* New York: Oxford University Press.
Levi-Strauss, Claude. 1969. *The Elementary Structures of Kinship.* Boston: Beacon Hill Press.
Levin, Michael. 1984. "The Earnings Gap and Family Choices." In *Equal Pay for UNequal Work,* ed. Phyllis Schlafly, 125–39. Washington, DC: Eagle Forum Education & Legal Defense Fund.
Levy, Frank, and Richard J. Murnane. 1992. "U.S. Earnings Levels and Earnings Inequality: A Review of Recent Trends and Proposed Explanations." *Journal of Economic Literature* 30, 3: 1333–81.

Lewis, H. Gregg. 1986. *Union Relative Wage Effects: A Survey.* Chicago: University of Chicago Press.
Lewis, Jane. 1984. *Women in England, 1870–1950: Sexual Divisions and Social Change.* Bloomington: Indiana University Press.
Lind, Michael. 1996. *Up From Conservatism.* New York: Simon and Schuster.
Littlejohn, Gary. Barry Smart, John Wakeford, and Nira Yuval-Davis. 1978. *Power and the State.* London: Croom Helm for the British Sociological Association.
Loader, Brian, and Roger Burrows. 1994. "Towards a Post-Fordist Welfare State? The Restructuring of Britain, Social Policy, and the Future of Welfare." In *Towards a Post-Fordist Welfare State?* ed. Roger Burrows and Brian Loader, 1–10. London: Routledge.
Lorber, Judith. 1994. *Paradoxes of Gender.* New Haven, CT: Yale University Press.
Luker, Kristen. 1984. *Abortion and the Politics of Motherhood.* Berkeley: University of California Press.
———. 1996. *Dubious Conceptions: The Politics of Teen Pregnancy.* Cambridge, MA: Harvard University Press.
Lund, Caroline. 1994. "Union Beats the 10–Hour Day at NUMMI." *Labor Notes* (September): 7.
McCann, Michael W. 1994. *Rights at Work: Pay Equity Reform and the Politics of Legal Mobilization.* Chicago: University of Chicago Press.
McCloskey, D.N. 1985. *The Rhetoric of Economics.* Madison: University of Wisconsin Press.
McCrate, Elaine. 1990. "Labor Market Segmentation and Relative Black/White Teenage Birth Rates." *Review of Black Political Economy* 18, 3: 37–53.
McDermott, Patricia. 1991. "Pay Equity in Canada: Assessing the Commitment to Reducing the Wage Gap." In *Just Wages: A Feminist Assessment of Pay Equity,* ed. Judy Fudge and Patricia McDermott, 21–32. Toronto: University of Toronto Press.
McDowell, Linda. 1991. "Life Without Father and Ford: The New Gender Order of Post-Fordism." *Transactions of the British Institute of Geographers* 16: 400–419.
MacKinnon, Catherine. 1989. *Toward a Feminist Theory of the State.* Cambridge, MA: Harvard University Press.
McLane, Louis. [1833] 1969. *Documents Relative to the Manufactures in the United States, Collected and Transmitted to the House of Representatives, In compliance with a resolution of January 19, 1832, by the Secretary of the Treasury, In Two Volumes.* New York: Augustus M. Kelley.
MacPherson, Stewart, and James Midgley. 1987. *Comparative Social Policy and the Third World.* New York: St. Martin's Press.
Malthus, Thomas. *An Essay on Population.* 1976 (1798). New York: W.W. Norton.
———. *An Essay on Population.* 1992 (1803). Donald Winch, editor. Cambridge: Cambridge University Press.
Malveaux, Julianne. 1985a. "Comparable Worth and Its Impact on Black Women." *Review of Black Political Economy* 13, 4: 4–27.
———. 1985b. "The Economic Interests of Black and White Women: Are They Similar?" *Review of Black Political Economy* 14, 1: 5–27.
Mandel, Bernard. 1955. "Samuel Gompers and the Negro Workers, 1886–1914." *Journal of Negro History* 40, 1: 34–60.
Mandel, E. 1975. *Late Capitalism.* Tr. J. De Bres. London: New Left Books.
Marcet, Mrs. (Jane Haldimand). 1806. *Conversations on Chemistry: In Which the Elements of That Science Are Familiarly Explained and Illustrated by Experiments.* London: Longman, Hurst, Rees, and Orme.
———. 1816. *Conversations on Political Economy: In Which the Elements of That*

Science Are Familiarly Explained. London: Longman, Hurst, Rees, Orme and Brown.

———. 1833. *John Hopkins's Notions on Political Economy.* Boston: Allen and Ticknor.

Martineau, Harriet. 1832. *Life in the Wilds.* Boston: L.C. Bowles.

Marx, K. 1954 [1867]. *Capital. Volume 1.* Moscow: Progress Publishers (tr. S. Moore and E. Aveling). 1954.

———. 1973 [1857–58]. *Grundrisse.* Tr. M. Nicolaus. London: NLR Allen Lane Penguin. Originally published as *Grundrisse der Kritik der politischen ōkonomie EuropÑische Verlagsanstalt,* 1953.

———. 1967. *Capital,* New York: International.

———. 1970. *A Contribution to the Critique of Political Economy.* New York: International.

———. 1978. "The German Ideology, Part I." in *The Marx-Engels Reader,* ed. Robert C. Tucker, 146–202. 2d ed. New York: W.W. Norton.

———. 1986a. *Capital: A Critique of Political Economy, Volume I.* Moscow: Progress Publishers.

———. 1986b. *Capital: A Critique of Political Economy, Volume III.* Moscow: Progress Publishers.

Mason, Patrick L. 1993. "Accumulation, Segmentation and the Discriminatory Process in the Market for Labor Power." *Review of Radical Political Economics* 25, 2: 1–25.

Massachusetts Bureau of Statistics of Labor. 1885. *Historical Review of Wages and Prices, 1752–1860.* Boston Public Library, Historical Government Records Department, Microfilm.

Matthaei, Julie A. 1982. *An Economic History of Women In America: Women's Work, the Sexual Division of Labor, and the Development of Capitalism.* New York: The Harvester Press.

———. 1995. "The Sexual Division of Labor, Sexuality, and Lesbian/Gay Liberation: Towards a Marxist-Feminist Analysis of Sexuality in U.S. Capitalism," *Review of Radical Political Economics* 27, 1: 1–37.

Maume, David J. 1991. "Child-care Expenditures and Women's Employment Turnover." *Social Forces* 70, 2 (December): 495–508.

May, Martha. 1982. "The Historical Problem of the Family Wage: The Ford Motor Company and the Five Dollar Day." In *Feminist Studies* 8 (summer): 399–424.

Metcalf, David. 1987. "Labour Market Flexibility and Jobs: A Survey of Evidence from OECD Countries with Special Reference to Europe." In *The Fight Against Unemployment: Macroeconomic Papers from the Centre for European Studies,* ed. Richard Layard and Lars Calmfors. Cambridge, MA: MIT Press.

Mill, James. 1826. *Elements of Political Economy.* 3rd ed. London: Baldwin, Cradock, and Joy.

Mill, John Stuart. 1834. "On Miss Martineau's Summary of Political Economy." *Monthly Repository.* 8: 318–22.

———. 1989 (1869). *The Subjection of Women.* Cambridge, MA: MIT Press.

Mishel, Lawrence, and Jared Bernstein. 1994. *The State of Working America: 1994–95.* Armonk, NY: M.E. Sharpe.

Mitter, Swasti. 1986. *Common Fate, Common Bond: Women in the Global Economy.* London: Pluto Press.

Mohr, Richard. 1994. *A More Perfect Union: Why Straight Americans Must Stand Up for Gay Rights.* Boston: Beacon Press.

Montgomery, David. 1984. "The Working Classes of the Pre-Industrial American City, 1780–1830." *Labor History* 9, 1.

More, Hannah. 1995 (1799). *Strictures on Female Education.* New York: Oxford University Press.
Morgan, Marjorie. 1994. *Manners, Morals, and Class in England, 1774–1858.* New York: St. Martin's Press.
Morris, Richard B. 1946. 1965. *Government and Labor in Early America.* New York: Harper and Row.
Motulsky, A.G. 1983. "Impact of Genetic Manipulation on Society and Medicine." *Science* 219: 135–40.
Nakamura, Takafusa. 1995. *The Postwar Japanese Economy: Its Development and Structure, 1937–1994.* (2nd ed.). Tokyo: University of Tokyo Press.
The Nation, 1996. "In Fact..." Vol. 262(24) (June 17): 7.
National Committee on Pay Equity. 1989. *Pay Equity Activity in the Public Sector, 1979–1989.* Washington, DC: NCPE.
———. 1993. *Erase the Bias: A Pay Equity Guide to Eliminating Race and Sex Bias from Wage Setting Systems.* Washington, DC: NCPE.
Nelson, Bruce A., Edward M. Opton, Jr., and Thomas E. Wilson. 1980. "Wage Discrimination and Title VII in the 1980s: The Case Against 'Comparable Worth.'" *Employee Relations Law Journal* 6, 3: 380–405.
Nicholson, Linda. 1986. *Gender and History: The Limits of Social Theory in the Age of the Family.* New York: Columbia University Press.
———, ed. 1990. *Feminism/Postmodernism.* London: Routledge.
North, Douglass C. 1974. *Growth and Welfare in the American Past: A New Economic History.* Englewood Cliffs, NJ: Prentice-Hall.
Northrup, Herbert E. 1984. "Comparable Worth and Realistic Wage Setting." In *Comparable Worth: Issue for the 80's,* ed. U.S. Commission on Civil Rights, 93–98. Washington, DC.
Nye, J.S. 1989. *Bound to Lead: The Changing Nature of American Power.* New York: Basic Books.
Offe, Claus. 1984. *Contradictions of the Welfare State.* Cambridge, MA: MIT Press.
O'Hara, Phillip Anthony. 1994. "An Institutionalist Review of Long Wave Theories: Schumpeterian Innovation, Modes of Regulation, and Social Structures of Accumulation." *Journal of Economic Issues* 28 (June): 489–500.
———. 1995. "Household Labor, the Family, and Macroeconomic Instability in the United States: 1940s-1990s." *Review of Social Economy* 53 (spring): 89–120.
Okker, Patricia. 1995. *Our Sister Editors.* Athens: University of Georgia Press.
Oliver, Melvin L., and Thomas M. Shapiro. 1995. *Black Wealth/White Wealth: A New Perspective on Racial Inequality.* New York: Routledge.
O'Neill, June. 1984a. "An Argument Against Comparable Worth." In *Comparable Worth: Issue for the 80's,* ed. U.S. Commission on Civil Rights, 177–86. Washington, DC.
———. 1984b. "Statement submitted by June O'Neill, Director, Program of Policy Research on Women and Families at the Urban Institute." In U.S., Congress, House, Committee on Post Office and Civil Service, Subcommittee on Compensation and Employee Benefits, *Options for Conducting a Pay Equity Study of Federal Pay and Classifications Systems,* 98th Cong. April 4, 261–64.
———. 1994. "The Shrinking Pay Gap." *The Wall Street Journal,* October 7, A10.
O'Neill, June, Michael Brien, and James Cunningham. 1989. "Effects of Comparable Worth Policy: Evidence from Washington State." *American Economic Review* 79, 2: 305–9.
Ono, Tsuneo. 1990. "The Maturing of the Labor–Management Relationship and a Macroeconomic Analysis of Wage Change." *Japanese Economic Studies* 18, 4: 65–91.

Organization for Economic Cooperation and Development (OECD). 1993a. *Employment Outlook.* Paris: Organisation for Economic Cooperation and Development.
———. 1993b. *Labour Force Statistics.* Paris: Organisation for Economic Cooperation and Development.
———. 1994a. *The OECD Jobs Study: Facts, Analysis, Strategies.* Paris: Organisation for Economic Cooperation and Development.
———. 1994b. *The OECD Jobs Study, Volume I.* Paris: Organisation for Economic Cooperation and Development.
Pagels, Elaine. 1988. *Adam, Eve, and the Serpent,* New York: Random House.
Palmer, Phyllis. 1989. *Domesticity and Dirt: Housewives and Domestic Servants in the United States. 1920–1945.* Philadelphia: Temple University Press.
Pateman, Carole. 1988. *The Sexual Contract.* Stanford, CA: Stanford University Press.
Paul, Ellen Frankel. 1989. *Equity and Gender: The Comparable Worth Debate.* New Brunswick, NJ: Transaction Publishers.
Pear, Robert. 1996. "A Computer Gap Is Likely to Slow Welfare Changes." *New York Times,* September 2, 1, 12.
Pearce, Diana. 1990. "Welfare Is Not for Women: Why the War on Poverty Cannot Conquer the Feminization of Poverty." In *Women, the State, and Welfare,* ed. Linda Gordon. Madison: University of Wisconsin Press.
Pease, Jane H., and William H. Pease. 1990. *Ladies, Women and Wenches: Choice and Constraint in Antebellum Charleston and Boston.* Chapel Hill: University of North Carolina Press.
Peplau, Letitia Anne. 1991. "Lesbian and Gay Relationships." In *Homosexuality: Research Implications for Public Policy,* eds. John C. Gonsiorek and James D. Weinrich 177–96. Newbury Park, CA: Sage.
Petchesky, Rosalind. 1979. " Dissolving the Hyphen: A Report on Marxist Feminist Groups 1–5." In *Capitalist Patriarchy and the Case for Socialist Feminism,* ed. Zillah Eisenstein, 373–90. New York: Monthly Review.
Peterson, Janice. 1992. "Public Policy and the Economic Status of Women in the United States." *Journal of Economic Issues* 26 (June): 441–48.
Peterson, Janice, and Doug Brown, eds. 1994. *The Economic Status of Women under Capitalism.* Brookfield, VT: Edward Elgar.
Peterson, Richard, and Jeremiah Sullivan, eds. 1990. "The Japanese Lifetime Employment System: Whither It Goest?" In *Advances in International Comparative Management: A Research Annual,* ed. S. Benjamin Prasad. Greenwich, CT and London: JAI Press.
Phelps, Edmund. 1972. "The Statistical Theory of Racism and Sexism." *American Economic Review* (September): 659–61.
Picchio del Mercato, Antonella. 1981. "Social Reproduction and the Basic Structure of Labour Markets." In *Dynamics of Labor Market Segmentation,* ed. Frank Wilkinson. New York: Academic Press.
Pinchbeck, Ivy. 1930. *Women Workers and the Industrial Revolution, 1750–1850.* New York: F.S. Crosts.
Piore, Michael. 1986. "Perspectives on Labor Market Flexibility." *Industrial Relations,* 25, 2: 146–66.
Piore, Michael J., and Charles F. Sabel. 1984. *The Second Industrial Divide: Possibilities for Prosperity.* New York: Basic Books.
Piven, Frances Fox, and Richard A. Cloward. 1971. *Regulating the Poor.* New York: Vintage Books.
Polanyi, Karl. 1944. *The Great Transformation: The Political and Economic Origins of Our Time.* Boston: Beacon Press.

Poovey, Mary. 1988. *Uneven Developments: The Ideological Work of Gender in Mid-Victorian England.* Chicago: University of Chicago Press.

———. 1995. *Making a Social Body: British Cultural Formation 1830–1864.* Chicago: University of Chicago Press.

Posner, Richard. 1992. *Sex and Reason.* Cambridge, MA: Harvard University Press.

Poulantzas, Nicos. 1975. *Political Power and Social Classes.* London: New Left Books.

Power, Marilyn. 1983. "From Home Production to Wage Labor: Women as a Reserve Army of Labor." *Review of Radical Political Economics* 15, 1: 71–91.

———. 1984. "Unity and Division Among Women: Feminist Theories of Gender and Class." *Economic Forum* 15, 1:39–67.

Power, Marilyn, and Sam Rosenberg. 1993. "Black Female Clerical Workers: Movement Toward Equality with White Women?" *Industrial Relations* 32, 2: 223–37.

Pratt, Mary Louise. 1992. *Imperial Eyes: Travel Writing and Transculturation.* New York: Routledge.

Priebe, John. 1972. *1970 Occupation and Industry Systems in Terms of Their 1960 Occupational and Industrial Elements.* Washington, DC: U.S. Bureau of the Census, Technical Paper No. 26.

Providence First Congregational Church Female Benevolent Society. 1837. "Report and Proposal to the Public on the Subject of Female Wages." Providence, RI: Committee of the Female Benevolent Society. Kress Collection. Baker Library at Harvard.

Pryme, George. 1816. *A Syllabus of a Course of Lectures on the Principles of Political Economy.* Cambridge: J. Smith.

Pursel, V.G, C.A. Pinkert, K.F. Miller, et al. 1989. "Genetic Engineering of Livestock." *Science* 244, 1281–87.

Quadagno, Jill. 1988. "From Old Age Assistance to Supplemental Security Income: The Political Economy of Relief in the South, 1935–72." In *The Politics of Social Policy in the United States,* ed. Margaret Weir, Ann Shola Orloff, and Theda Skocpol. Princeton, NJ: Princeton University Press.

———. 1994. *The Color of Welfare: How Racism Undermined the War on Poverty.* New York: Oxford University Press.

Quick, Paddy. 1992. "Capitalism and the Origins of Domestic Labor." *Review of Radical Political Economics* 24, 2 (summer).

Rabkin, Jeremy. 1984. "Comparable Worth as Civil Rights Policy: Potentials for Disaster." In *Comparable Worth: Issue for the 80's,* ed. U.S. Commission on Civil Rights, 187–95. Washington, DC.

Raines, L.J. 1992. "The Mouse that Roared." In F. Grosveld and G. Kollios, eds., *Transgenic Animals.* London: Academic Press.

Redclift, M.R. 1984. *Development and the Environmental Crisis: Red or Green Alternatives?* London: Methuen.

———. 1987. *Sustainable Development: Exploring the Contradictions.* London and New York: Methuen.

Redclift, M.R., and E. Mingione, eds. 1985. *Beyond Employment, Household, Gender and Subsistence.* Oxford: Basil Blackwell.

Reich, Michael. 1981. *Racial Inequality: A Political-Economic Analysis.* Princeton, NJ: Princeton University Press.

Renner, Karl. 1978. *Austro-Marxism.* Oxford: Clarendon Press.

Reskin, Barbara F., and Heidi I. Hartmann, eds. 1986. *Women's Work, Men's Work: Sex Segregation on the Job.* Washington, DC: National Academy Press.

Reskin, Barbara R., and Patricia A. Roos. 1990. *Job Queues, Gender Queues: Explaining Women's Inroads into Male Occupations.* Philadelphia: Temple University Press.

Rhoads, Steven E. 1993a. *Incomparable Worth: Pay Equity Meets the Market.* New York: Cambridge University Press.
———. 1993b. "Pay Equity Won't Go Away." *Across the Board* (July/August): 37–41.
———. 1993c. "Would Decentralized Comparable Worth Work? The Case of the United Kingdom." *Regulation: The Cato Review of Business and Government* 3: 65–70.
Rich, Adrienne. 1983. "Compulsory Heterosexuality and Lesbian Existence." In *Powers of Desire,* ed. Ann Snitow, Christine Stansell, and Sharon Thompson, 177–205. New York: Monthly Review Press.
Roback, Jennifer. 1986. *A Matter of Choice: A Critique of Comparable Worth by a Skeptical Feminist.* New York: Priority Press.
Robson, Ruthann. 1992. *Lesbian (Out)Law: Survival Under the Rule of Law.* Ithaca, NY: Firebrand Books.
———. 1994. "Resisting the Family: Repositioning Lesbians in Legal Theory." *Signs: Journal of Women in Culture and Society* 19, 4: 975–95.
Rollins, Judith. 1985. *Between Women: Domestics and Their Employers.* Philadelphia: Temple University Press.
Romero, Mary. 1988. "Day Work in the Suburbs: The Work Experience of Chicana Private Housekeepers." In *The Worth of Women's Work: A Qualitative Synthesis,* ed. Anne Statham, Eleanor M. Miller, and Hans O. Mauksch, 77–91. Albany: State University of New York Press.
———. 1992. *Maid in the U.S.A.* London: Routledge.
Rose, Nancy. 1995. *Workfare or Fair Work: Women, Welfare, and Government Work Programs.* New Brunswick, NJ: Rutgers University Press.
Rose, Sonya O. 1992. *Limited Livelihoods: Gender and Class in Nineteenth-Century England.* Berkeley: University of California Press.
Rosecrance, R.N. 1986. *The Rise of the Trading State: Commerce and Conquest in the Modern World.* New York: Basic Books.
Rosenberg, Sam. 1991. "From Segmentation to Flexibility: A Selective Survey." *Review of Radical Political Economics* 23 (spring/summer): 71–79.
Rothenberg, Winnifred B. 1985. "The Emergence of a Capital Market in Rural Massachusetts, 1730–1838." *Journal of Economic History* 45, 4: 781–808.
Rubenstein, William R., ed. 1993. *Lesbians, Gay Men, and the Law.* New York: New Press.
Rubery, Jill, ed. 1988. *Women and Recession.* London and New York: Routledge & Kegan Paul.
Rubin, Gayle. 1975. "The Traffic in Women: Notes on the 'Political Economy' of Sex." In *Toward an Anthropology of Women,* ed. Rayna Reiter, 157–210. New York: Monthly Review Press.
Rubin, Robert E., Ronald Brown, Robert B. Reich, Joseph E. Stiglitz, and Laura D'Andrea Tyson. 1996. "What's a Minimum Wage Job Worth? Up to a Living Wage." *Wall Street Journal,* April 1.
Rutten, Tim. 1991. "Inner Cities in Need of Living Wage." *Los Angeles Times,* August 2.
Ryan, Cheyney C. 1981. "The Fiends of Commerce: Romantic and Marxist Criticisms of Classical Political Economy." *History of Political Economy* 13: 80–94.
Ryan, Mary. 1981. *Cradle of the Middle Class.* Cambridge: Cambridge University Press.
———. 1983. *Womanhood in American: From Colonial Times to the Present.* 3rd ed. New York: Franklin Watts.
———. 1990. *Women in Public: Between Banners and Ballots, 1825–1880.* Baltimore: Johns Hopkins University Press.

Sacks, Karen Brodkin. 1988. *Caring by the Hour: Women, Work, and Organizing at Duke Medical Center.* Urbana: University of Illinois Press.
Said, Edward. 1993. *Culture and Imperialism.* New York: Vintage.
Sanger, David. 1992. "Women in Japan Job Market Find the Door Closing Again." *New York Times,* December 1, A1, A10.
Sapiro, Virginia. 1990. "The Gender Basis of American Social Policy." In *Women, the State, and Welfare,* ed. Linda Gordon. Madison: University of Wisconsin Press.
Sargent, Lydia, ed. 1981. *Women and Revolution: A Discussion of the Unhappy Marriage of Marxism and Feminism.* Boston: South End Press.
Sawicki, Jana. 1991. *Disciplining Foucault.* New York: Routledge.
Schafer, Todd, and Jeff Faux, eds. 1996. *Reclaiming Prosperity: A Blueprint for Progressive Economic Reform.* Armonk, NY: M.E. Sharpe.
Schettkat, Ronald. 1990. "Adjustment Processes in the Economy: Labor Market Dynamics in the Federal Republic of West Germany." In *Labor Market Adjustments to Structural Change and Technological Progress,* ed. Eileen Appelbaum and Ronald Schettkat. New York: Praeger.
Scheuermann, Mona. 1993. *Her Bread to Earn: Women, Money and Society from Defoe to Austen.* Lexington: University Press of Kentucky.
Schlafly, Phyllis. 1985. "Statement of Phyllis Schlafly, President, Eagle Forum." In U.S. Congress, House, Committee on Post Office and Civil Service, Subcommittee on Compensation and Employee Benefits, *Options for Conducting a Pay Equity Study of Federal Pay and Classifications Systems.* 98th Cong. April 4, 1984, 265–85.
Scoresby, William, D.D. 1845. *American Factories and Their Female Operatives: With an Appeal on Behalf of the British Factory Population, and Suggestions for the Improvement of Their Condition.* London: Longman, Brown, Green, & Longman. Kress Collection. Baker Library at Harvard.
Scott, A.M. 1986. "Rethinking Petty Commodity Production." *Social Analysis* 20, special issue series.
Scott, Joan Wallach. 1988. *Gender and the Politics of History.* New York: Columbia University Press.
Scott, Joan W., and Louise A. Tilly. 1975. "Women's Work and the Family in Nineteenth-Century Europe." *Comparative Studies in Society and History* 17, 1: 36–64.
Scrope, G. Poulett. 1831. "Malthus and Sadler on Population." *Quarterly Review* 45 (April): 97–145.
———. 1833. *Quarterly Review* 49 (April): 136–52.
Seccombe, Wally. 1974. "The Housewife and Her Labor Under Capitalism." *New Left Review* 83.
———. 1992. *A Millennium of Family Change.* London: Verso.
———. 1993. *Weathering the Storm.* London: Verso.
Sedgwick, Eve Kosofsky. 1990. *Epistemology of the Closet.* Berkeley: University of California Press.
Seidman, Steven. 1993. "Identity and Politics in a 'Postmodern' Gay Culture: Some Historical and Conceptual Notes." In *Fear of a Queer Planet: Queer Politics and Social Theory,* ed. Michael Warner, 105–42. Minneapolis: University of Minnesota Press.
Sen, Gita. 1980. "The Sexual Division of Labor and the Working Class Family: Towards a Conceptual Synthesis of Class Relations and the Subordination of Women." *Review of Radical Political Economics* 12, 2.
Sen, Gita, and Caren Grown. 1987. *Development, Crises, and Alternative Visions: Third World Women's Perspectives.* New York: Monthly Review Press.

Senior, Nassau. 1827. "Political Economy." *Westminster Review* 8 (July): 183, 189.
Shaiken, Harley. 1984. *Work Transformed: Automation and Labor in the Computer Age.* Lexington, MA: Lexington Books.
Shaikh, Anwar. 1980. "Marxian Competition Versus Perfect Competition: Further Comments on the So-called Choice of Technique." *Cambridge Journal of Economics* 4: 75–83.
Shammas, Carole. 1993. "A New Look at Long Term Trends in Wealth Inequality in the United States." *American Historical Review* (April): 412–31.
Shank, Susan E. 1988. "Women and the Labor Market: The Link Grows Stronger." *Monthly Labor Review* 111, 3: 3–9.
Shanley, Mary Lyndon. 1989. *Feminism, Marriage, and the Law in Victorian England, 1850–1895.* Princeton, NJ: Princeton University Press.
Shaw, M. 1991. *Post-Military Society.* Cambridge: Polity Press.
Sherman, Suzanne, ed. 1992. *Lesbian and Gay Marriage: Private Commitments, Public Ceremonies.* Philadelphia: Temple University Press.
Shiva, V. 1988. *Staying Alive: Women, Ecology, and Survival in India.* London: Zed Press.
Showalter, Elaine. 1985. *The Female Malady.* New York: Penguin.
———. 1990. *Sexual Anarchy: Gender and Culture at the Fin De Siecle.* New York: Viking.
Simmler, Lucy. 1990. "The Landless Worker: An Index of Economic and Social Change in Chester County, Pennsylvania, 1750–1820." *The Pennsylvania Magazine of History & Bibliography* 114, 2: 163–99.
Simmons, Christina. 1991. "Companionate Marriage and the Lesbian Threat." In *Women and Power in American History: A Reader, Vol. II from 1870,* ed. Kathryn Kish Sklar and Thomas Dublin. Englewood Cliffs, NJ: Prentice-Hall.
Skinner, Q. 1978. *The Foundations of Modern Political Thought.* 2 vols. Cambridge: Cambridge University Press.
Sklar, Kathryn Kish. 1973. *Catharine Beecher: A Study in American Domesticity,* New Haven, CT: Yale University Press.
———. 1991. "Why Were Most Politically Active Women Opposed to the ERA in the 1920's?" In *Women and Power in American History: A Reader, Vol. II.,* ed. Sklar and Dublin, 175–82. Englewood Cliffs, NJ: Prentice-Hall.
———. 1995. *Florence Kelley and the Nation's Work.* New Haven, CT: Yale University Press.
Sklar, Kathryn Kish, and Thomas Dublin, eds. 1991. *Women and Power in American History.* Vols. 1 and 2. Englewood Cliffs, NJ: Prentice-Hall.
Skocpol, Theda. 1992. *Protecting Soldiers and Mothers.* Cambridge, MA: The Belknap Press of Harvard University Press.
Slaughter, Jane. 1995. "Auto Union's Partnership with Saturn in Doubt." *Labor Notes* (January): 3.
Slottje, Daniel J. 1989. *The Structure of Earnings and the Measurement of Income Inequality in the U.S.* Amsterdam: North-Holland.
Smith, Adam. 1991. *The Wealth of Nations.* New York: Knopf.
Smith, Robert S. 1988. "Comparable Worth: Limited Coverage and the Exacerbation of Inequality." *Industrial and Labor Relations Review* 41, 1: 227–39.
Smith-Rosenberg, Carroll. 1985. *Disorderly Conduct.* New York: Knopf.
Sorensen, Elaine. 1987. "Effect of Comparable Worth Policies on Earnings. *Industrial Relations* 26, 3: 227–39.
———. 1989a. "Measuring the Effect of Occupational Sex and Race Composition on

Earnings." In *Pay Equity: Empirical Inquiries,* ed. Robert T. Michael, Heidi I. Hartmann, and Brigid O'Farrell, 49–60. Washington, DC: National Academy Press.
———. 1989b. "The Wage Effects of Occupational Sex Composition: A Review and New Findings." In *Comparable Worth: Analyses and Evidence,* ed. M. Anne Hill and Mark R. Killingsworth, 57–79. Ithaca, NY: ILR Press.
———. 1990. "The Crowding Hypothesis and Comparable Worth." *Journal of Human Resources* 25, 1: 55–89.
———. 1994. *Comparable Worth: Is It a Worthy Policy?* Princeton, NJ: Princeton University Press.
Sorrentino, Constance. 1995. "International Employment Indicators, 1983–93." *Monthly Labor Review* 118, 8: 31–50.
Spallone, P. 1992. *Generation Games: Genetic Engineering and the Future for Our Lives.* London: The Women's Press.
Spalter-Roth, Roberta, and Beverly Burr, Heidi Hartmann, and Lois Shaw. 1995. *Welfare that Works: The Working Lives of AFDC Recipients.* Washington, DC: Institute for Women's Policy Research.
Standing, Guy. 1989. "Global Feminization Through Flexible Labor." *World Development* 17 (July): 1077–95.
Staves, Susan. 1990. *Married Women's Separate Property in England, 1660–1833.* Cambridge, MA: Harvard University Press.
Steinberg, Ronnie. 1986. "The Comparable Worth Debate." *New Politics* 1 (spring): 108–26.
———. 1990. "Social Construction of Skill: Gender, Power, and Comparable Worth." *Work and Occupations* 17, 4: 449–82.
———. 1992. "Gendered Instructions: Cultural Lag and Gender Bias in the Hay System of Job Evaluation." *Work and Occupations* 19, 4: 387–423.
Sterling, Dorothy, ed. 1984. *We Are Your Sisters: Black Women in the Nineteenth Century.* New York: W.W. Norton.
Stocking, George W., Jr. 1987. *Victorian Anthropology.* New York: Free Press.
Stoddard, Thomas. 1989. "Why Gay People Should Seek the Right to Marry." *Out/Look* 6 (Fall): 9–13. (Reprinted in Rubenstein 1993 and Sherman 1992.)
Stone, Lawrence. 1977. *The Family, Sex and Marriage in England, 1500–1800.* New York: Harper & Row.
Stone, Lawrence, and Jeanne C. Fawtier Stone. 1984. *An Open Elite? England 1540–1880.* Oxford: Clarendon Press.
Strassmann, Diana. 1993. "The Stories of Economics and the Power of the Storyteller." *History of Political Economy* 25, 1: 145–63.
Strassmann, Diana, and Livia Polanyi. 1995. "The Economist as Storyteller: What the Texts Reveal." In *Out of the Margin: Feminist Perspectives on Economic Theory,* ed. Edith Kuiper and Jolande Sap, 129–50. London: Routledge.
Straughan, R. 1989. *The Genetic Manipulation of Plants, Animals and Microbes.* London: National Consumer Council.
Tachibanaki, Toshiaki. 1987. "Labour Market Flexibility in Japan in Comparison with Europe and the U.S." *European Economic Review* 31 (April): 647–84.
Taira, Koji. 1985. "The Labor Force Survey and Unemployment: A Philosophical Note." *Japanese Economic Studies* 14, 1: 3–33.
Talbot, Margaret. 1996. "Les Tres Riches Heures de Martha Stewart." *The New Republic,* May 13, 30–35.
Taylor, Barbara. 1983. *Eve and the New Jerusalem.* New York: Pantheon.
Thomas, Clarence. 1985. "Statement by Chairman Clarence Thomas on First EEOC

Comparable Worth Decision." Washington, DC: Equal Employment Opportunity Commission. June 17.
Thompson, Noel W. 1984. *The People's Science.* Cambridge: Cambridge University Press.
Thorne, Barrie. 1992. "Feminism and the Family: Two Decades of Thought." In *Rethinking the Family: Some Feminist Questions,* rev. ed., ed. Barrie Thorne with Marilyn Yalom. Boston: Northeastern University Press.
Tickamyer, Ann R., and Kathleen M. Blee. 1990. "The Racial Convergence Thesis in Women's Intergenerational Occupational Mobility." *Social Science Quarterly* 71, 4: 711–28.
Trattner, Walter I. 1984. *From Poor Law to Welfare State: A History of Social Welfare in America.* New York: The Free Press.
Treas, Judith. 1983. "Postwar Determinants of Family Income Inequality." *American Sociological Review* 48, 2: 546–59.
Treiman, Donald J., and Heidi I. Hartmann, eds. 1981. *Women, Work, and Wages: Equal Pay for Jobs of Equal Value.* Washington, DC: National Academy Press.
Tukey, John W. 1977. *Exploratory Data Analysis.* Reading, MA: Addison-Wesley.
Tyson, James L. 1996."'Living Wage' Drive Accelerates in Cities." *Christian Science Monitor,* April 10.
Uchitelle, Louis. 1996. "Some Cities Pressuring Employers to Raise Wages of Working Poor." *New York Times,* April 9.
Uhlenberg, Peter. 1978. "Changing Configurations of the Life Course." In *Transitions: The Family and the Life Course in Historical Perspective,* ed. Tamara H. Hareven, 65–95. New York, San Francisco, London: Academic Press.
Ulrich, Laurel Thatcher. 1991. "A Friendly Neighbor: Social Dimensions of Daily Work in Northern Colonial New England." In *Women and Power in American History: A Reader Vol. I to 1880,* ed. Sklar and Dublin, 37–50. Englewood Cliffs, NJ: Prentice-Hall.
United States Bureau of the Census, Census of Population. 1973. *1969 Occupational Characteristics.* Subject Report PC(2)-7A. Washington, DC.
———. 1992. *Money Income of Households, Families, and Persons in the U.S.* Current Population Reports Series p-60, #167. Washington, DC.
United States Bureau of Labor Statistics. 1993. *Monthly Labor Review.* Washington, DC: Government Printing Office. November.
United States Congress. House. 1994. 103rd Congress, H.R. 3734, Title 1, Section 101.10.
United States Department of Commerce. 1949. *Historical Statistics of the United States, 1789–1945,* a Supplement to the *Statistical Abstract of the United States.*
United States Department of Labor, Bureau of Labor Statistics. *Employment and Earnings.* Various issues.
———. Office of Policy Planning and Research. 1965. *The Negro Family, The Case for National Action.* Washington, DC: Government Printing Office.
United States Office of Personnel Management. 1987. *Comparable Worth for Federal Jobs: A Wrong Turn Off the Road Toward Pay Equity and Women's Career Advancement.* Washington, DC. September.
Valenze, Deborah. 1995. *The First Industrial Women,* New York: Oxford University Press.
Vogel, Lise. 1983. *Marxism and the Oppression of Women.* New Brunswick, NJ: Rutgers University Press.
Wagman, Barnet. 1995. "Occupation, Power and the Origins of Labor Segmentation in the United States, 1870–1910." *Review of Radical Political Economics* 27 (March): 1–24.

Wagman, Barnet, and Nancy Folbre. 1988. "The Feminization of Inequality: Some New Patterns." *Challenge* (November/December): 56–59.

Wajcman, Judy. 1991. "Patriarchy, Technology, and Conceptions of Skill." *Work and Occupations* 18, 1: 29–45.

Walby, Sylvia. 1986. *Patriarchy at Work: Patriarchal and Capitalist Relations in Employment.* Minneapolis: University of Minnesota Press.

Walkowitz, Judith. 1980. *Prostitution and Victorian Society,* Cambridge: Cambridge University Press.

———. 1992. *City of Dreadful Delight.* Chicago: University of Chicago Press.

Ware, Norman. 1924. *The Industrial Worker, 1840–1860. The Reaction of American Industrial Society to the Advance of the Industrial Revolution.* Boston and New York: Houghton Mifflin Company, The Riverside Press Cambridge.

Warren, George F., and Frank A. Pearson. 1933. *Prices.* New York: John Wiley & Sons.

Waterman, A.M.C. 1991. *Revolution, Economics and Religion: Christian Political Economy, 1798–1833.* Cambridge: Cambridge University Press.

Watt, Ian. 1957. *The Rise of the Novel.* Berkeley: University of California Press.

Webb, R.K. 1955. *The British Working Class Reader, 1790–2848.* London: Allen and Unwin.

Weinbaum, Batya, and Amy Bridges. 1979. "The Other Side of the Pay Check: Monopoly Capital and the Structure of Consumption." In *Capitalist Patriarchy and the Case for Socialist Feminism,* ed. Z.R. Eisenstein. New York: Monthly Review.

Weisskopf, Thomas E. 1994. "Alternative Social Structure of Accumulation Approaches to the Analysis of Capitalist Booms and Crises." In *Social Structures of Accumulation: The Political Economy of Growth and Crisis,* ed. David M. Kotz, Terrence McDonough, and Michael Reich, 146–72. Cambridge: Cambridge University Press.

Welter, Barbara. 1966. "The Cult of True Womanhood: 1820–1860." *American Quarterly* 18 (summer).

Weston, Kath. 1991. *Families We Choose: Lesbians, Gays, Kinship.* New York: Columbia University Press.

White, M.V. 1987. "Robinson Crusoe." In *The New Palgrave Dictionary of Economics, volume 4,* ed. John Eatwell, Murray Milgate, and Peter Newman, 217–18. London: The Macmillan Press.

Williams, Fiona. 1994. "Social Relations, Welfare, and the Post-Fordism Debate." In *Towards a Post-Fordist Welfare State?* ed. Roger Burrows and Brian Loader, 49–73. London: Routledge.

Williams, Patricia J. 1991. *The Alchemy of Race and Rights.* Cambridge, MA: Harvard University Press.

Williams, Raymond. 1987. *Culture and Society: Coleridge to Orwell.* London: Hogarth Press.

Williams, Rhonda. 1991. "Competition, Discrimination, and Differential Wage Rates: On the Continued Relevance of Marxian Theory to the Analysis of Earnings and Employment Inequality." In *New Approach to Economic and Social Analyses of Discrimination,* ed. Richard R. Cornwall and Phanindra V. Wunnava. New York: Praeger.

Williams, Rhonda M. 1993. "Race, Deconstruction, and the Emergent Agenda of Feminist Economic Theory." In *Beyond Economic Man: Feminist Theory and Economics,* ed. Marianne A. Ferber and Julie A. Nelson, 144–53. Chicago: University of Chicago Press.

Williams, Rhonda, and Peggie R. Smith. 1990. "What Else Do Unions Do?: Race and Gender in Local 35." *Review of Black Political Economy* 18, 3: 59–77.

Williams, Robert E., and Lorence L. Kessler. 1984. *A Closer Look at Comparable Worth.* Washington, DC: National Foundation for the Study of Employment Policy.

Williamson, Jeffrey G., and Peter H. Lindert. 1980. *American Inequality: A Macroeconomic History.* New York: Academic Press.

Wilson, William Julius, and Kathryn M. Neckerman. 1986. "Poverty and Family Structure: The Widening Gap between Evidence and Public Policy Issues." In *Fighting Poverty, What Works and What Doesn't,* ed. Sheldon H. Danziger and Daniel H. Weinberg, 232–59. Cambridge, MA: Harvard University Press, 232–59.

Wolff, Edward. 1995. *Top Heavy.* New York: Twentieth Century Fund Report.

Yoon, Young-Hee, and Roberta Spalter-Roth. 1995. *Unemployment Insurance: Barriers to Access for Women and Part-time Workers.* Washington, DC: National Commission for Employment Policy.

Zalokar, Nadja. 1990. *The Economic Status of Black Women: An Exploratory Investigation.* Staff Report, United States Commission on Civil Rights. Washington, DC.

Zavella, Patricia. 1991. "Mujeres in Factories: Race and Class Perspectives on Women, Work, and Family." In *Gender at the Crossroads of Knowledge: Feminist Anthropology in the Postmodern Era,* ed. Micaela di Leonardo. Berkeley: University of California Press.

Zinn, Maxine Baca. 1987. "Structural Transformation and Minority Families." In *Women, Households, and the Economy,* ed. Lourdes Benería and Catharine R. Stimpson, 155–71. New Brunswick, NJ: Rutgers University Press.

Zinn, Maxine Baca, and Bonnie Thornton Dill. 1994. *Women of Color in U.S. Society.* Philadelphia: Temple University Press.

About the Editors and Contributors

Ellen Mutari is a visiting scholar and assistant professor at the Labor Studies Program of Rutgers University. She has taught at the New School for Social Research and James Madison College of Michigan State University. Her research addresses the relationship between gender relations and economic restructuring, historically and contemporarily. She has published in *Feminist Economics, Journal of Economic Issues,* and *Review of Radical Political Economics.*

Heather Boushey is completing her doctorate in economics at the New School for Social Research. Her work is on labor market inequality and social policy. She has taught courses on labor economics and Marxian economic theory.

William Fraher IV works for the Washington State Department of Corrections, Division of Correctional Industries, where he performs research on current, internal, and external markets for possible business creation and/or expansion. He received his master's degree in economics at the New School for Social Research in 1996. His main areas of interest are class and gender and how the process of globalization is affecting women around the world.

M.V. Lee Badgett is a labor economist and an assistant professor in the School of Public Affairs at the University of Maryland College Park. She has also taught lesbian and gay studies at Yale University, and is currently serving as the executive director of the Institute for Gay and Lesbian Strategic Studies, a national think tank. Her work on sexual orientation includes studies of workplace discrimination against lesbians and gay men and studies of gay family issues. Her articles have appeared in books, magazines, and academic journals. She is currently writing a book on the economic issues of lesbians and gay men.

Teresa Brennan is the author of *The Interpretation of the Flesh* and *History after Lacan*. She has a new book called *Okonomie fur die Erde* (*Economy for the Earth*), just published in Germany. She is also the editor of *Between Feminism and Psychoanalysis* and *Vision in Context* (with Martin Jay), and general editor (with Susan James) of the Oxford Readings in Feminism series.

Margaret S. Coleman received a Ph.D. in economics from the New School in May 1996. Her current project comparing nineteenth-century poor laws in England and the United States has been awarded a research grant by the Vincentians. She is both an adjunct professor at Saint John's University and a technician at NYNEX.

Brian Cooper is a Diamond Postdoctoral Fellow at the New School for Social Research. The author of several essays and articles on the relationship between economics and literary theory, he is currently finishing work on a book called *Family Fictions and Family Facts: Harriet Martineau, Adolphe Quetelet and the Population Question in England, 1798–1859*.

Ann Davis is currently assistant professor of economics at Marist College and director of the Marist College Bureau of Economic Research. Davis consults with regional groups concerning economic development strategies, in addition to her research on the economics of gender. She has served on the editorial board of the *Review of Radical Political Economics*.

Deborah M. Figart is associate professor of economics at Richard Stockton College. Her research interests include discrimination by gender and race, poverty and low-wage labor markets, and public sector industrial relations. She has published in *Feminist Economics, Industrial Relations, Work and Occupations, Review of Radical Political Economics,* and other journals. Her new book (with Peggy Kahn), *Contesting the Market: Pay Equity and the Politics of Economic Restructuring,* is published by Wayne State University Press.

David Kucera is assistant director of the Center for Economic Policy Analysis at the New School for Social Research. He received his Ph.D. in economics at the New School with a dissertation titled "Labor Adjustment in Japan and the Former West Germany." He has taught labor economics at St. Francis College. Among his publications is a paper on the effects of mass production and mass marketing on prices and wages in Japanese manufacturing, published in *Transformational Growth and the Business Cycle.*

June Lapidus is associate professor of economics at Roosevelt University in Chicago. Her research is on gender and labor markets, with particular emphasis on comparable worth and temporary work. She has also been a member of the Center for Popular Economics since 1983. Her work has appeared in *International Contributions to Labor Studies, Review of Radical Political Economics, Feminist Economics,* and *Work and Occupations.*

Marilyn Power is a faculty member in economics at Sarah Lawrence College. Her research and writing focus on inequality by race, class, and gender; the effects of public policy on women in the labor force; and the interconnecting issues of work and family. Her most recent project is on the social determination of wages for women, with particular reference to childcare workers.

Sam Rosenberg is professor of economics at Roosevelt University. He is the editor of *The State and the Labor Market* (Plenum Press) and is currently conducting research on labor market segmentation and low-wage labor markets in Chicago.

Index

A

Aaronson, Stephanie, 197
Abbott, Grace, 186n.12
Abraham, Katherine, 134, 136, 144
Abramovitz, Mimi, 182
Acker, Joan, 188
Addams, Jane, 100
Adler, David E., 119
Affirmative action, 186n.5
African Americans. *See* Race
Aglietta, Michel, 118
Aid to Families with Dependent Children, 15, 178, 180, 183, 186n.6
Albelda, Randy, 118, 130n.3, 151, 172, 174, 195
Aldrich, Mark, 191
Althusser, Louis, 6
Amariglio, Jack, 25
Amott, Teresa, 9
Andersen, Margaret, 5
Anderson, Cynthia D., 188
Anderson, Robert, 64, 77n.9
Appelbaum, Eileen, 118
Aries, Philippe, 102
Aristotle, 30
Armstrong, Nancy, 28, 29, 31, 32
Armstrong, Pat, 14, 120
Atack, Jeremy, 48
Atkinson, Anthony B., 194
Austen, Jane, 10, 33

B

Babysitting, 163
Badgett, M.V. Lee, 11-12, 61-76, 67, 72, 73, 74, 118, 125
Bakker, Isabella, 13, 115, 116, 120, 124, 130n.7
Balibar, E., 89
Baron, James N., 188
Barrett, Michèle, 7, 8, 93, 108, 110
Baty, S. Paige, 102
Becker, Gary, 63, 66, 70, 71, 72, 73, 77n.9
Beecher, Catherine, 99
Beechey, Veronica, 7
Beller, Andrea H., 191
Beneria, Lourdes, 6, 7, 92
Benston, Margaret, 5
Berger, Brigitte, 123
Bergmann, Barbara R., 63, 67, 122, 172
Bernstein, Jared, 189
Bernstein, Michael A., 116, 119
Beron, Kurt, 191
Beware the U.S. Model, 116
Bisexuals. *See* Lesbians, gays and bisexuals
Black women. *See* Race
Blank, Rebecca, 134
Blau, Francine D., 189, 191
Blewett, Mary H., 44, 45, 55, 56, 58n.3
Block, Fred, 3, 121
Bluestone, Barry, 105, 188, 189

Blumstein, Philip, 70-71
Bordo, Susan, 94, 103
Boris, Eileen, 103
Bose, Christine, 11
Boston, Thomas, 172
Botwinick, Howard, 172
Boushey, Heather, 3-16, 15, 16, 170-185
Bowles, Samuel, 109
Brady, Ray, 57
Brantlinger, Patrick, 25
Brennan, Teresa, 12, 78-90, 91n.3
Brenner, Johanna, 186n.4, 190
Bridges, William P., 188
Briggs, Rex, 72
Brodie, Janine, 116
Brodsky, Melvin, 122, 135
Brody, Michael, 126
Brown, Doug, 9, 121
Brown, Helen Gurley, 103
Bruegel, Irene, 5, 119
Buchele, Robert, 191
Buffer work force, 132, 135-136, 143-146
Burawoy, Michael, 108
Burk, Martha, 129
Burke, Phyllis, 77n.7
Burrows, Roger, 121
Burtless, Gary, 189
Buswell, Carol, 188

C

Cagatay, Nilüfer, 120
Cameron, Barbara, 119
Capitalism
  family structure and, 6-7, 12-13
  patriarchy and, 92
  stages of, 90-91n.1
  state monopoly, 85-86, 90n.1
  wage and employment inequality under, 172-176
  women's roles in, 104-111
Carey, Henry, 49
Carey, Mathew, 45, 47, 48, 52-53, 56
Carney, Larry, 136

Cato Institute, 122
Child-rearing
  division of labor and, 126, 183
  in gay family, 72
  self-interest and, 88-89
  work/family conflicts and, 158-160, 166
Children's Bureau, 182
Clark, Anna, 99, 109
Clarke, A., 90
Class
  behavioral codes of, 32, 35, 98
  economic restructuring and, 125
  family wage and, 125
  gender and, 92-93, 99-111
  population pressure and, 23, 26
  property and, 33
  race and, 161-163
  sexuality and, 93
Clinton, Bill, 184
Cloward, Richard A., 177, 180, 182
Cobble, Dorothy Sue, 169n.14
Cockburn, Cynthia, 8
Cole, Arthur H., 47
Coleman, Margaret, 11, 42-58
Colley, Linda, 32
Colonial economy, 43-44, 46-47
Colonialism, 7, 23, 32-33
Colquhoun, Patrick, 41n.5
Comparable worth
  defined, 204n.1
  See also Pay equity
Conduct books, 29, 31-32
Conrad, Cecilia A., 199
Contract with America, 104-105, 184
Conversations on Political Economy (Marcet), 34, 36
Cooper, Brian, 10, 13, 21-41
Cott, Nancy, 99, 102
Cotton, Jeremiah, 193
County of Washington, Oregon vs Gunther, 116
Cowan, Ruth S., 102
Crow, Duncan, 102, 104
Cult of domesticity, 97-100
Cult of the true woman, 102

Culture
  of domesticity, 93, 97-100,
    104-107, 109-110
  feminization of, 100
Curtin, Michael, 32, 41n.4
Cushman, John H., Jr., 105

D

Dalla Costa, M., 91n.3
Davidoff, Leonore, 29, 30, 98, 108
Davis, Ann, 11, 12-13, 92-111
Defoe, Daniel, 10, 21-22
Deindustrialization, 120, 128
Delphy, C., 91n.3
DeParle, Jason, 105
Deregulation, 121
Dickens, Charles, 24-25
Dill, Bonnie Thornton, 7
Discouraged workers, 132, 134, 145-146
Di Stefano, Christine, 93
Division of labor
  gender-based, 7, 10, 22, 24, 37, 39, 67, 70, 126-127
  in homosexual couples, 70-71
Domestic economy
  and political economy, 10, 30-31
  separate spheres of, 29-32, 93, 98, 126-127
Domestic ideology, gender roles and, 93, 97-100, 104-107, 109-110, 125
Domestic labor
  capitalism and, 107-108
  ideology and, 101-102
  Marxist theory and, 5, 94, 96-97
  surplus value and, 5, 91n.3
  in utopian narratives, 10, 24, 37, 39-40, 40
Domestic partnership movement, 63, 73-75
Domestics (servants), 51-52, 59-60, 163, 165-166
Domestic woman, 10, 25-26, 29-32
Douglas, Ann, 100

Douglas, S. J., 103
Dual systems theory, 6-7, 12, 92
Dublin, Thomas, 44, 52, 53, 55, 56, 59n.9, 104
DuBois, Ellen, 104

E

Eagle Forum, 123, 126
Earle, Peter, 31
Economic man, 10, 21, 41
Economic Policy Institute, 116, 190
Economic restructuring, 115-120
Edgeworth, Maria, 21-22, 32-33
Education
  mass, 22, 34-35
  occupational mobility and, 160-161, 166-167
Edwards, Linda, 136
Edwards, Richard, 101, 108, 118, 119, 130n.3
Ehrenberg, Ronald, 191
Ehrenreich, Barbara, 102, 103, 104, 105
Eisenstein, Zillah, 6
El Cheikh, Nabil, 191
Elements of Political Economy (Mill), 30
Embargo Act, 45
Employment benefits, domestic partnership and, 74
Employment discrimination. *See* Labor market discrimination
Employment flexibility, 121-122
England, Paula, 188, 191
Equal Employment Advisory Council, 124
Equal Pay Act, 194
Equal Pay for UNequal Work, 126
Esping-Andersen, Gøsta, 177
Essay on Population, An (Malthus), 28
Essays in Practical Education (Edgeworth), 32
Etiquette books, 32, 41n.4

Ettelbrick, Paula, 74
Ewen, Stuart, 102

F

Factory work
  mill girls, 49-51
  sweat shops, 57
  transition to, 44-45
Faludi, Susan, 45
Family structure
  black family, 158-160, 183
  capitalism and, 6-7, 12-13
  diversity of forms, 8, 11-12, 69
  feminist reconceptualizing of, 69, 73
  of lesbians, gays and bisexuals, 61-63, 66, 67-75
  children in, 72
  domestic partnership and, 63, 73-75
  specialization in, 70-71
  stability of, 72, 77n.9
  in nineteenth century, 26-41
  occupational mobility and, 158-160
  wage inequality and, 189
Family wage, 97, 101, 116, 119, 124-125, 128-129, 186n.4, 189
Fanon, Frantz, 174
Farkas, George, 191
Farley, Harriet, 48, 49
Faux, Jeff, 116, 121
Feminine Mystique (Friedan), 104
Feminist economics
  development of, 4-9
  gender-based analysis of, 63, 64-67
  neoclassical economics and, 3-4
  sexual orientation and, 69, 73, 76
  universalizing tendency in, 62
Feminization, and economic restructuring, 119-120, 128-129, 130n.7
Ferber, Marianne A., 3, 62
Ferdinand, Theodore, 53
Fichtenbaum, Rudy, 193
Fielding, Henry, 28

Figart, Deborah M., 11, 13, 15-16, 115-129, 128, 129, 188-204, 190, 193, 197
Fine, Ben, 94, 100, 102
Flax, Jane, 109, 110
Folbre, Nancy, 5, 9, 62, 93, 94, 108, 189, 200
Fontana, Biancamaria, 34
Fordism, 118, 121, 135
Ford Motor Company, wage policy at, 125
Foucault, Michel, 26, 93, 101
Fraad, 100, 103, 110
Fraser, Nancy, 117
Friedan, Betty, 100, 104
Friedman-Goldstein, Leslie, 56
Fuchs, Victor, 172

G

Galenson, David W., 47, 59n.6
Gallatin, Albert, 58n.1
Gardiner, Jean, 5, 91n.3
Garrett, G., 91n.2
Garza, Melita Marie, 129
Gays. *See* Lesbians, gays and bisexuals
Gender
  as analytic category, 8-9, 62, 115
  capitalism and, 104-11
  class and, 92-93, 99-111
  division of labor, 7, 10, 22, 24, 37, 39, 67, 70, 126-127
  economic restructuring and, 118-120, 121-122, 124-129
  neocolonialism and, 86-89
  separate spheres ideology of, 13, 93
  sexuality and, 64-67
  welfare system and, 178-179, 181-184
  See also Labor force participation, female; Labor market discrimination
Gender roles
  domestic ideology and, 93, 97-100, 104-107, 109-110

Gender roles *(continued)*
   in nineteenth century, 10, 29-32, 98-99, 109, 125
   pay equity and, 124-128
   sexual orientation and, 65, 70-71
Geoghegan, Thomas, 129
Gerhart, Barry, 191
Gilbert, Nigel, 121
Gilfoyle, Timothy J., 49, 54, 59n.10
Gilman, Charlotte Perkins, 108
Gini coefficient, 194, 198, 200, 202
Gintis, Herbert, 109
Gisborne, Thomas, 32
Gittleman, Maury, 172
Glenn, Evelyn Nakano, 8, 150, 163, 174, 179
Goffman, Irving, 102, 106
Goldin, Claudia, 11, 102, 120
Gordon, David M., 100, 101, 108, 117, 118, 119, 130n.3
Gordon, Linda, 117, 181, 182, 186n.13
Gordon, Robert, 134
Gossett, Charles, 73
Gove, Philip, 22
Gramm, Wendy Lee, 124
Grappard, Ulla, 21
Greenwood, Daphne, 122
Grown, Caren, 7, 8
Grubb, W. Norton, 189, 198-199, 204n.4
Grub, Farley, 59n.6
Gutman, Herbert G., 44, 45, 46, 48, 49, 52, 56
Gyimah-Brempong, Kwabina, 193

H

Hagen, Elizabeth, 13, 116, 120, 189
Hale, Sarah, 99
Hall, Catherine, 29, 30
Hard Times (Dickens), 24-25
Harrison, Bennett, 105, 188, 189
Harrison, J., 5, 91n.3
Harrison, Rachel, 27

Harth, Erica, 27, 28
Hartmann, Heidi, 5-6, 8, 92, 125, 129, 172, 174, 188, 197
Harvard Law Review, 65, 71, 72
Harvey, David, 121
Hildebrand, George, 123, 124
Hill, Marilyn Wood, 49, 54, 59n.9
Hillsborough, Earl of, 27
Hilton, Boyd, 25
Himmelweit, Susan, 5
Hobsbawm, E. J., 82-83
Holmes, Steven A., 104
Homer, Steven, 65
Homosexuality. *See* Lesbians, gays and bisexuals
hooks, bell, 7
Horrell, Sara, 11
Hospital attendants, 163
Household production, 44, 90
Houseman, Susan, 134, 136, 144
Housework. *See* Domestic labor
Howell, Chris, 116
Howell, David, 172
Humphries, Jane, 5, 6-7, 8, 11, 91n.3, 99, 174, 185n.2
Hunt, Margaret, 33

I

Illustrations of Political Economy (Martineau), 30, 36
Indentured servants, 46-47, 59n.6
Individualism, economic, 32
Industrialization, 44-45
Industry
   deindustrialization, 120, 128, 189
   Fordism, 118, 121, 135
   service sector, 14, 150-168, 189
   See also Factory work
Institutionalist theory, 9

J

Jacobs, Jerry A., 192
Jacobson, Paul H., 52
Janiewski, Dolores, 178, 179, 184

Japan, labor market flexibility in, 131-149
Jefferson, Thomas, 45
Jenkins, Sarah, 188
Jenkins, Stephen, 194
Jenson, Jane, 13, 116, 120, 128, 189
Jervis, Robert, 91n.2
Jessop, Bob, 116
Job evaluation, 130n.2
John Hopkins's Notions on Political Economy (Marcet), 35, 38
Johnson, George, 191, 195
Joseph, Gloria, 7
Just-in-time production, 131, 135

K

Kahn, Lawrence M., 189, 197
Kahn, Peggy, 128
Karoly, Lynn, 189, 194, 197, 198, 200
Katz, Michael B., 45, 47, 102, 178
Kawashima, Yoko, 136
Kelley, Florence, 100
Kelso, Robert W., 46, 47
Kerber, Linda, 99
Kessler, Lorance L., 126
Kessler-Harris, Alice, 45, 46, 48, 49, 50, 56, 58n.2, 107, 120, 121, 125
Keynesian economics, 118
Kilbourne, Barbara, 191
Killingsworth, Mark R., 191
King, Mary C., 151
Kirschenman, Joleen, 172
Klamer, Arjo, 25
Kotz, David M., 14, 109
Koven, Seth, 100, 104
Kowaleski-Wallace, Elizabeth, 98, 100, 109
Krugman, Paul, 105
Kuchera, David, 14, 16, 131-149
Kuhn, Sarah, 189
Kuiper, Edith, 3
Kuttner, Robert, 129
Kuznets, Simon, 48

L

Labor aristocracy, 82-83
Labor force participation, female
  as buffer work force, 132, 135-136, 143-146, 185n.2
  domestic ideology and, reassertion of, 104-107
  dual systems approach to, 7
  feminization process in, 119-120, 128-129, 130n.7
  in household production, 44, 90
  labor market flexibility and, 121-122, 132-149
  in low-paid jobs, 129, 150-168, 179, 189
  in nineteenth century, 11, 42-58
    age and marital status, 55-56
    cyclical pattern of, 56-58
    domestic ideology and, 99-100
    economic conditions and, 47-49
    factory work, 49-51
    industrialization and, 44-45
    non-free labor tradition and, 46-47
    occupational categories, 49, 51-55
    rural economy, 43-44
    social framework for, 45-46
  patterns of, 54-55, 58, 100-101, 120
  undercounting of, 56-57
  in wartime, 56
  See also Occupations, female; Pay equity; Wages
Labor market discrimination, 15
  in capitalist system, 172-176
  against lesbians and gays, 65
  by unions, 185-186n.4
  wage inequality and, 172-173, 174, 175, 188-189
  welfare system in, 170-171, 178-179, 181, 184-185
Labor market flexibility
  functional, 121, 135
  gender and, 121-122
  numerical, 121, 135-136
  pay equity and, 14, 120-124

Labor market flexibility *(continued)*
  unemployment and, 131-149
Labor market segmentation, 130n.3
Labor migration, 12, 84, 88, 89-90
Labor reproduction, 12, 87-88
Labor theory of value, 5, 12, 16n.3, 37-38, 78-84
  methodology of, 94-97
Labor unions, 185-186n.4, 195
Lalli, Michael, 53
Lam, Alice, 136
Lange, P., 91n.2
Langland, Elizabeth, 32, 41n.4
Lapidus, June, 15-16, 129, 188-204, 190, 193
Larson, Kathryn, 61, 63, 71
Lebergott, Stanley, 45, 52
Lee, Everett S., 53
Lemann, Nicholas, 105, 180
Lemons, J. Stanley, 102
Lenin, 83
Lerner, Gerda, 92
Lesbians, gays and bisexuals
  employment discrimination against, 65
  family structure of, 61-63, 66, 67-75
    children in, 72
    domestic partnership and, 63, 73-75
    specialization in, 70-71
    stability of, 72, 77n.9
  gender-based analysis and, 64-67
Levin, Michael, 126
Levy, Frank, 189, 194, 199
Life and Adventures of Robinson Crusoe, The (Defoe), 10, 21-22, 37
Lifetime employment system, in Japan, 136
Life in the Wilds (Martineau), 10, 22, 23-24, 36-38, 40
Lind, Michael, 106
Lindert, Peter H., 48
Living wage movement, 129
Lorber, Judith, 8

Loury, Glenn, 187n.15
Lowell mills, 50-51
Luker, Kristen, 104, 106

M

McCloskey, D. N., 25
McCrate, Elaine, 169n.11
McDonough, Terrence, 13
McDowell, Linda, 116, 119, 120, 121, 125
MacKinnon, Catherine, 93, 103
McLane Report, 42, 45, 49, 50, 51, 55, 58n.2, 60
Malthus, Thomas, 24, 31
  moral restraint doctrine of, 25, 28-29
  population theory of, 23, 35-36
Malthusian economics, 25
Malveaux, Julianne, 151, 190
Mandel, E., 90n.1
Mansfield Park (Austen), 33
Marcet, Jane Haldiman, 10, 22, 25-26, 34, 35, 36, 38-40, 40
Marital status, labor force participation and, 55-56
Marriage
  age of, 52
  defined, 70
  domestic partnership and, 63
  property settlement in, 26, 27
  same-sex, 65, 68
  state regulation of, 27, 28
Marriage Act of 1753, 27, 28
Martineau, Harriet, 10, 22, 25-26, 30, 36, 40
Marx, Karl, 110
  capitalist stages of, 90n.1
  on domestic labor, 5, 94, 96-97
  labor market analysis of, 172-173
  labor theory of value, 5, 12, 16n.3, 37-38, 78-84, 86, 94
  methodology of, 94-97
Marxist feminists, 17n.5, 92-93
Mason, Patrick L., 172, 175
Matthaei, Julie A., 9, 48

May, Martha, 125
Metcalf, David, 132
Michel, Sonya, 100, 104
Mill, James, 30, 35
Mill, John Stuart, 30-31, 36
Mill girls, 49-51
Minimum wage, 129
Mishel, Lawrence, 189
Mitter, Swasti, 115, 119
Mohr, Richard, 68
Mohun, Simon, 5
Montgomery, David, 48, 50
Moral restraint doctrine, 28-29
Moral science, political economy as, 25-41
More, Hannah, 32, 34, 98, 100
Morgan, Marjorie, 31
Morris, Richard B., 46, 47, 59n.6
Mort, Frank, 27
Moynihan, Daniel, 183
Murnane, Richard J., 189, 194, 199
Mutari, Ellen, 3-16, 11, 13, 115-129

N

Nakamura, Takafusa, 148
National Longitudinal Survey (NLS), 152, 168n.3
Neckerman, Kathryn M., 106, 172
Negro Family, The (Moynihan), 183
Nelson, Bruce A., 127
Nelson, Julie A., 3, 62
Nelson, Robert L., 188
Neoclassical economics, 3-4
Neocolonialism, 84-90
Nicholson, Linda, 92, 93, 94, 107, 110
North, Douglass C., 48
Northrup, Herbert E., 123
Nye, J. S., 91n.2

O

Occupations, female
 feminization, 189
 mobility and, 14, 150-168

Occupations, female *(continued)*
 in nineteenth century, 49, 51-55
 and pay equity, 117, 128, 191-194
 segregated, 151, 188, 191
O'Hara, Phillip A., 101-102, 109, 116, 118
O'Kelly, Charlotte, 136
Okker, Patricia, 99, 102
Oliver, Melvin L., 181
O'Neill, June, 123, 126, 127
Ono, Tsuneo, 136
Opton, Edward M., Jr., 127
Organization for Economic Cooperation and Development (OECD), 122, 131-132, 134
Outwork production, 55
Owen, William, 24
Özler, Sule, 120

P

Pagels, Elaine, 98
Pamela (Richardson), 28, 29
Part-time work, 6, 121, 135, 136
Passell, Peter, 48
Pateman, Carole, 31, 92, 93, 109
Patriarchy, 6, 8, 9, 92
Paul, Alice, 100
Paul, Ellen Frankel, 122, 123, 126, 127
Pay equity, 13-14, 15-16, 188
 court decisions on, 116-117
 gender roles and, 124-128
 labor market flexibility and, 120-124
 opposition to, 117, 126-128, 189-190
 potential effect of, 190-204
 race and, 203-204
 See also Wages
Pearce, Diana, 178
Pear, Robert, 106
Pearson, Frank A., 47
Pease, Jane H., 49, 53
Pease, William H., 49, 53
Peplau, Letitia Anne, 70
Perrons, Diane, 119

Personal Responsibility and Work
 Opportunity Reconciliation Act,
 184
Petchesky, Rosalind, 92
Peterson, Janice, 9, 122
Peterson, Richard, 136
Petrie, Gordon, 183
Phelps, Edmund, 174
Pinchbeck, Ivy, 59n.12
Piore, Michael J., 135
Piven, Frances Fox, 177, 181, 182
Polanyi, Karl, 93, 101, 176
Political activism, 104
Political economy
 feminist, development of, 4-9
 in nineteenth century, 10, 21-41
 restructuring, 115-129
 sexual orientation and, 61-76
Pollert, Anna, 121
Poor Laws of 1601, 176
Poor relief. *See* Welfare system
Poovey, Mary, 98, 104, 109
Population pressure, 23, 26
Posner, Richard, 64, 76n.3, 77n.9
Postindustrial economy, 121
Postmodernism, 17n.6
Post-structuralism, 9
Power, Marilyn, 5, 14-15, 150-68
Primogeniture, 27
Progressive movement, 182
Prolife movement, 104
Property rights, 26, 27, 98
Prostitution, 53-54
Pryme, G., 34

Q

Quadagno, Jill, 179, 180, 183,
 186n.9
Quality circles, 135

R

Rabkin, Jeremy, 126
Race
 class and, 161-163

Race *(continued)*
 colonialism and, 23, 32-33, 36
 earnings and, 151
 economic restructuring and, 125
 educational level and, 160-161
 employment discrimination and,
  174-176
 family structure and, 158-160, 183
 labor migration and, 84, 89-90
 occupational mobility and, 14,
  150-168
 pay equity and, 203-204
 socialist feminism and, 7
 voting rights and, 186n.9
 welfare system and, 170-171, 179,
  180-181, 183, 187n.15
Ramas, Maria, 186n.4
Reclaiming Prosperity, 190
Reddy, Ceallaigh, 13, 116, 120, 189
Reed, Ralph, 105
Regulation theory, 115, 118, 119
Reich, Michael, 14, 101, 108, 118,
 119, 130n.3, 172
Reich, Robert, 57
Reserve army of labor, 172-173,
 185n.2
Reskin, Barbara F., 172, 189
Resnick, Stephen, 25, 100, 103,
 110
Rhoads, Steven E., 117, 122, 123
Ricardo, David, 34, 35
Rich, Adrienne, 64, 66
Richardson, Pamela, 28
Roback, Jennifer, 126, 127
Robertson, Pat, 105
Robson, Ruthann, 68, 71
Roldán, Martha, 7, 92
Rollins, Judith, 163
Romero, Mary, 165
Roos, Patricia A., 189
Rose, Nancy, 183
Rose, Sonya O., 99, 109, 125
Rosecrance, R. N., 91n.2
Rosenberg, Sam, 14-15, 121,
 150-168
Rothenberg, Winnifred B., 48

Rubery, Jill, 6, 7, 13, 132, 174, 185n.2
Rubin, Gayle, 92
Rubin, Robert E., 129
Rural economy, 43-44, 48
Rutten, Tim, 129
Ryan, Mary, 25, 45, 46, 48, 49, 52, 56, 104, 109

S

Sacks, Karen Brodkin, 107
Same-sex marriage, 65, 68
Sanger, David, 146
Sap, Jolande, 3
Sapiro, Virginia, 181-182, 186n.6
Sargent, Lydia, 6
Schettkat, Ronald, 134-135
Schlafly, Phyllis, 100, 123, 126-127
Schwartz, Pepper, 70-71
Scoresby, William D. D., 48, 49, 50-51
Scott, Joan Wallach, 8, 9, 11
Scrope, G. Poulett, 23
Seamstresses, 52-53
Seccombe, Wally, 5, 94, 99, 100, 101, 108
Sedgwick, Eve Kosofsky, 65-66
Seidman, Steven, 66
Sen, Gita, 7, 8, 186n.4
Senior, Nassau, 35
Separate spheres ideology, 13, 93
Servants (domestics), 51-52, 59-60, 163, 165-166
Service sector
  expansion of, 189
  occupational mobility in, 14, 150-168
Sexuality
  class and, 93
  economic analysis of, 11-12, 62
  gender and, 64-67
  norms of, 102-103
  regulation of, 27-29, 105-106, 183-184

Sexual orientation. *See* Lesbians, gays and bisexuals
Shaiken, Harley, 108
Shaikh, Anwar, 172
Shamela (Fielding), 28
Shammas, Carole, 48
Shank, Susan E., 55
Shanley, Mary Lyndon, 98, 104
Shapiro, Thomas M., 181
Shipwreck narratives, 10, 22
Shiva, V., 90
Showalter, Elaine, 102
Simmons, Christina, 102
Single mothers, 158-160
Sklar, Kathryn K., 99, 100, 102, 104
Skocpol, Theda, 182
Slaves, 46
Smith, Abbot E., 46
Smith, Adam, 22, 25, 123
Smith, Peggie R., 175
Smith, Robert, 191
Smith, William B., 47
Smith-Rosenberg, Carroll, 102, 104
Socialist feminism, 6-7, 17n.5
Social reproduction, 6, 88-89, 174
Social Security Act, 176-177, 179, 183, 186n.6
Social Structure of Accumulation (SSA), 101, 109, 115, 118, 119, 130n.3
Social welfare movement, 104
Solon, Gary, 191, 195
Sorensen, Elaine, 188, 191, 192, 193, 195
Sorrentino, Constance, 146
Sowell, Thomas, 187n.15
Spalter-Roth, Roberta, 187n.14
Spivak, Gayatri Chakravorty, 8
Standing, Guy, 119, 120, 121
State control, neocolonialism and, 85-86
Staves, Susan, 27, 98, 104
Steinberg, Ronnie, 122, 188, 192
Steinem, Gloria, 100
Sterling, Dorothy, 46
Stewart, Martha, 107

Stocking, George W., Jr., 33
Stoddard, Thomas, 68
Stone, Jeanne C. F., 26
Stone, Lawrence, 26
Strassmann, Diana, 25
Strict settlement, 27
Subjection of Women, The (Mill), 30-31
Sullivan, Jeremiah, 136
Supply-side economics, 123-124
Supreme Court, U.S., and pay equity, 116
Sweat shops, 57
Syllabus of a Course of Lectures on the Principles of Political Economy (Pryme), 34

T

Tachibanaki, Toshiaki, 134, 136
Talbot, Margaret, 107
Taylor, Barbara, 98, 99
Teachers, 53
Tench Coxe Report, 50, 58n.1
Theil-Entropy Index, 194-195, 198
Thomas, Clarence, 123
Thompson, Noel W., 35
"Three Giants, The" (Marcet), 10, 22, 23, 24, 38-40
Tilly, Chris, 118, 130n.3
Tilly, Louise A., 11
Tomaskovic-Devey, Donald, 188
Trattner, Walter I., 176
Treas, Judith, 195
Treiman, Donald J., 188
Tyson, James L., 129

U

Uchitelle, Louis, 129
Uhlenberg, Peter, 52
Ulrich, Laurel T., 46
Underconsumptionist theory, 119, 130n.5
Unemployment
  in capitalist system, 172-173

Unemployment *(continued)*
  and labor market flexibility, 131, 132, 133-136
Utilitarianism, 24-25

V

Valenze, Deborah, 98, 100, 109
Virtuous circle concept, 118
Virtuous love, 25, 26-29, 38

W

Wages
  family, 97, 101, 116, 119, 121, 124-125, 128-129, 186n.4, 189
  flexibility, 121, 122-123, 134
  inequality, 172-173, 174, 175, 188-189
  labor theory of value, 95-96
  living, 129
  of mill girls, 49
  race and, 151
  unionization and, 195
  See also Pay equity
Wagman, Barnet, 189, 200
Waitresses, 163, 166-167
Wajcman, Judy, 188
Walby, Sylvia, 6
Walkowitz, Judith, 104, 106
Wallerstein, I., 89
Ware, Norman, 45, 46, 47, 49, 50, 54, 86n.2
Warren, George F., 47
Waterman, A. M. C., 25
Watt, Ian, 32
Webb, R. K., 35
Weir, Dorothea, 191
Welfare system, 15
  evolution of, 176-184
  labor market discrimination through, 172-176, 178-179, 184-185
  purpose of, 184
  reform, 105-106, 128, 129, 170, 184

Welter, Barbara, 102
West Germany, labor market flexibility in, 131-149
Weston, Kate, 67, 68
White, M. V., 21, 22
Williams, Fiona, 116, 120
Williams, Raymond, 24, 25
Williams, Rhonda M., 11-12, 62, 118, 125, 172, 175
Williams, Robert E., 126
Williamson, Jeffrey G., 48
Wilson, Robert H., 189, 198-199, 204n.4
Wilson, Thomas E., 127
Wilson, William Julius, 106
Wolff, Edward, 105
Wolff, Richard, 25, 100, 103, 110
Wollstonecraft, Mary, 100
Women and Recession (Rubery), 132, 137

Y

Yoon, Young-Hee, 187n.14

Z

Zalokar, Nadja, 151
Zinn, Maxine Baca, 7, 125